TONIGHT!

Dan Watters, Writer
and Caspar Wijngaard, Artist

With:

Aditya Bidikar: Letterer

Tom Muller: Designer

Erika Schnatz: Production Artist

PRESENT:

IMAGE COMICS, INC.
Todd McFarlane: President
Jim Valentino: Vice President
Marc Silvestri: Chief Executive Officer
Erik Larsen: Chief Financial Officer
Robert Kirkman: Chief Operating Officer

Eric Stephenson: Publisher / Chief Creative Officer
Nicole Lapalme: Controller
Leanna Caunter: Accounting Analyst
Sue Korpela: Accounting & HR Manager
Marla Eizik: Talent Liaison
Jeff Boison: Director of Sales & Publishing Planning
Dirk Wood: Director of International Sales & Licensing
Alex Cox: Director of Direct Market Sales
Chloe Ramos: Book Market & Library Sales Manager
Emilio Bautista: Digital Sales Coordinator
Jon Schlaffman: Specialty Sales Coordinator
Kat Salazar: Director of PR & Marketing
Drew Fitzgerald: Marketing Content Associate
Heather Doornink: Production Director
Drew Gill: Art Director
Hilary DiLoreto: Print Manager
Tricia Ramos: Traffic Manager
Melissa Gifford: Content Manager
Erika Schnatz: Senior Production Artist
Ryan Brewer: Production Artist
Deanna Phelps: Production Artist

Tara Ferguson: White Noise marketing

HOME SICK PILOTS

Home Sick Pilots
created by
Dan Watters and Caspar Wijngaard

Originally published as HOME SICK PILOTS #6–10

HOME SICK PILOTS, VOL. 2: I WANNA BE A WALKING WEAPON. November 2021. Published by Image Comics, Inc. Office of publication: PO BOX 14457, Portland, OR 97293. Copyright © 2021 Dan Watters & Caspar Wijngaard. All rights reserved. Contains material originally published in single magazine form as HOME SICK PILOTS #6-10. HOME SICK PILOTS, and the likenesses of all characters herein or hereon are trademarks of Dan Watters & Caspar Wijngaard, unless expressly indicated. "Image" and the Image Comics logos are registered trademarks of Image Comics, Inc. No part of this publication may be reproduced or transmitted in any form or by any means (except for short excerpts for journalistic or review purposes), without the express written permission of Dan Watters & Caspar Wijngaard or Image Comics, Inc. All names, characters, events, and places herein are entirely fictional. Any resemblance to actual persons (living or dead), events, or places, without satiric intent, is coincidental. Printed in the USA. All inquiries: licensing@imagecomics.com.

Standard ISBN: 978-1-5343-2052-9

**Kowabunga Exclusive
ISBN: 978-1-5343-2241-7**

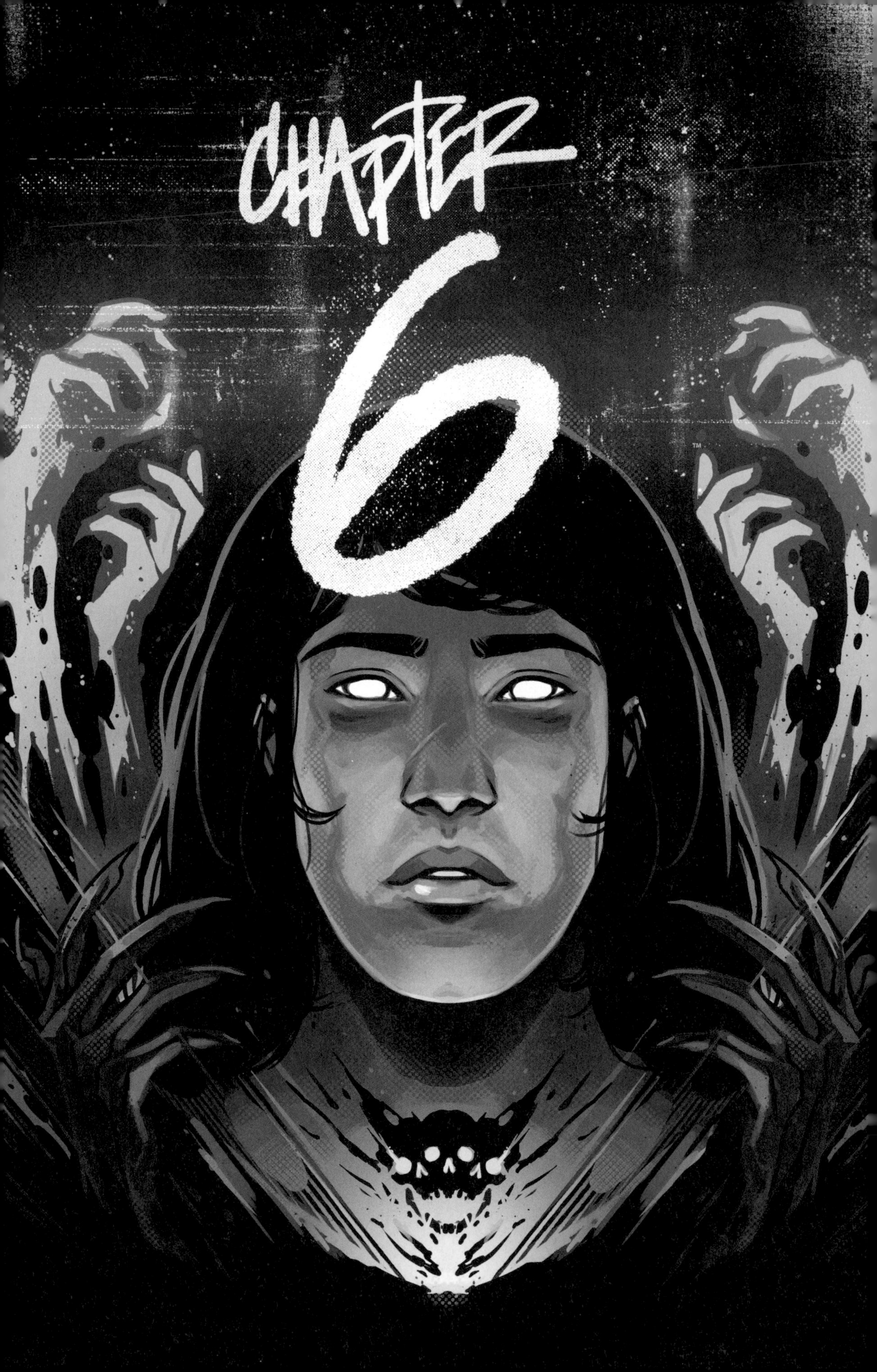
CHAPTER
6

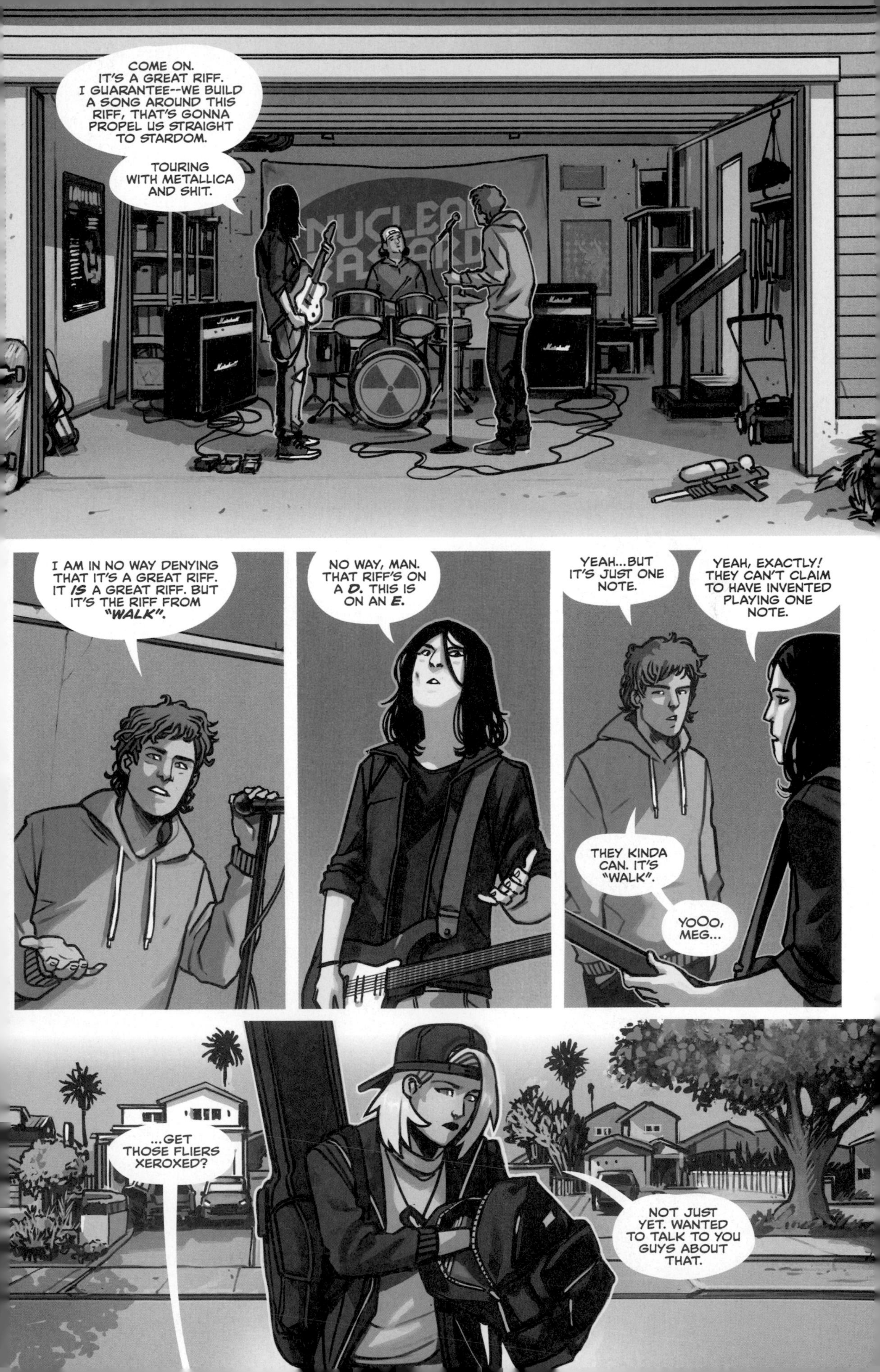
COME ON. IT'S A GREAT RIFF. I GUARANTEE--WE BUILD A SONG AROUND THIS RIFF, THAT'S GONNA PROPEL US STRAIGHT TO STARDOM.
TOURING WITH METALLICA AND SHIT.
NUCLEAR BASTARDS
I AM IN NO WAY DENYING THAT IT'S A GREAT RIFF. IT *IS* A GREAT RIFF. BUT IT'S THE RIFF FROM *"WALK"*.
NO WAY, MAN. THAT RIFF'S ON A *D*. THIS IS ON AN *E*.
YEAH...BUT IT'S JUST ONE NOTE.
YEAH, EXACTLY! THEY CAN'T CLAIM TO HAVE INVENTED PLAYING ONE NOTE.
THEY KINDA CAN. IT'S "WALK".
YOOO, MEG...
...GET THOSE FLIERS XEROXED?
NOT JUST YET. WANTED TO TALK TO YOU GUYS ABOUT THAT.

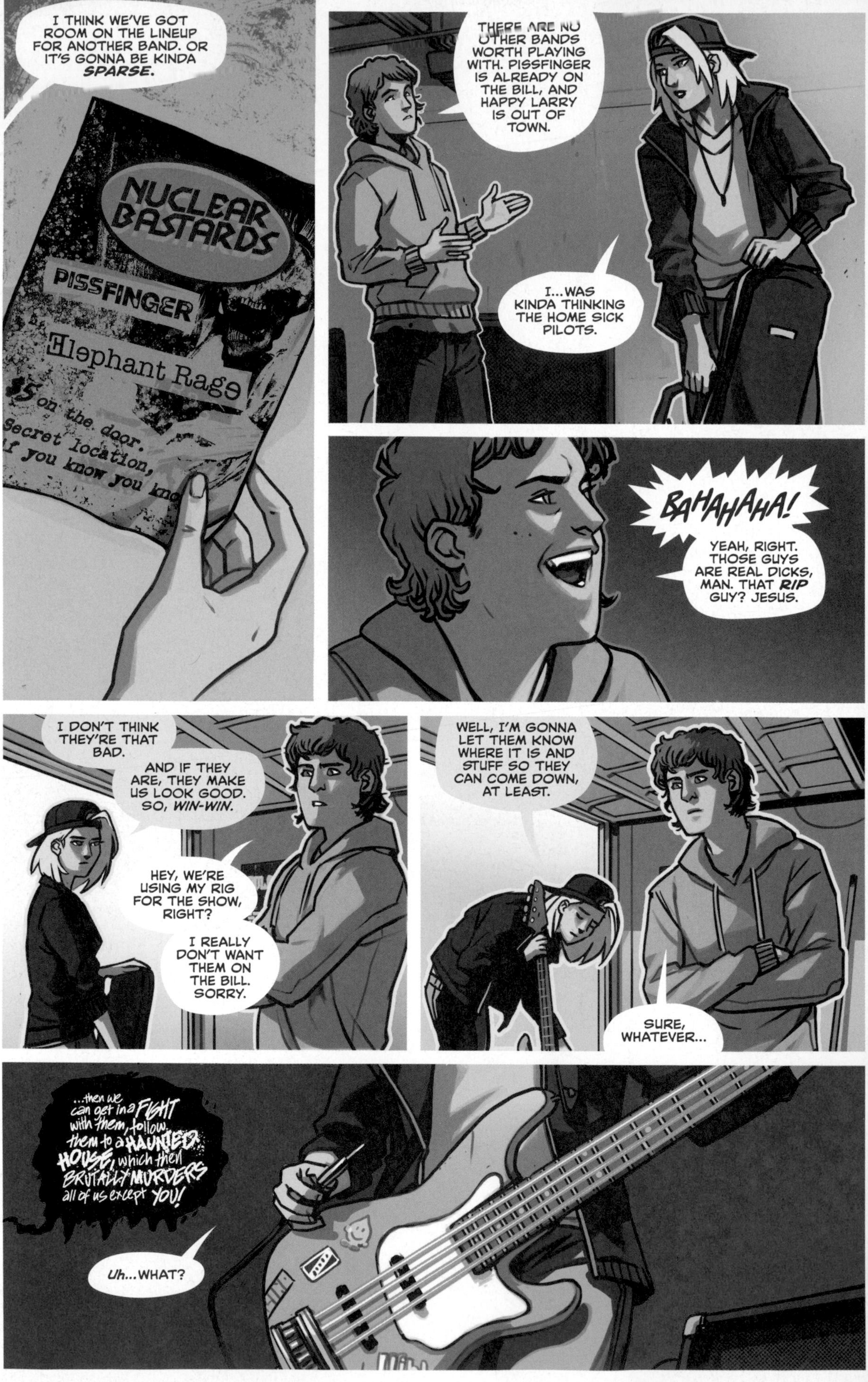

I THINK WE'VE GOT ROOM ON THE LINEUP FOR ANOTHER BAND. OR IT'S GONNA BE KINDA *SPARSE*.
NUCLEAR BASTARDS
PISSFINGER
Elephant Rage
$5 on the door.
Secret location,
if you know you kno
THERE ARE NO OTHER BANDS WORTH PLAYING WITH. PISSFINGER IS ALREADY ON THE BILL, AND HAPPY LARRY IS OUT OF TOWN.
I...WAS KINDA THINKING THE HOME SICK PILOTS.
BAHAHAHA!
YEAH, RIGHT. THOSE GUYS ARE REAL DICKS, MAN. THAT *RIP* GUY? JESUS.
I DON'T THINK THEY'RE THAT BAD.
AND IF THEY ARE, THEY MAKE US LOOK GOOD. SO, *WIN-WIN*.
HEY, WE'RE USING MY RIG FOR THE SHOW, RIGHT?
I REALLY DON'T WANT THEM ON THE BILL. SORRY.
WELL, I'M GONNA LET THEM KNOW WHERE IT IS AND STUFF SO THEY CAN COME DOWN, AT LEAST.
SURE, WHATEVER...
...then we can get in a FIGHT with them, follow them to a HAUNTED HOUSE, which then BRUTALLY MURDERS all of us except YOU!
Uh...WHAT?

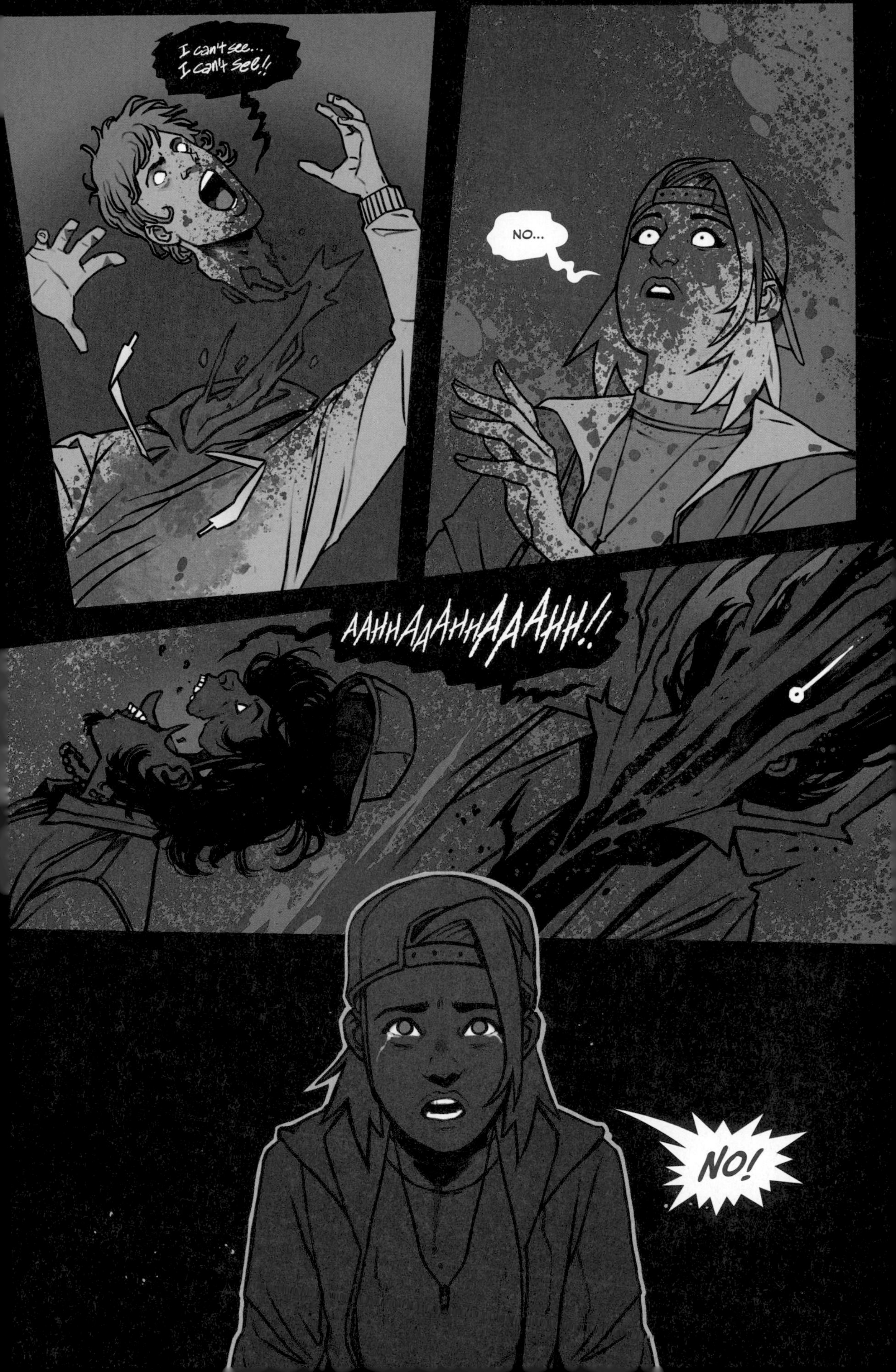
I can't see...
I can't see!!
NO...
AAHHAAAHHAAAHH!!
NO!

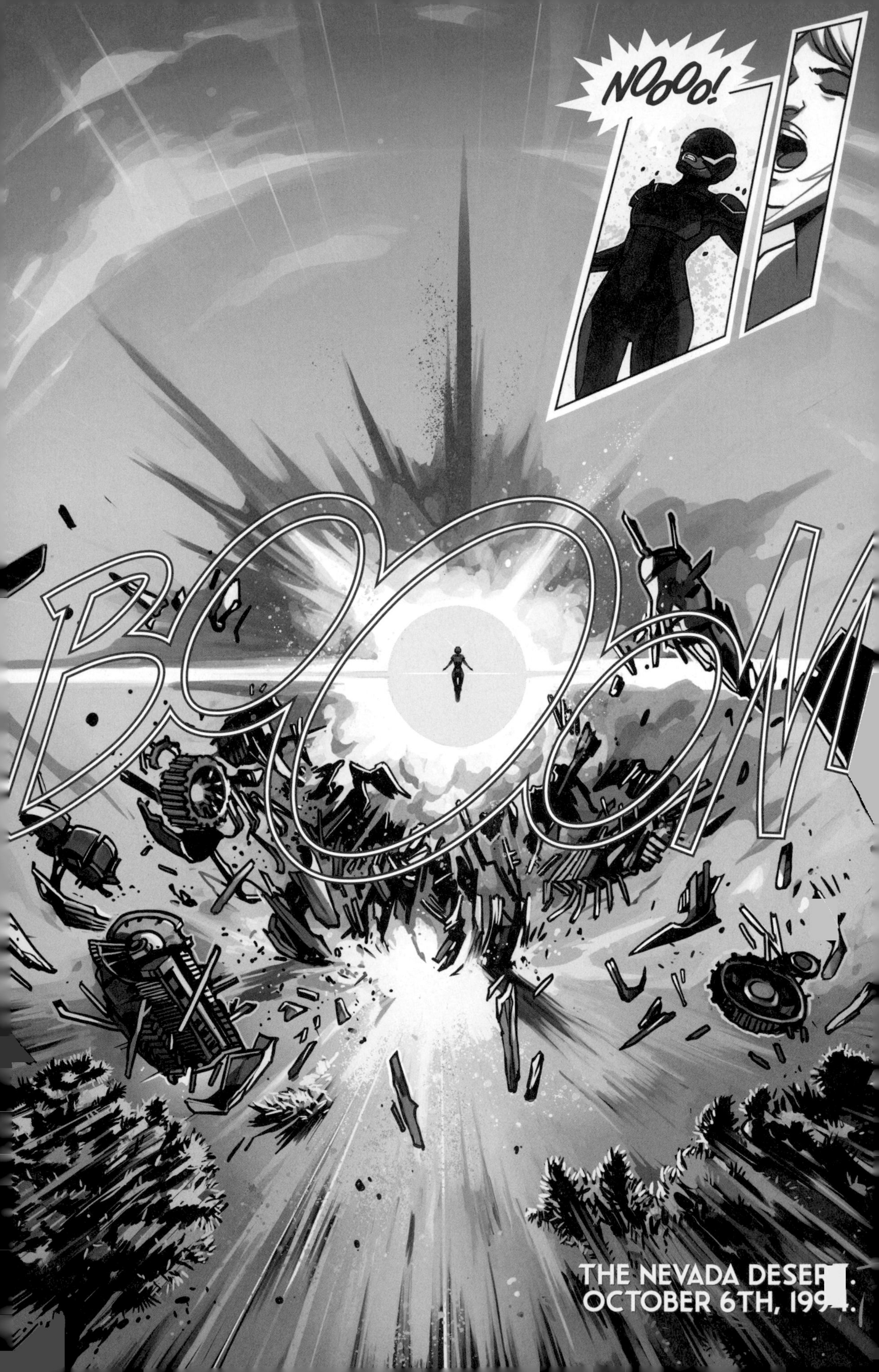

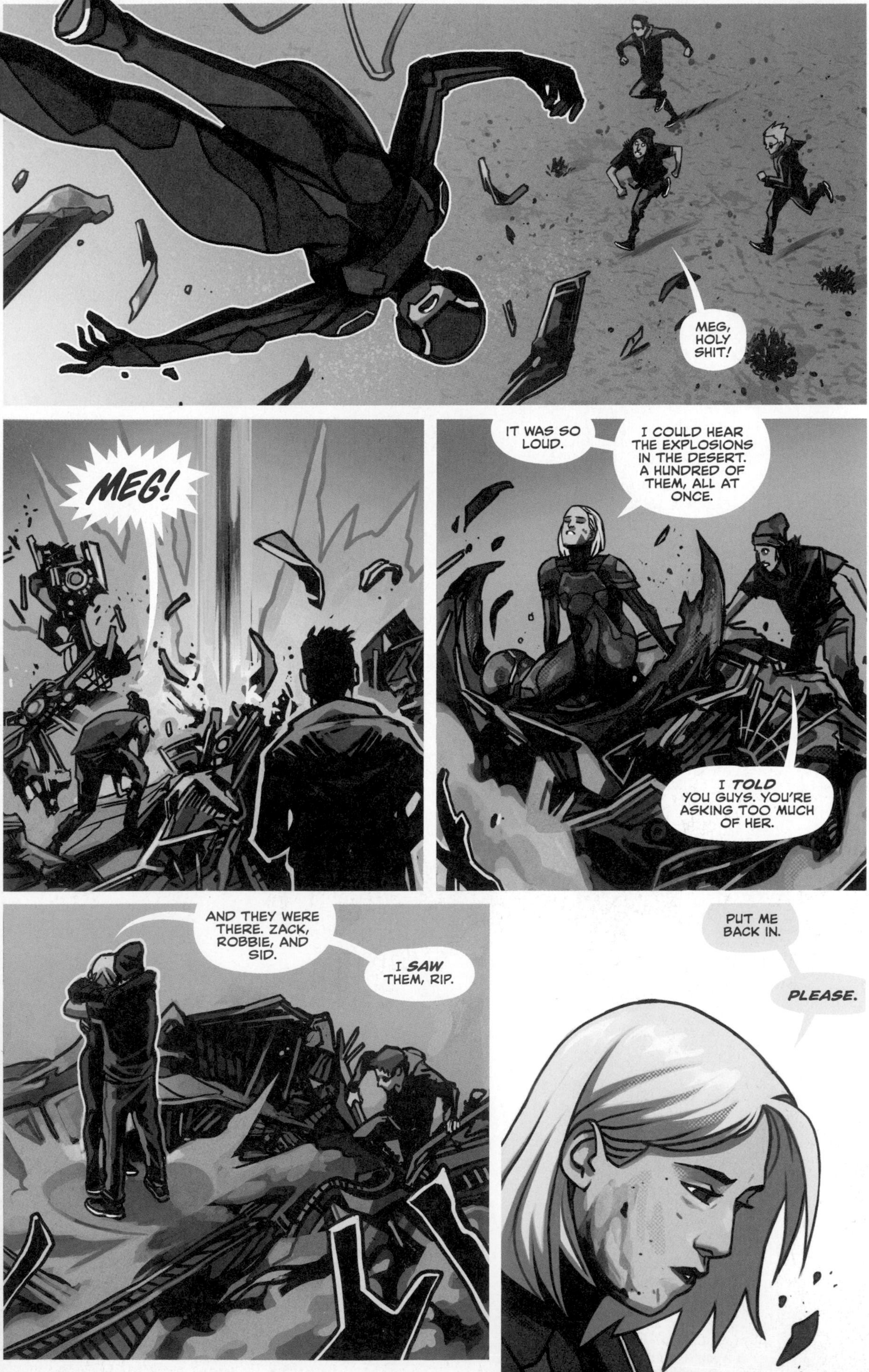
MEG, HOLY SHIT!
MEG!
IT WAS SO LOUD.
I COULD HEAR THE EXPLOSIONS IN THE DESERT. A HUNDRED OF THEM, ALL AT ONCE.
I TOLD YOU GUYS. YOU'RE ASKING TOO MUCH OF HER.
AND THEY WERE THERE. ZACK, ROBBIE, AND SID.
I SAW THEM, RIP.
PUT ME BACK IN.
PLEASE.

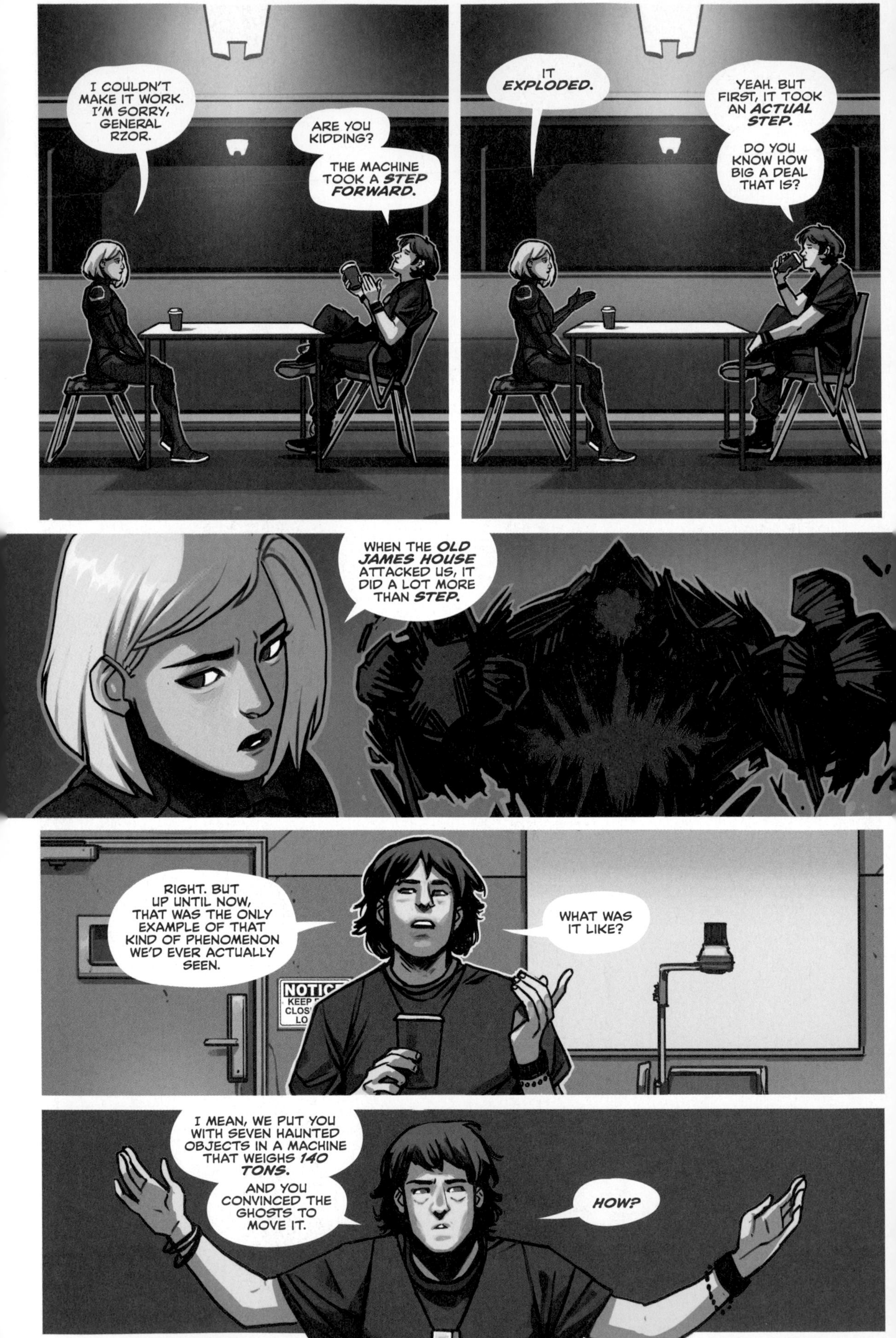
I COULDN'T MAKE IT WORK. I'M SORRY, GENERAL RZOR.
ARE YOU KIDDING?
THE MACHINE TOOK A **STEP FORWARD.**
IT **EXPLODED.**
YEAH. BUT FIRST, IT TOOK AN **ACTUAL STEP.**
DO YOU KNOW HOW BIG A DEAL THAT IS?
WHEN THE **OLD JAMES HOUSE** ATTACKED US, IT DID A LOT MORE THAN **STEP.**
RIGHT. BUT UP UNTIL NOW, THAT WAS THE ONLY EXAMPLE OF THAT KIND OF PHENOMENON WE'D EVER ACTUALLY SEEN.
WHAT WAS IT LIKE?
NOTICE
I MEAN, WE PUT YOU WITH SEVEN HAUNTED OBJECTS IN A MACHINE THAT WEIGHS **140 TONS.**
AND YOU CONVINCED THE GHOSTS TO MOVE IT.
HOW?

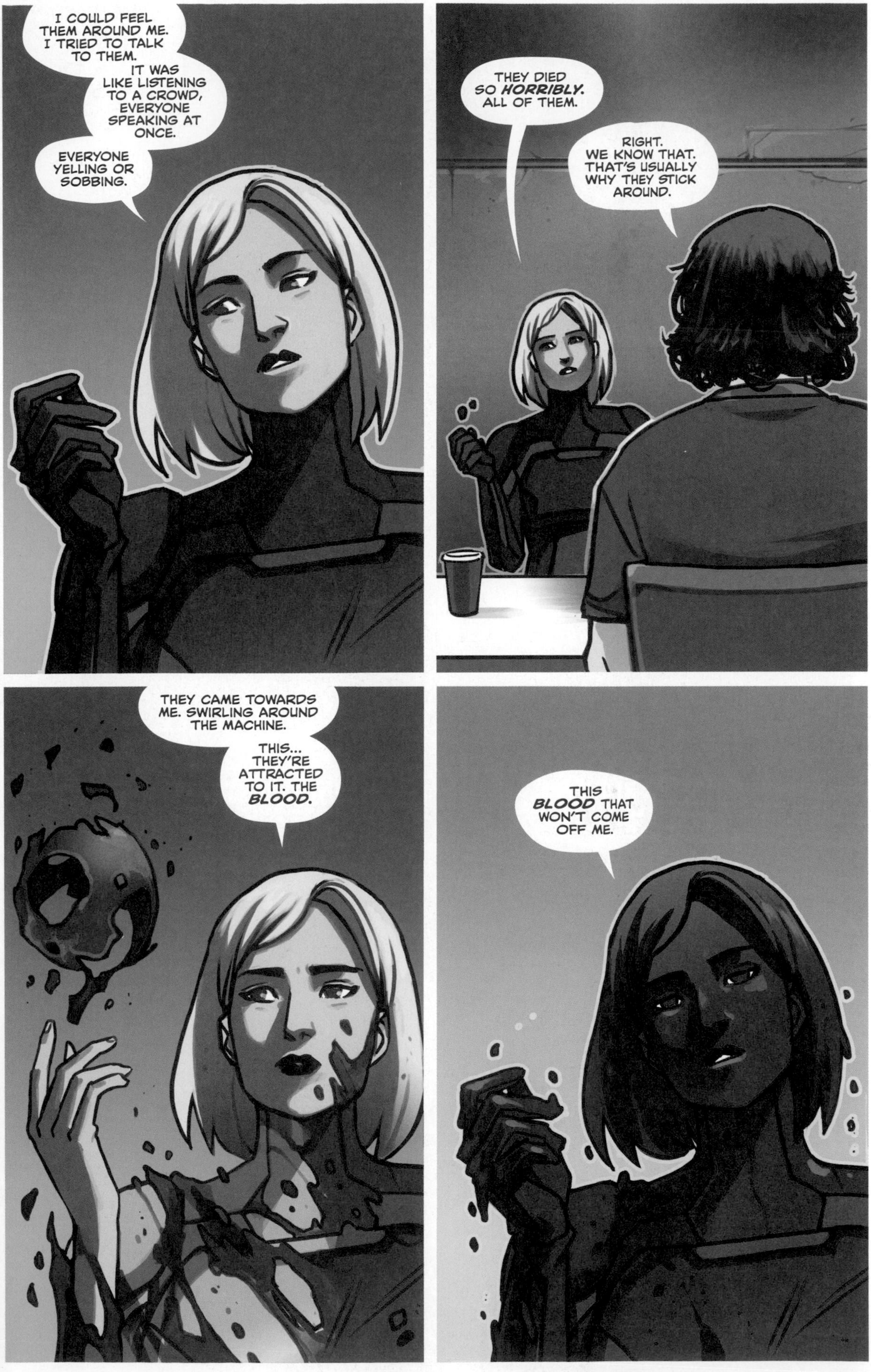
I COULD FEEL THEM AROUND ME. I TRIED TO TALK TO THEM.
IT WAS LIKE LISTENING TO A CROWD, EVERYONE SPEAKING AT ONCE.
EVERYONE YELLING OR SOBBING.
THEY DIED SO ***HORRIBLY.*** ALL OF THEM.
RIGHT. WE KNOW THAT. THAT'S USUALLY WHY THEY STICK AROUND.
THEY CAME TOWARDS ME. SWIRLING AROUND THE MACHINE.
THIS... THEY'RE ATTRACTED TO IT. THE ***BLOOD.***
THIS ***BLOOD*** THAT WON'T COME OFF ME.

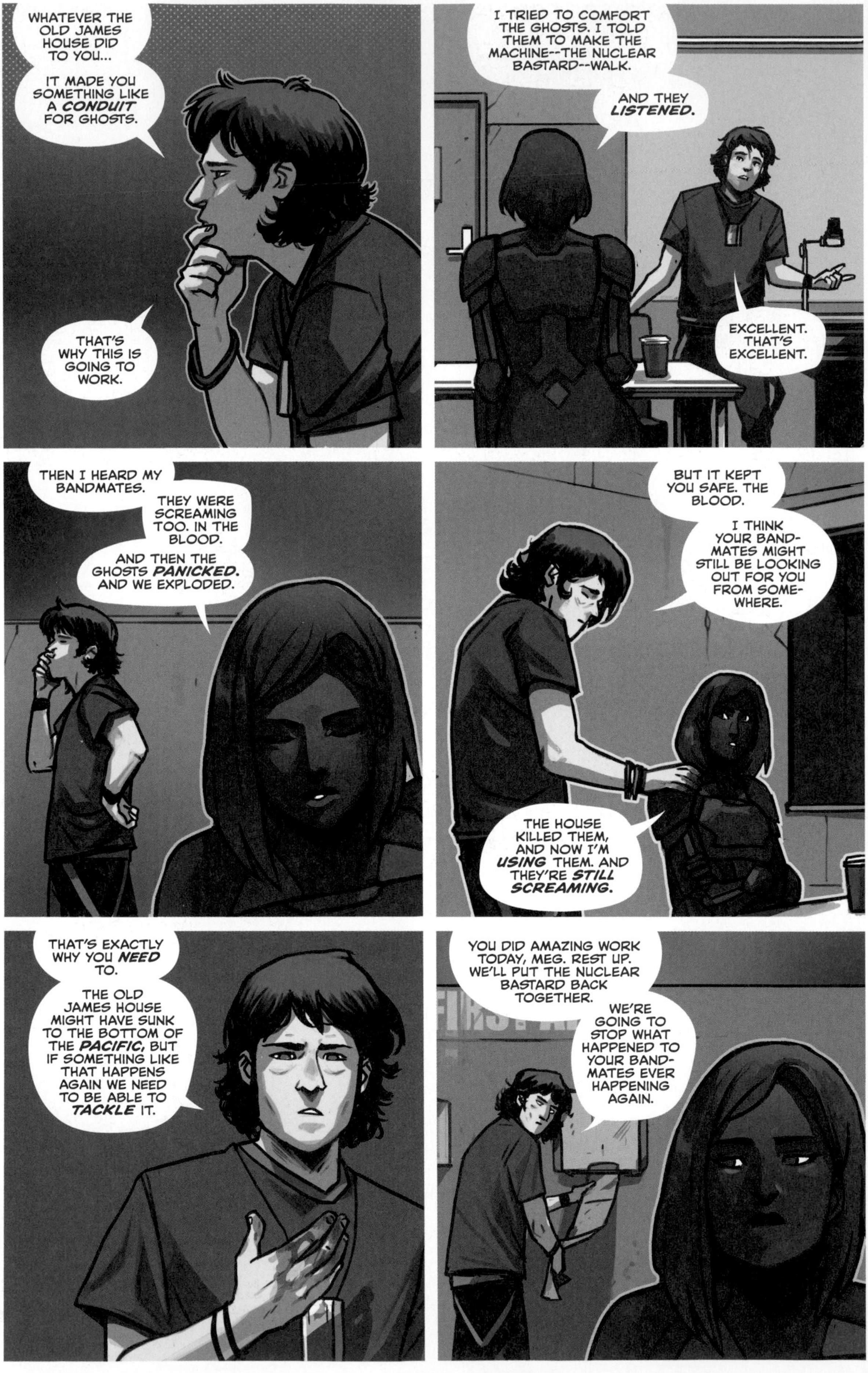
WHATEVER THE OLD JAMES HOUSE DID TO YOU...
IT MADE YOU SOMETHING LIKE A CONDUIT FOR GHOSTS.
THAT'S WHY THIS IS GOING TO WORK.
I TRIED TO COMFORT THE GHOSTS. I TOLD THEM TO MAKE THE MACHINE--THE NUCLEAR BASTARD--WALK.
AND THEY LISTENED.
EXCELLENT. THAT'S EXCELLENT.
THEN I HEARD MY BANDMATES.
THEY WERE SCREAMING TOO. IN THE BLOOD.
AND THEN THE GHOSTS PANICKED. AND WE EXPLODED.
BUT IT KEPT YOU SAFE. THE BLOOD.
I THINK YOUR BAND-MATES MIGHT STILL BE LOOKING OUT FOR YOU FROM SOME-WHERE.
THE HOUSE KILLED THEM, AND NOW I'M USING THEM. AND THEY'RE STILL SCREAMING.
THAT'S EXACTLY WHY YOU NEED TO.
THE OLD JAMES HOUSE MIGHT HAVE SUNK TO THE BOTTOM OF THE PACIFIC, BUT IF SOMETHING LIKE THAT HAPPENS AGAIN WE NEED TO BE ABLE TO TACKLE IT.
YOU DID AMAZING WORK TODAY, MEG. REST UP. WE'LL PUT THE NUCLEAR BASTARD BACK TOGETHER.
WE'RE GOING TO STOP WHAT HAPPENED TO YOUR BAND-MATES EVER HAPPENING AGAIN.

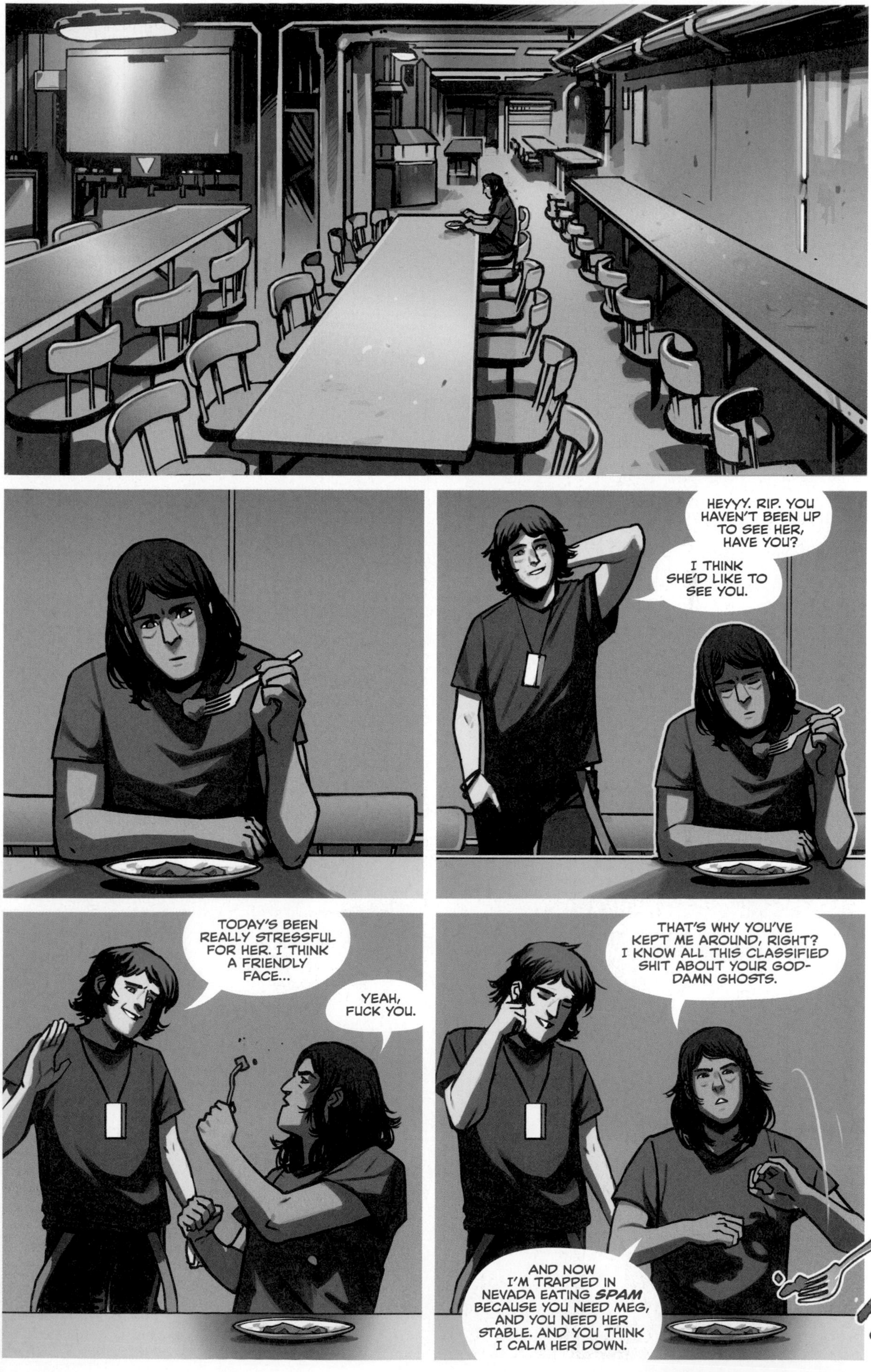
HEYYY. RIP. YOU HAVEN'T BEEN UP TO SEE HER, HAVE YOU?
I THINK SHE'D LIKE TO SEE YOU.
TODAY'S BEEN REALLY STRESSFUL FOR HER. I THINK A FRIENDLY FACE...
YEAH, FUCK YOU.
THAT'S WHY YOU'VE KEPT ME AROUND, RIGHT? I KNOW ALL THIS CLASSIFIED SHIT ABOUT YOUR GOD-DAMN GHOSTS.
AND NOW I'M TRAPPED IN NEVADA EATING SPAM BECAUSE YOU NEED MEG, AND YOU NEED HER STABLE. AND YOU THINK I CALM HER DOWN.

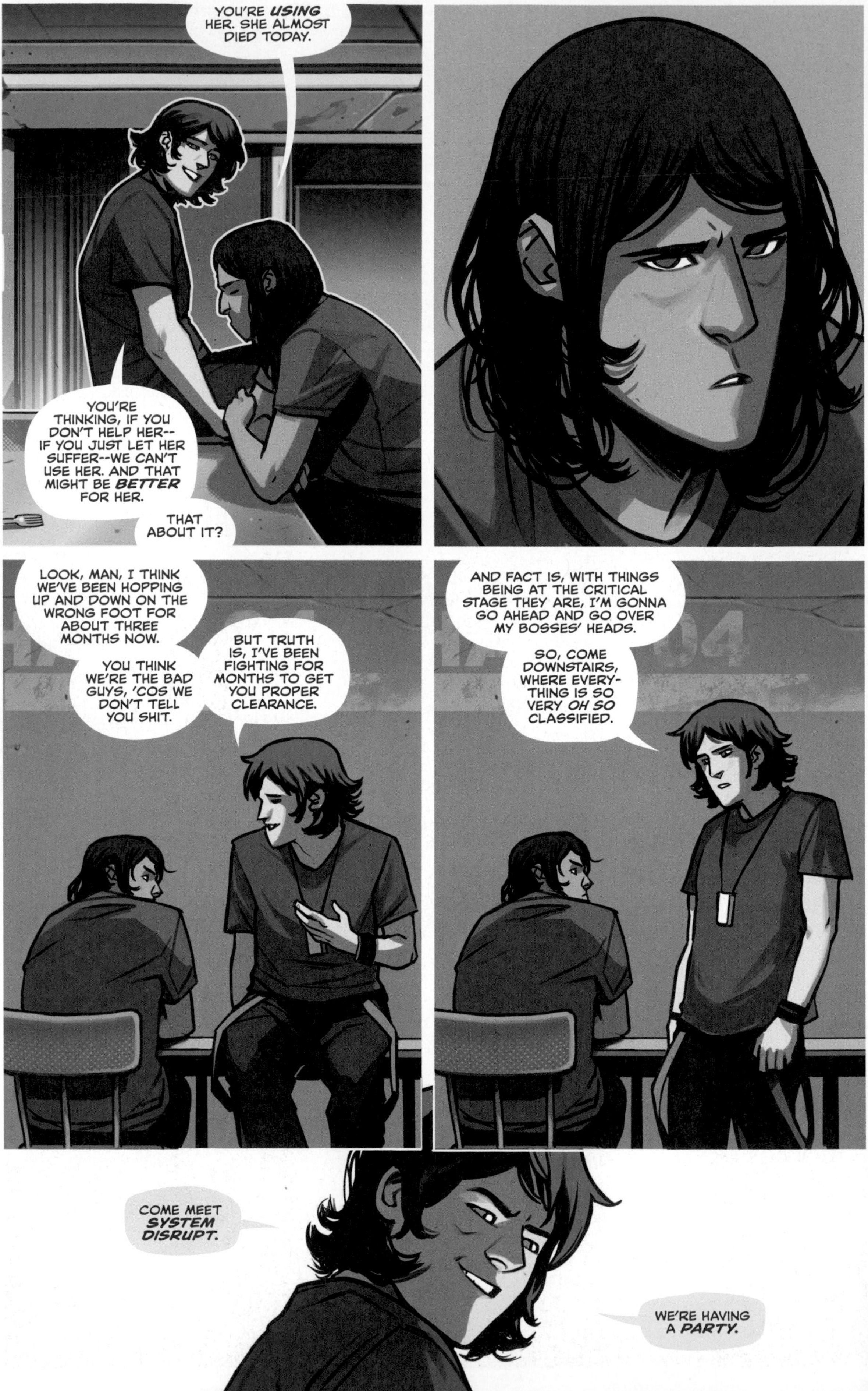
YOU'RE USING HER. SHE ALMOST DIED TODAY.
YOU'RE THINKING, IF YOU DON'T HELP HER--IF YOU JUST LET HER SUFFER--WE CAN'T USE HER. AND THAT MIGHT BE BETTER FOR HER.
THAT ABOUT IT?
LOOK, MAN, I THINK WE'VE BEEN HOPPING UP AND DOWN ON THE WRONG FOOT FOR ABOUT THREE MONTHS NOW.
YOU THINK WE'RE THE BAD GUYS, 'COS WE DON'T TELL YOU SHIT.
BUT TRUTH IS, I'VE BEEN FIGHTING FOR MONTHS TO GET YOU PROPER CLEARANCE.
AND FACT IS, WITH THINGS BEING AT THE CRITICAL STAGE THEY ARE, I'M GONNA GO AHEAD AND GO OVER MY BOSSES' HEADS.
SO, COME DOWNSTAIRS, WHERE EVERYTHING IS SO VERY OH SO CLASSIFIED.
COME MEET SYSTEM DISRUPT.
WE'RE HAVING A PARTY.

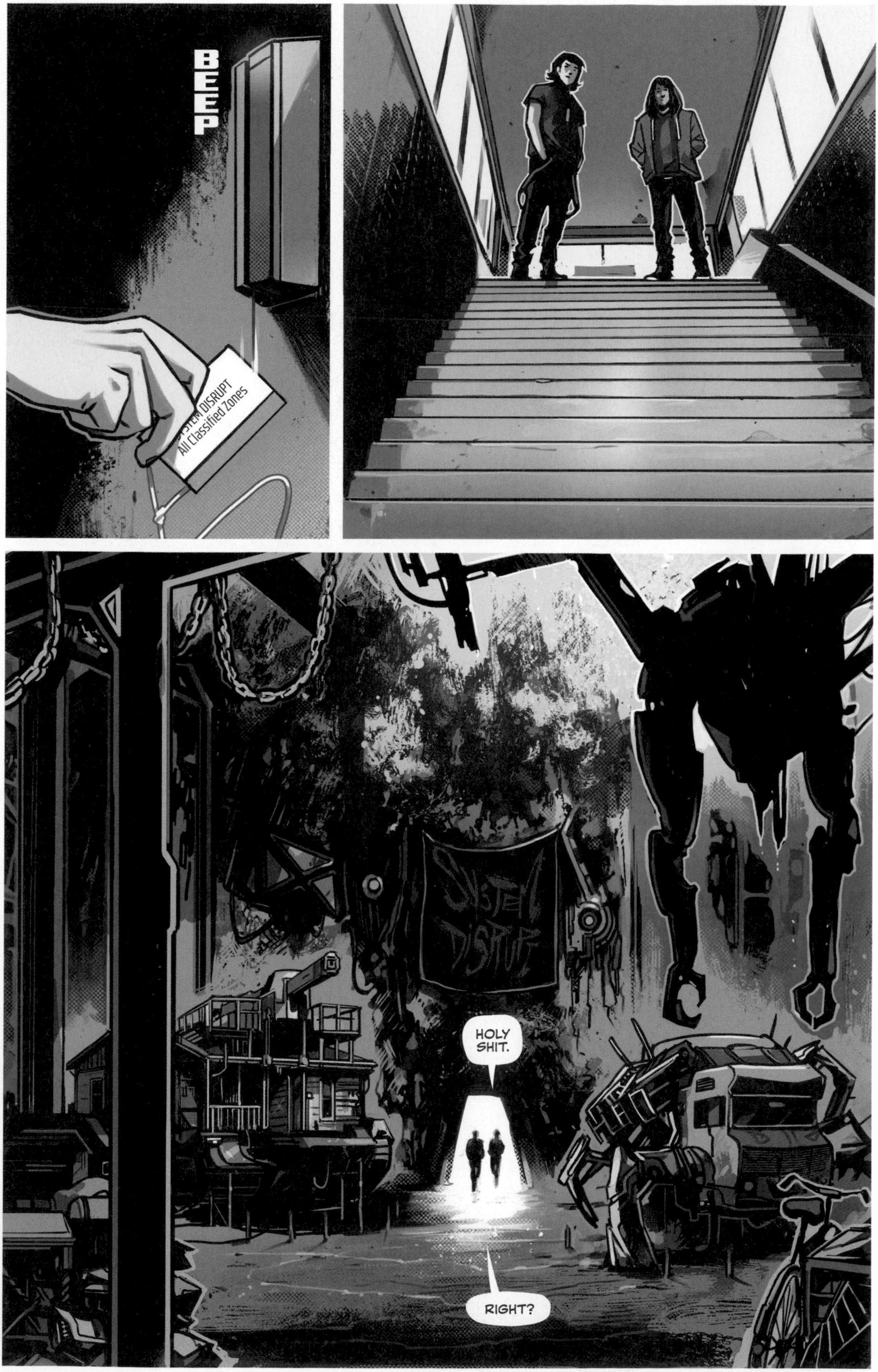
BEEP
SYSTEM DISRUPT
All Classified Zones
HOLY SHIT.
RIGHT?

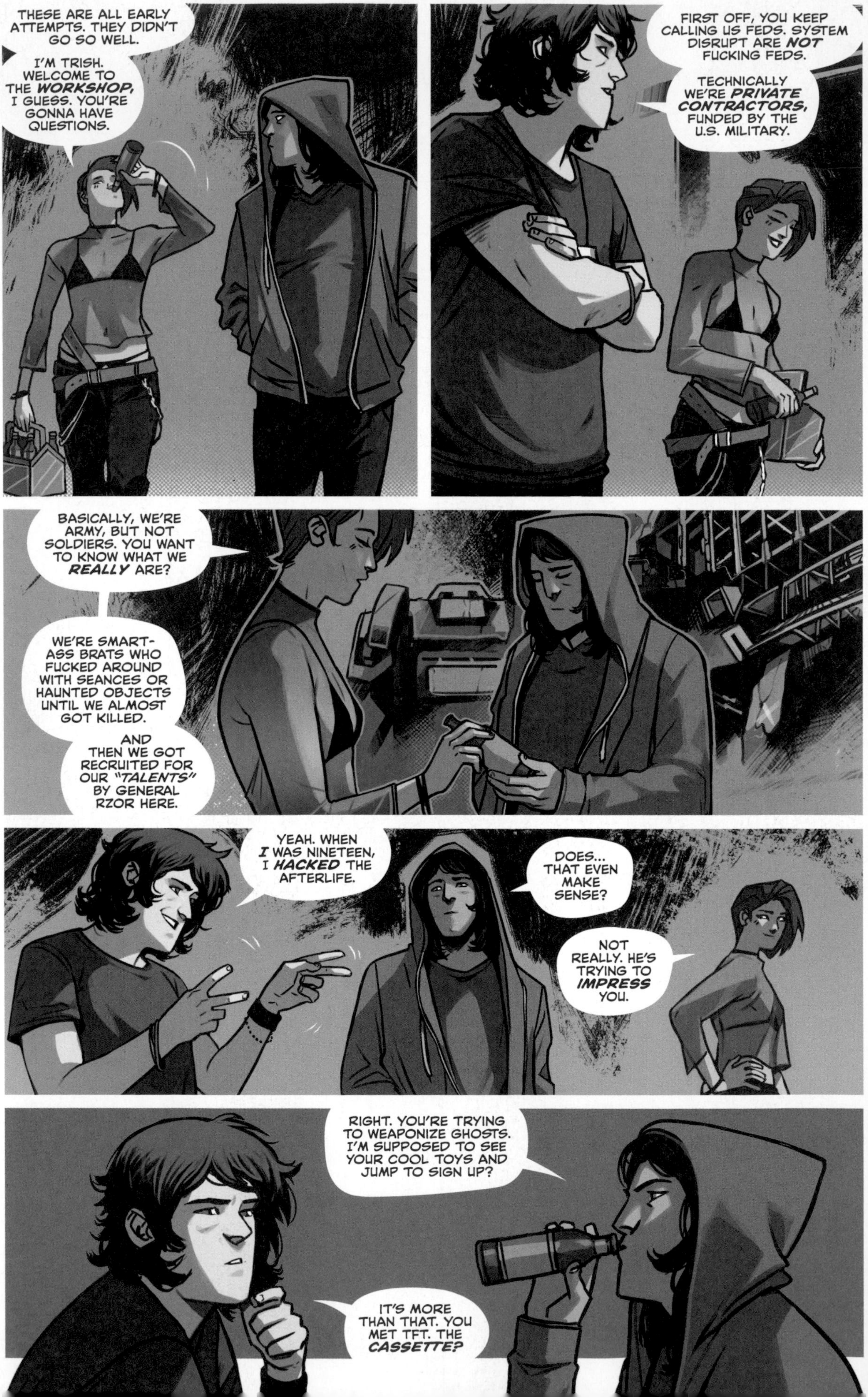
THESE ARE ALL EARLY ATTEMPTS. THEY DIDN'T GO SO WELL.
I'M TRISH. WELCOME TO THE WORKSHOP, I GUESS. YOU'RE GONNA HAVE QUESTIONS.
FIRST OFF, YOU KEEP CALLING US FEDS. SYSTEM DISRUPT ARE NOT FUCKING FEDS.
TECHNICALLY WE'RE PRIVATE CONTRACTORS, FUNDED BY THE U.S. MILITARY.
BASICALLY, WE'RE ARMY, BUT NOT SOLDIERS. YOU WANT TO KNOW WHAT WE REALLY ARE?
WE'RE SMART-ASS BRATS WHO FUCKED AROUND WITH SEANCES OR HAUNTED OBJECTS UNTIL WE ALMOST GOT KILLED.
AND THEN WE GOT RECRUITED FOR OUR "TALENTS" BY GENERAL RZOR HERE.
YEAH. WHEN I WAS NINETEEN, I HACKED THE AFTERLIFE.
DOES... THAT EVEN MAKE SENSE?
NOT REALLY. HE'S TRYING TO IMPRESS YOU.
RIGHT. YOU'RE TRYING TO WEAPONIZE GHOSTS. I'M SUPPOSED TO SEE YOUR COOL TOYS AND JUMP TO SIGN UP?
IT'S MORE THAN THAT. YOU MET TFT. THE CASSETTE?

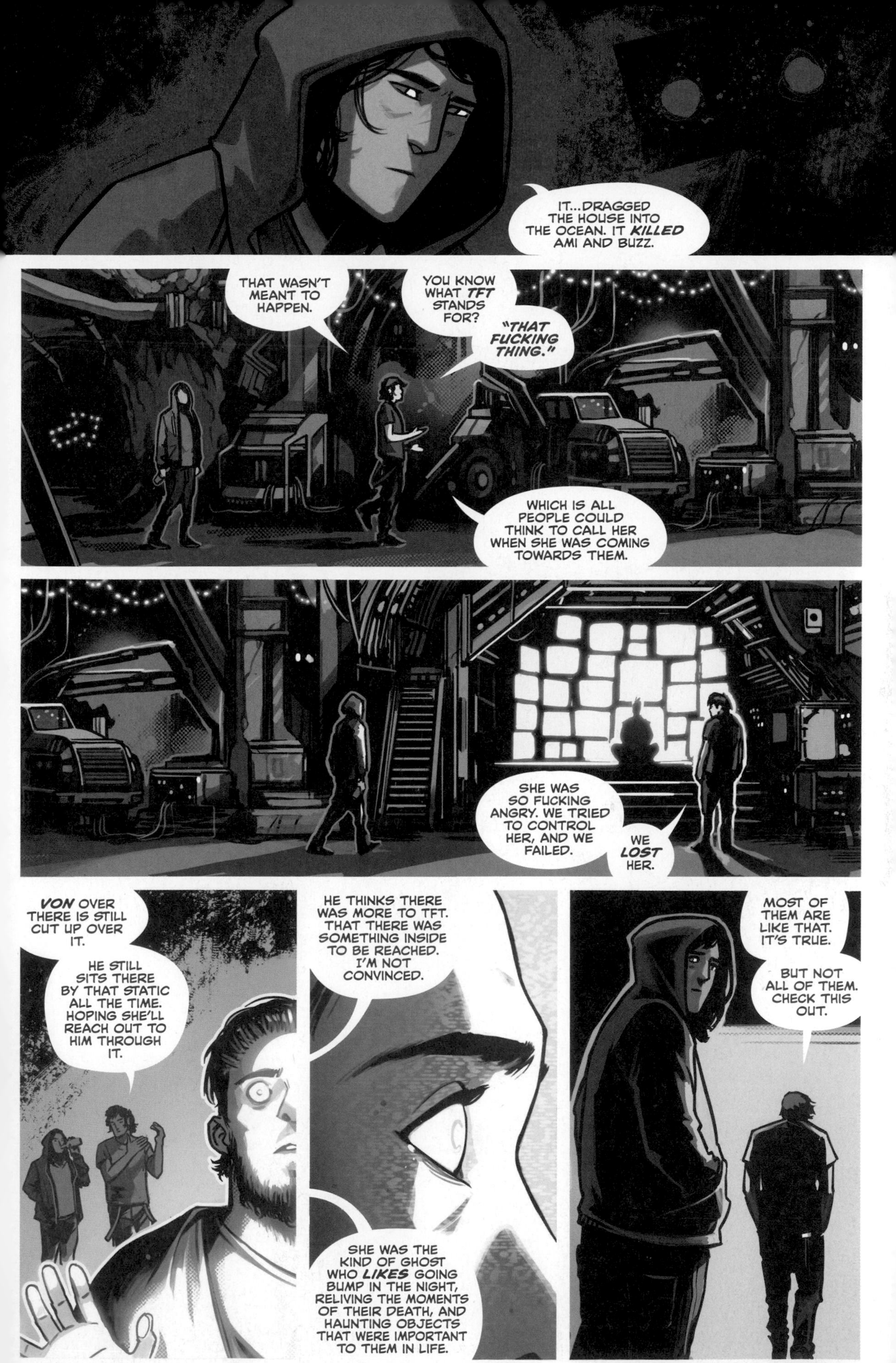
IT...DRAGGED THE HOUSE INTO THE OCEAN. IT *KILLED* AMI AND BUZZ.
THAT WASN'T MEANT TO HAPPEN.
YOU KNOW WHAT *TFT* STANDS FOR?
"THAT FUCKING THING."
WHICH IS ALL PEOPLE COULD THINK TO CALL HER WHEN SHE WAS COMING TOWARDS THEM.
SHE WAS SO FUCKING ANGRY. WE TRIED TO CONTROL HER, AND WE FAILED.
WE *LOST* HER.
VON OVER THERE IS STILL CUT UP OVER IT.
HE STILL SITS THERE BY THAT STATIC ALL THE TIME. HOPING SHE'LL REACH OUT TO HIM THROUGH IT.
HE THINKS THERE WAS MORE TO TFT. THAT THERE WAS SOMETHING INSIDE TO BE REACHED. I'M NOT CONVINCED.
SHE WAS THE KIND OF GHOST WHO *LIKES* GOING BUMP IN THE NIGHT, RELIVING THE MOMENTS OF THEIR DEATH, AND HAUNTING OBJECTS THAT WERE IMPORTANT TO THEM IN LIFE.
MOST OF THEM ARE LIKE THAT. IT'S TRUE.
BUT NOT ALL OF THEM. CHECK THIS OUT.

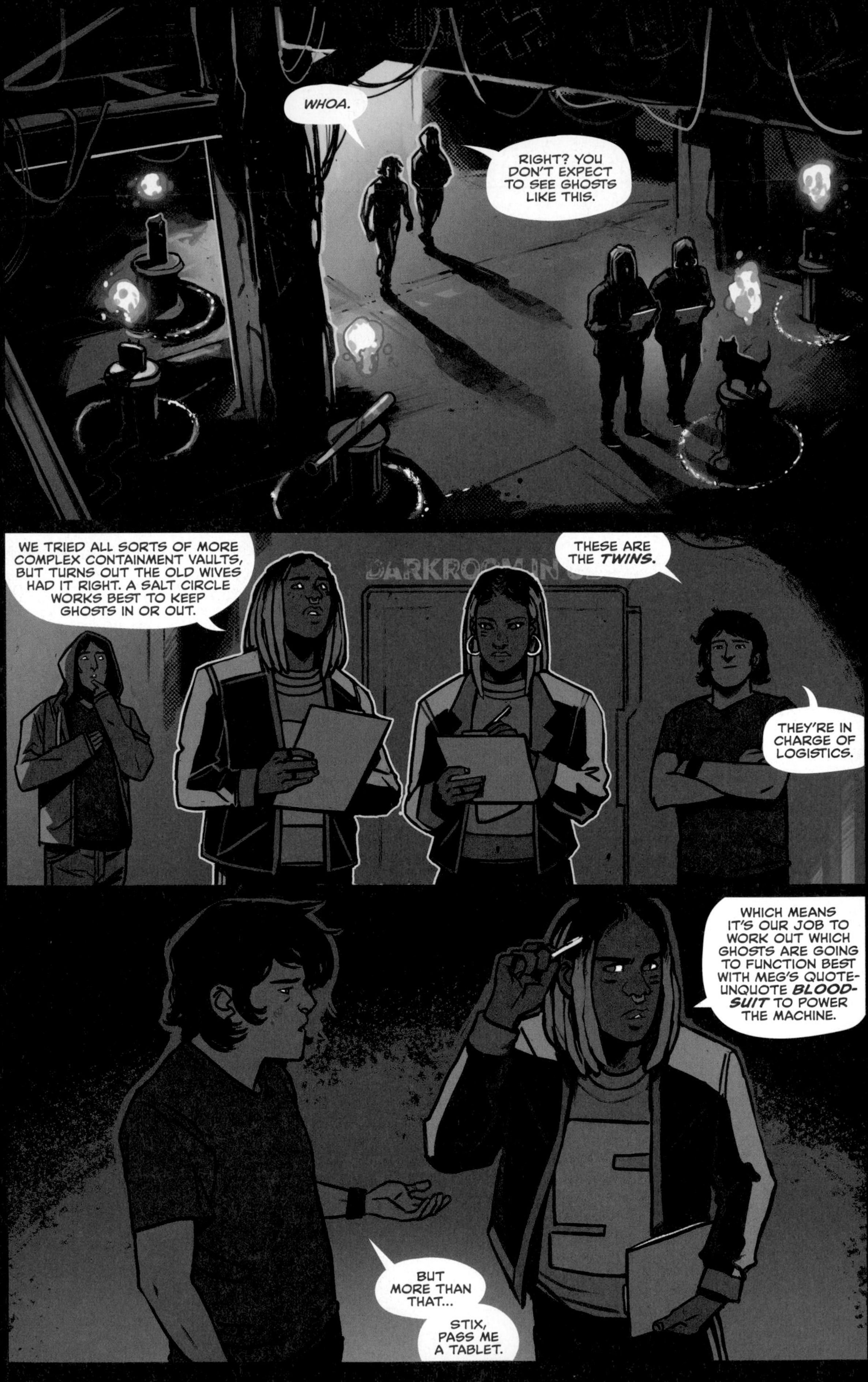
WHOA.
RIGHT? YOU DON'T EXPECT TO SEE GHOSTS LIKE THIS.
WE TRIED ALL SORTS OF MORE COMPLEX CONTAINMENT VAULTS, BUT TURNS OUT THE OLD WIVES HAD IT RIGHT. A SALT CIRCLE WORKS BEST TO KEEP GHOSTS IN OR OUT.
THESE ARE THE *TWINS.*
THEY'RE IN CHARGE OF LOGISTICS.
WHICH MEANS IT'S OUR JOB TO WORK OUT WHICH GHOSTS ARE GOING TO FUNCTION BEST WITH MEG'S QUOTE-UNQUOTE ***BLOOD-SUIT*** TO POWER THE MACHINE.
BUT MORE THAN THAT...
STIX, PASS ME A TABLET.

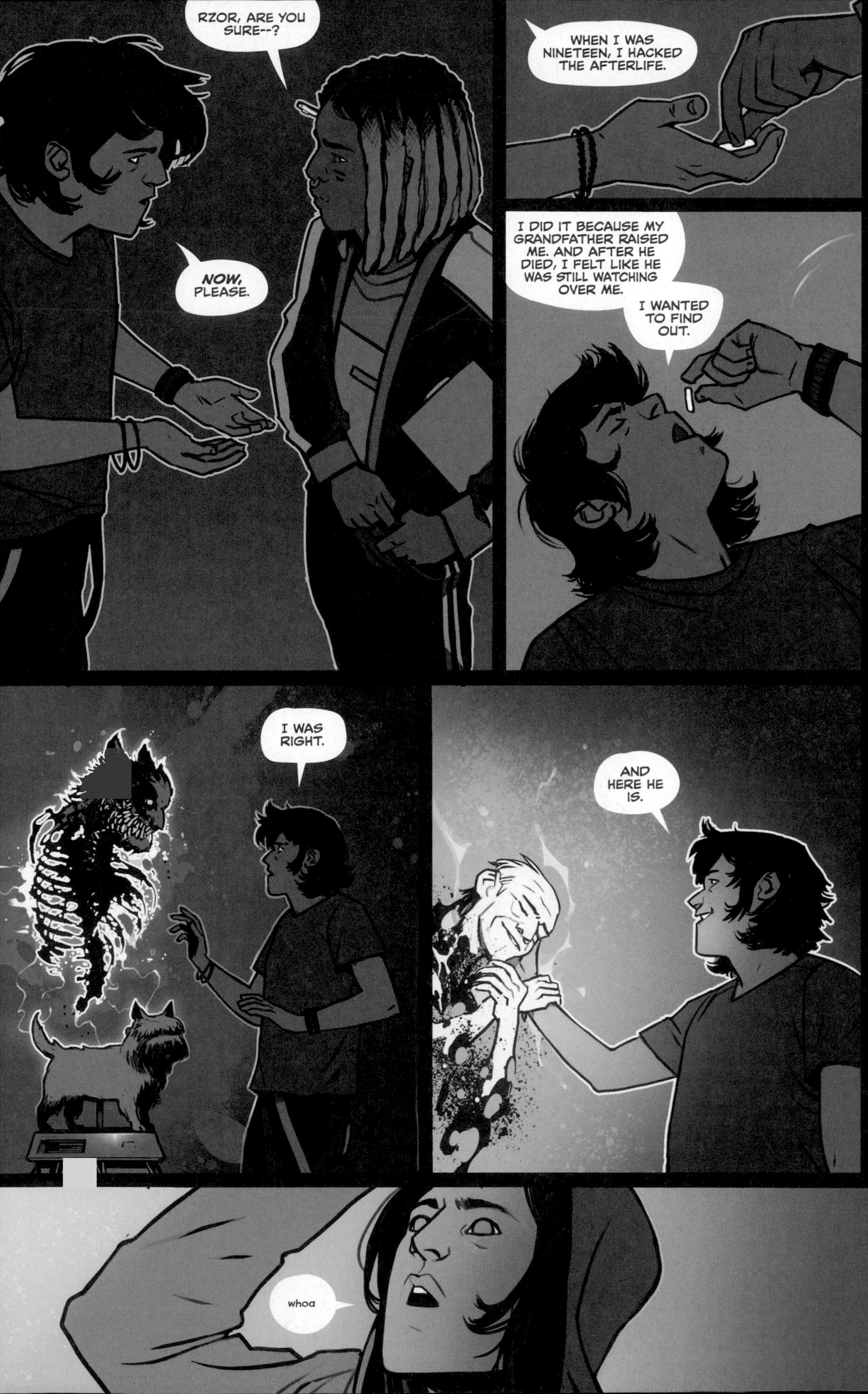
RZOR, ARE YOU SURE--?
NOW, PLEASE.
WHEN I WAS NINETEEN, I HACKED THE AFTERLIFE.
I DID IT BECAUSE MY GRANDFATHER RAISED ME. AND AFTER HE DIED, I FELT LIKE HE WAS STILL WATCHING OVER ME.
I WANTED TO FIND OUT.
I WAS RIGHT.
AND HERE HE IS.
whoa

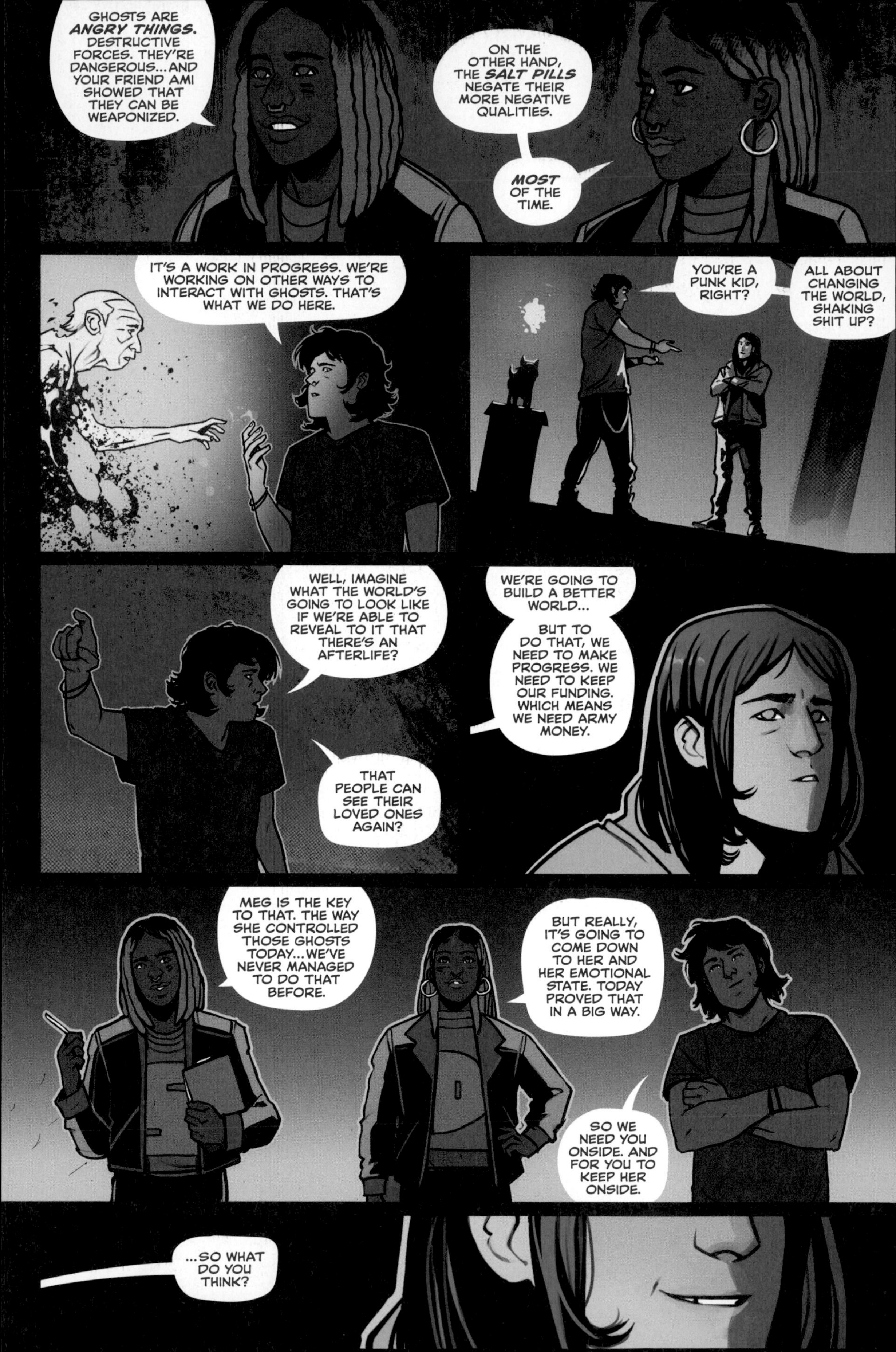
GHOSTS ARE ANGRY THINGS. DESTRUCTIVE FORCES. THEY'RE DANGEROUS...AND YOUR FRIEND AMI SHOWED THAT THEY CAN BE WEAPONIZED.
ON THE OTHER HAND, THE SALT PILLS NEGATE THEIR MORE NEGATIVE QUALITIES.
MOST OF THE TIME.
IT'S A WORK IN PROGRESS. WE'RE WORKING ON OTHER WAYS TO INTERACT WITH GHOSTS. THAT'S WHAT WE DO HERE.
YOU'RE A PUNK KID, RIGHT?
ALL ABOUT CHANGING THE WORLD, SHAKING SHIT UP?
WELL, IMAGINE WHAT THE WORLD'S GOING TO LOOK LIKE IF WE'RE ABLE TO REVEAL TO IT THAT THERE'S AN AFTERLIFE?
THAT PEOPLE CAN SEE THEIR LOVED ONES AGAIN?
WE'RE GOING TO BUILD A BETTER WORLD...
BUT TO DO THAT, WE NEED TO MAKE PROGRESS. WE NEED TO KEEP OUR FUNDING. WHICH MEANS WE NEED ARMY MONEY.
MEG IS THE KEY TO THAT. THE WAY SHE CONTROLLED THOSE GHOSTS TODAY...WE'VE NEVER MANAGED TO DO THAT BEFORE.
BUT REALLY, IT'S GOING TO COME DOWN TO HER AND HER EMOTIONAL STATE. TODAY PROVED THAT IN A BIG WAY.
SO WE NEED YOU ONSIDE. AND FOR YOU TO KEEP HER ONSIDE.
...SO WHAT DO YOU THINK?

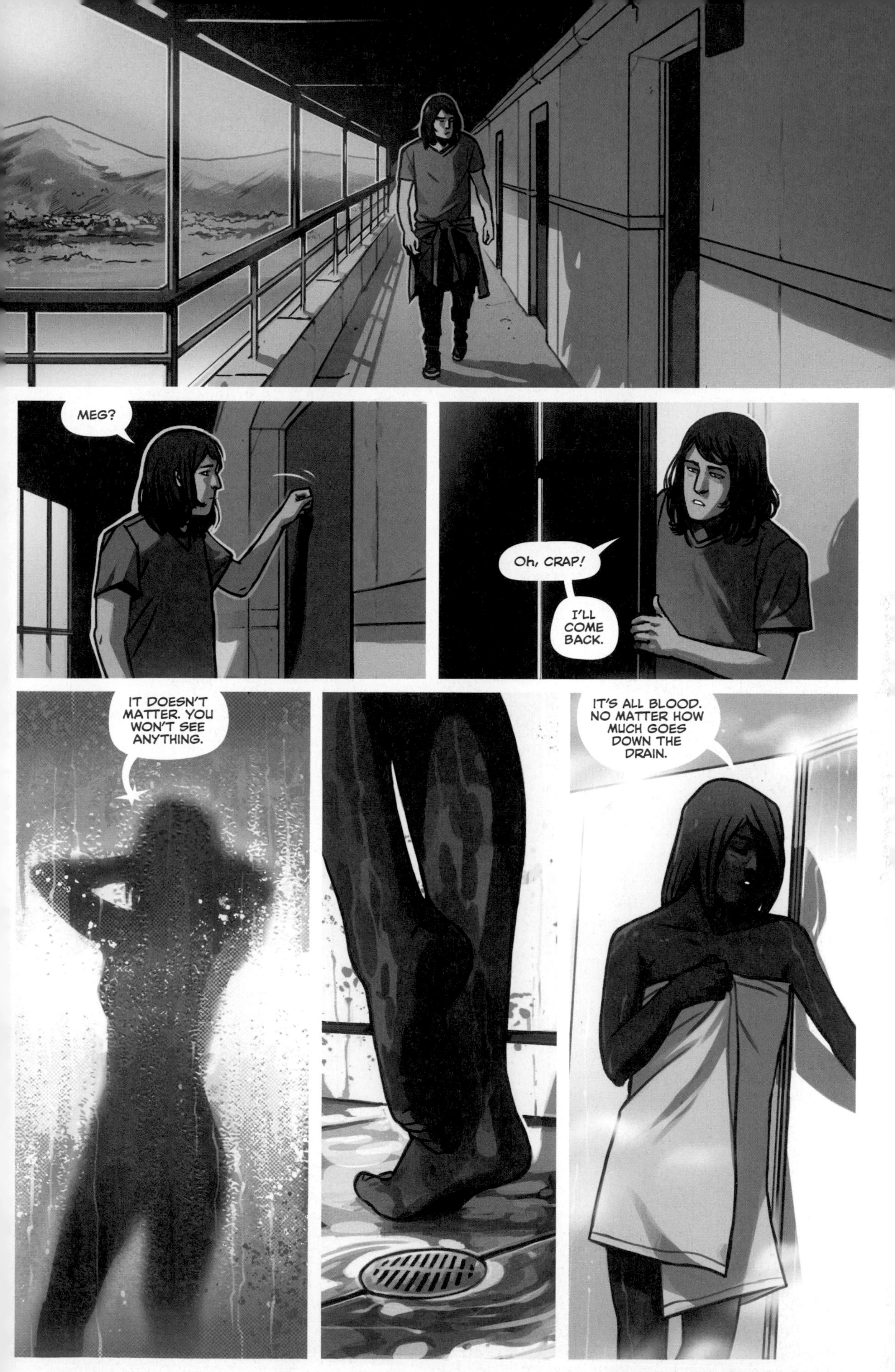
MEG?
Oh, CRAP!
I'LL COME BACK.
IT DOESN'T MATTER. YOU WON'T SEE ANYTHING.
IT'S ALL BLOOD. NO MATTER HOW MUCH GOES DOWN THE DRAIN.

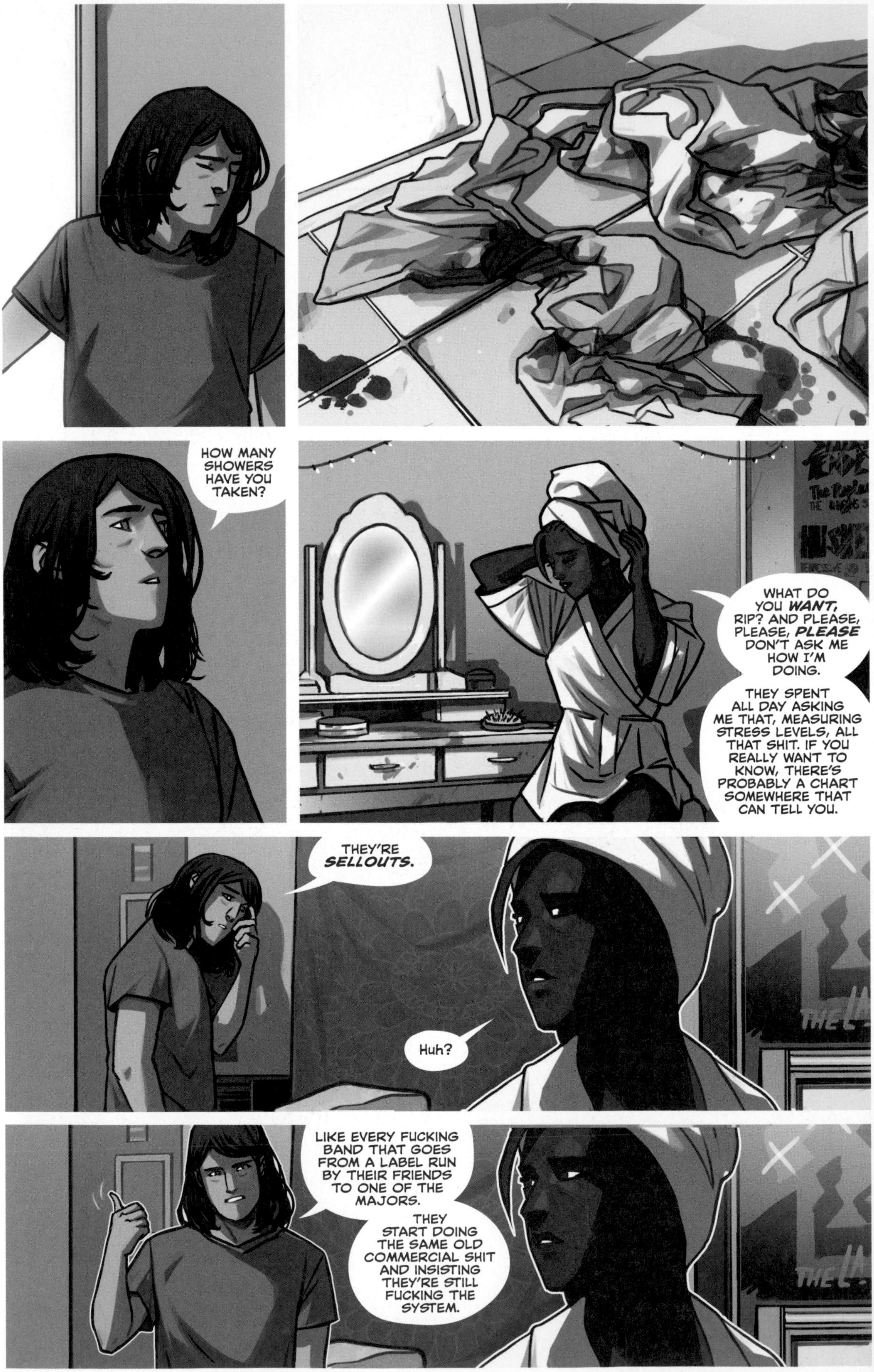
HOW MANY SHOWERS HAVE YOU TAKEN?
WHAT DO YOU *WANT,* RIP? AND PLEASE, PLEASE, *PLEASE* DON'T ASK ME HOW I'M DOING.
THEY SPENT ALL DAY ASKING ME THAT, MEASURING STRESS LEVELS, ALL THAT SHIT. IF YOU REALLY WANT TO KNOW, THERE'S PROBABLY A CHART SOMEWHERE THAT CAN TELL YOU.
THEY'RE *SELLOUTS.*
Huh?
LIKE EVERY FUCKING BAND THAT GOES FROM A LABEL RUN BY THEIR FRIENDS TO ONE OF THE MAJORS.
THEY START DOING THE SAME OLD COMMERCIAL SHIT AND INSISTING THEY'RE STILL FUCKING THE SYSTEM.

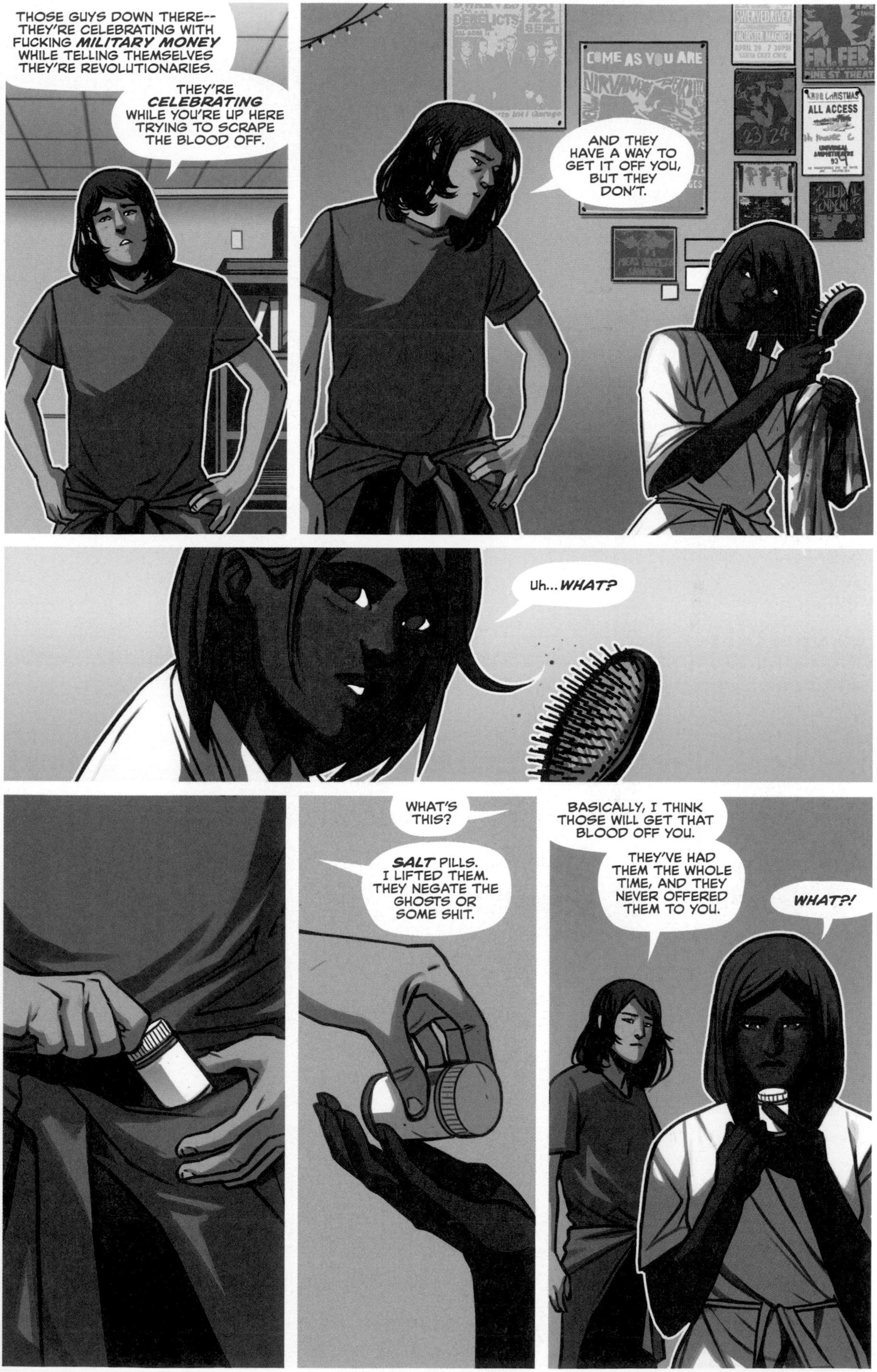
THOSE GUYS DOWN THERE-- THEY'RE CELEBRATING WITH FUCKING ***MILITARY MONEY*** WHILE TELLING THEMSELVES THEY'RE REVOLUTIONARIES.
THEY'RE ***CELEBRATING*** WHILE YOU'RE UP HERE TRYING TO SCRAPE THE BLOOD OFF.
DERELICTS
SWERVEDRIVER
COME AS YOU ARE
FRI. FEB.
ALL ACCESS
AND THEY HAVE A WAY TO GET IT OFF YOU, BUT THEY DON'T.
Uh... ***WHAT?***
WHAT'S THIS?
SALT PILLS. I LIFTED THEM. THEY NEGATE THE GHOSTS OR SOME SHIT.
BASICALLY, I THINK THOSE WILL GET THAT BLOOD OFF YOU.
THEY'VE HAD THEM THE WHOLE TIME, AND THEY NEVER OFFERED THEM TO YOU.
WHAT?!

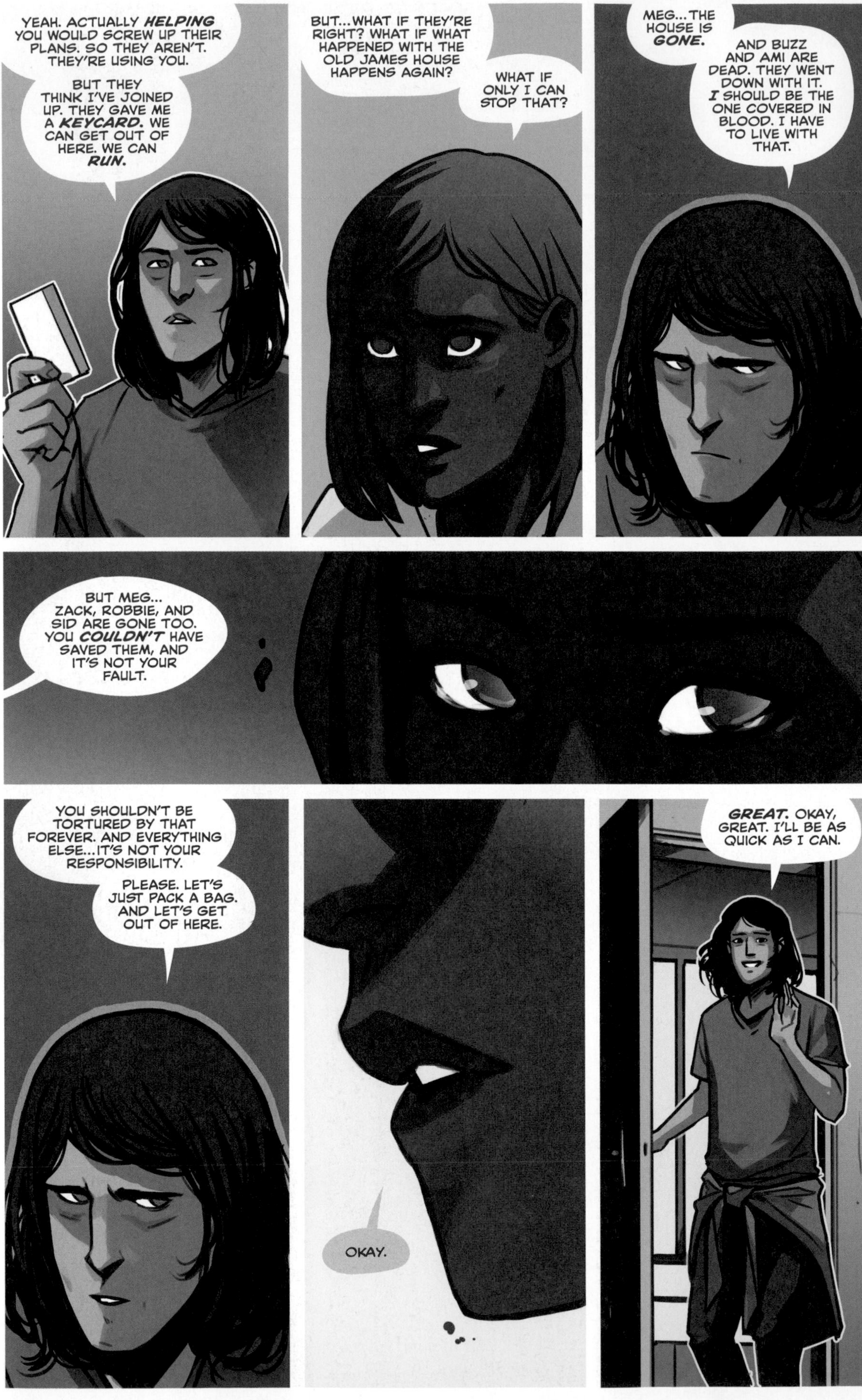
YEAH. ACTUALLY HELPING YOU WOULD SCREW UP THEIR PLANS. SO THEY AREN'T. THEY'RE USING YOU.
BUT THEY THINK I'VE JOINED UP. THEY GAVE ME A KEYCARD. WE CAN GET OUT OF HERE. WE CAN RUN.
BUT...WHAT IF THEY'RE RIGHT? WHAT IF WHAT HAPPENED WITH THE OLD JAMES HOUSE HAPPENS AGAIN?
WHAT IF ONLY I CAN STOP THAT?
MEG...THE HOUSE IS GONE.
AND BUZZ AND AMI ARE DEAD. THEY WENT DOWN WITH IT. I SHOULD BE THE ONE COVERED IN BLOOD. I HAVE TO LIVE WITH THAT.
BUT MEG... ZACK, ROBBIE, AND SID ARE GONE TOO. YOU COULDN'T HAVE SAVED THEM, AND IT'S NOT YOUR FAULT.
YOU SHOULDN'T BE TORTURED BY THAT FOREVER. AND EVERYTHING ELSE...IT'S NOT YOUR RESPONSIBILITY.
PLEASE. LET'S JUST PACK A BAG. AND LET'S GET OUT OF HERE.
OKAY.
GREAT. OKAY, GREAT. I'LL BE AS QUICK AS I CAN.

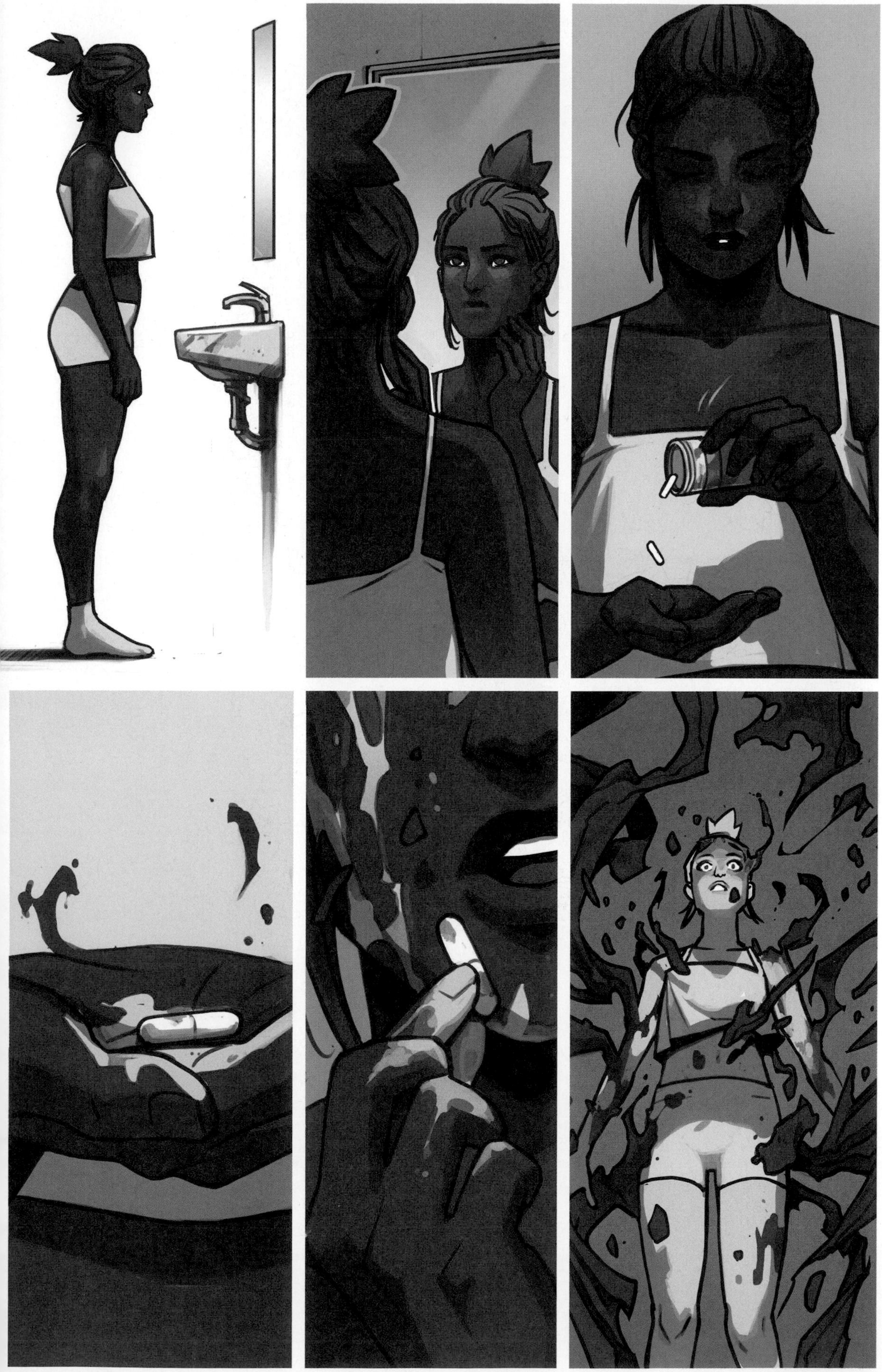

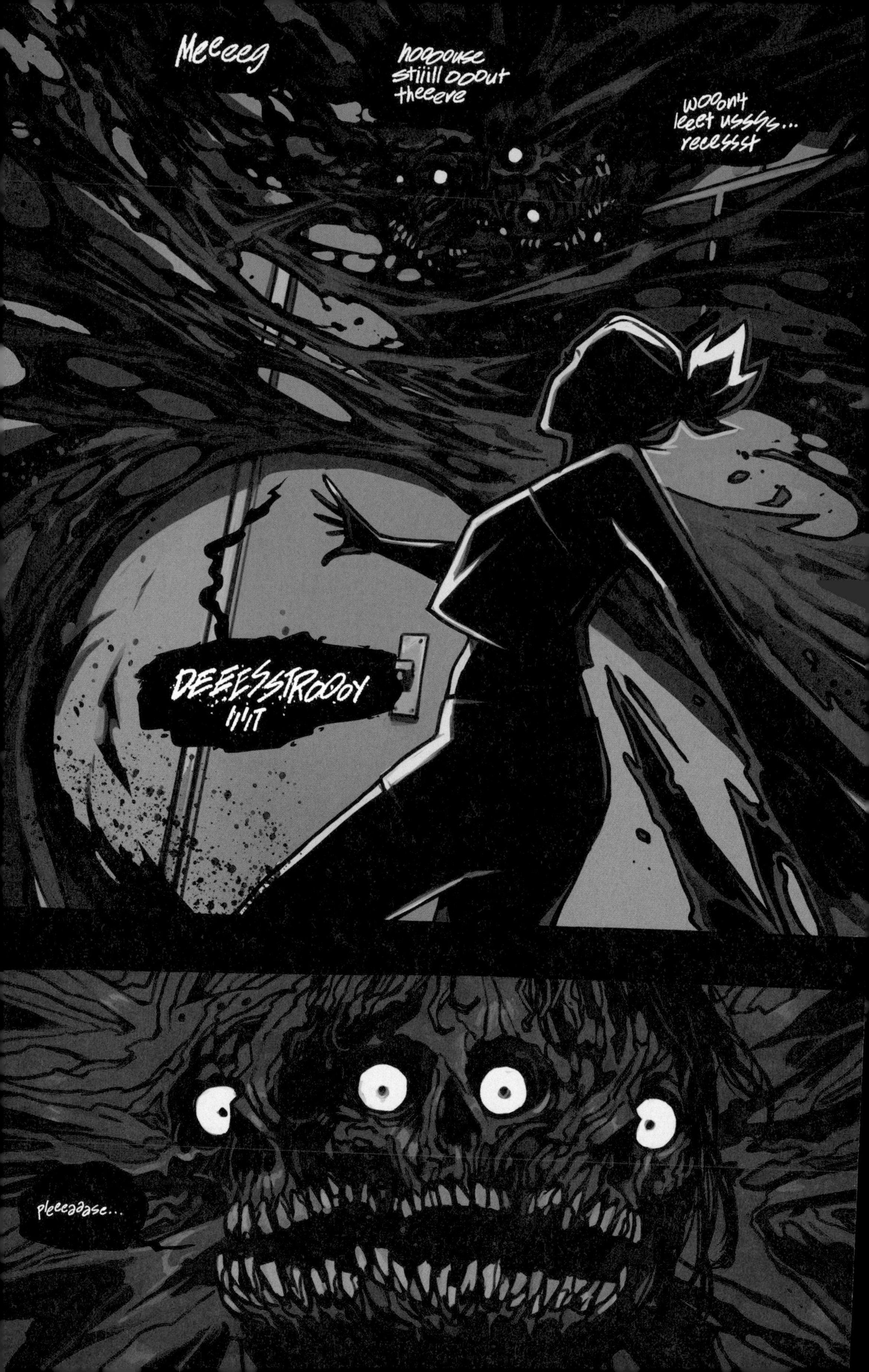
Meeeeg
hoooouse stiiiill ooout theeere
wooon't leeet ussss... reeessst
DEEESSTROOOY IIIT
pleeeaaase...

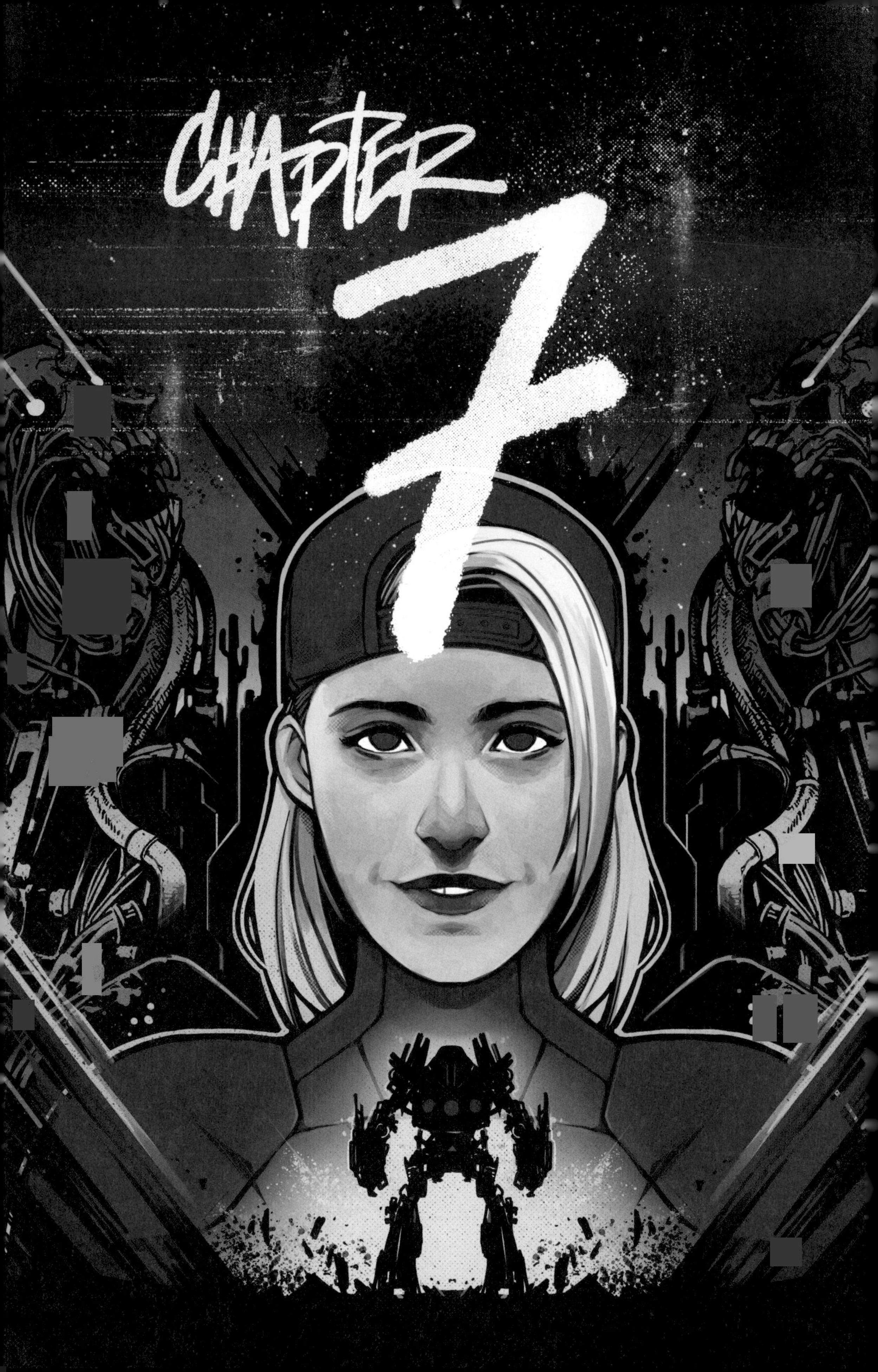
CHAPTER
7

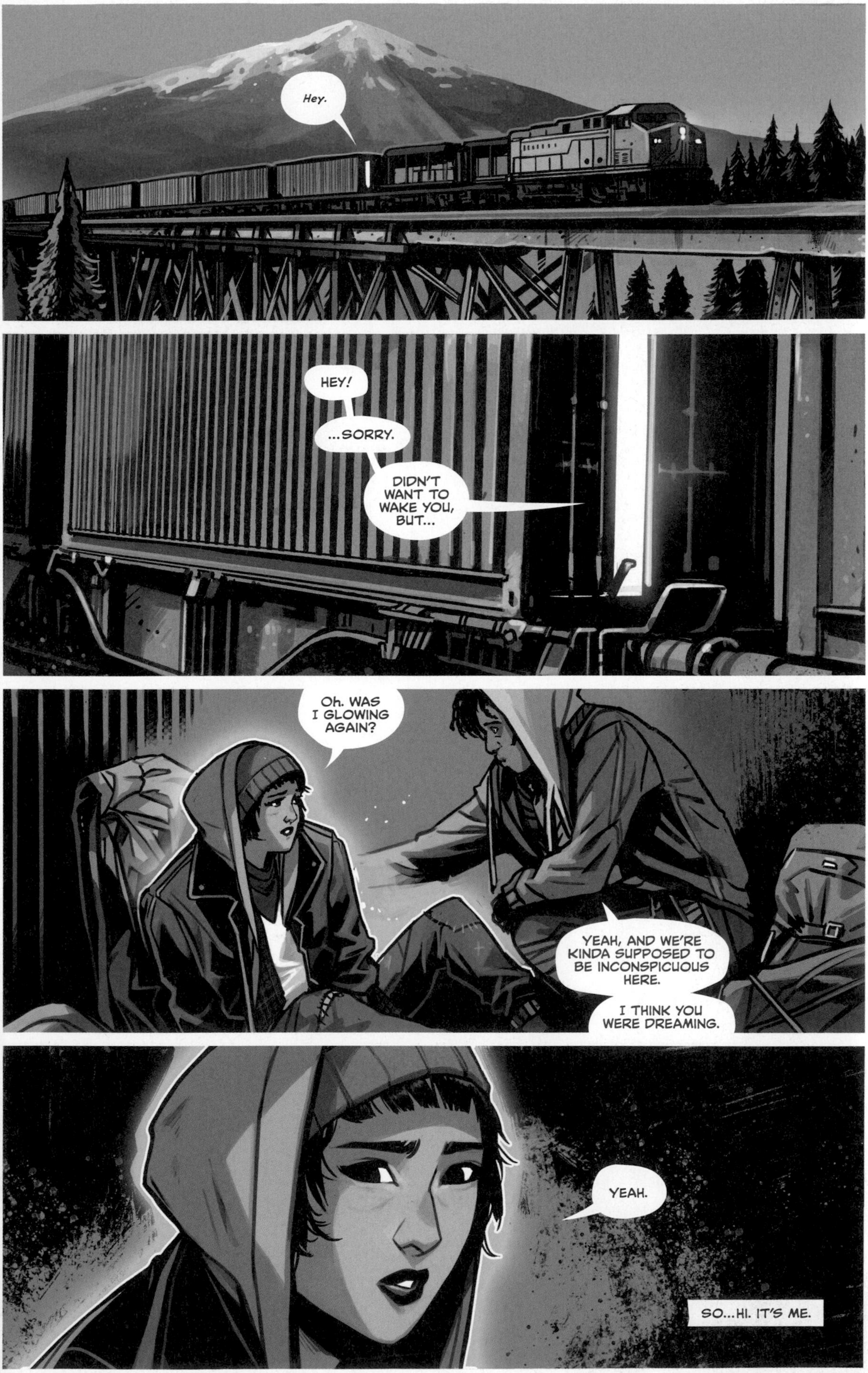
Hey.
HEY!
...SORRY.
DIDN'T WANT TO WAKE YOU, BUT...
Oh. WAS I GLOWING AGAIN?
YEAH, AND WE'RE KINDA SUPPOSED TO BE INCONSPICUOUS HERE.
I THINK YOU WERE DREAMING.
YEAH.
SO...HI. IT'S ME.

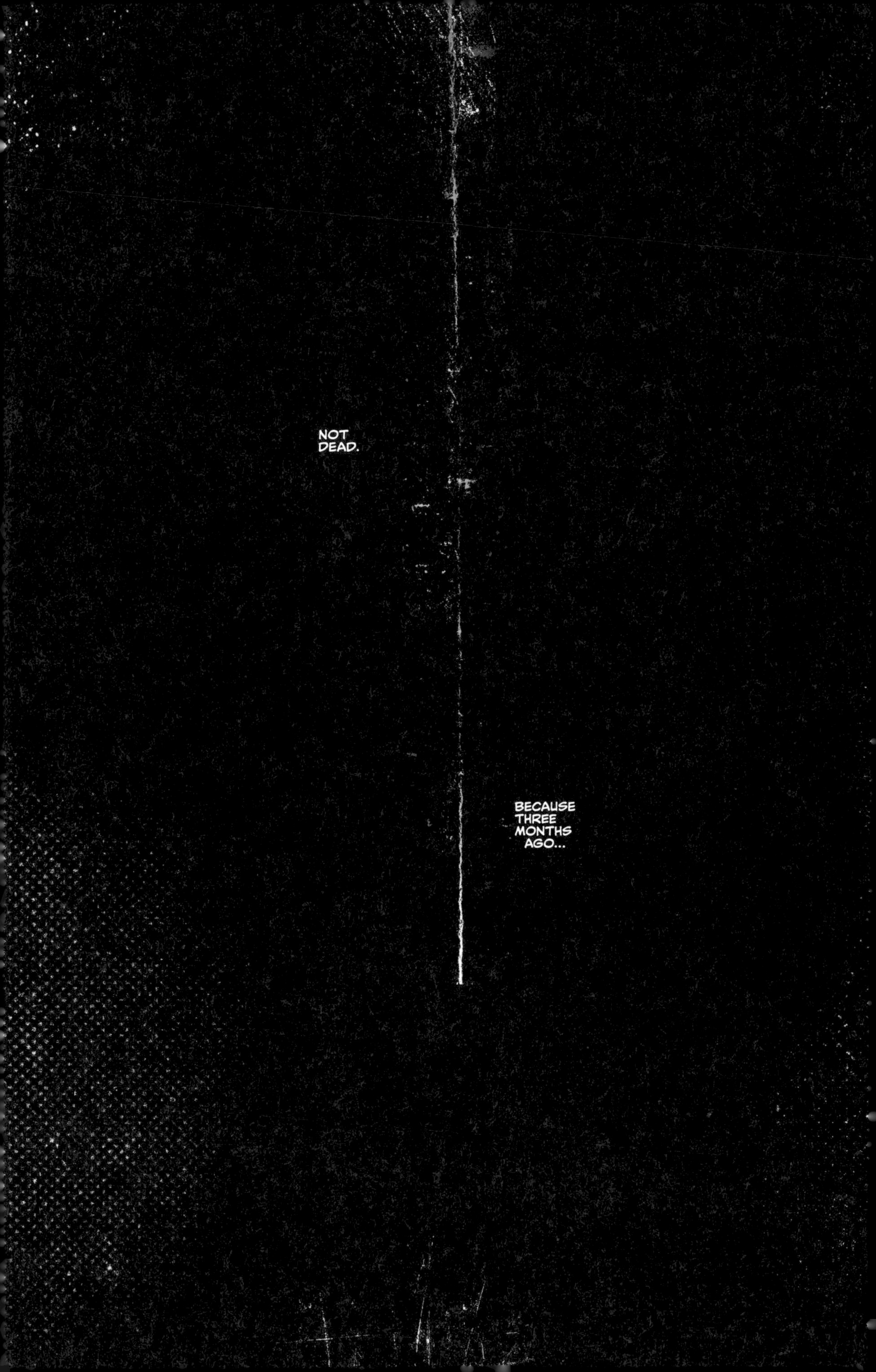
NOT DEAD.
BECAUSE THREE MONTHS AGO...

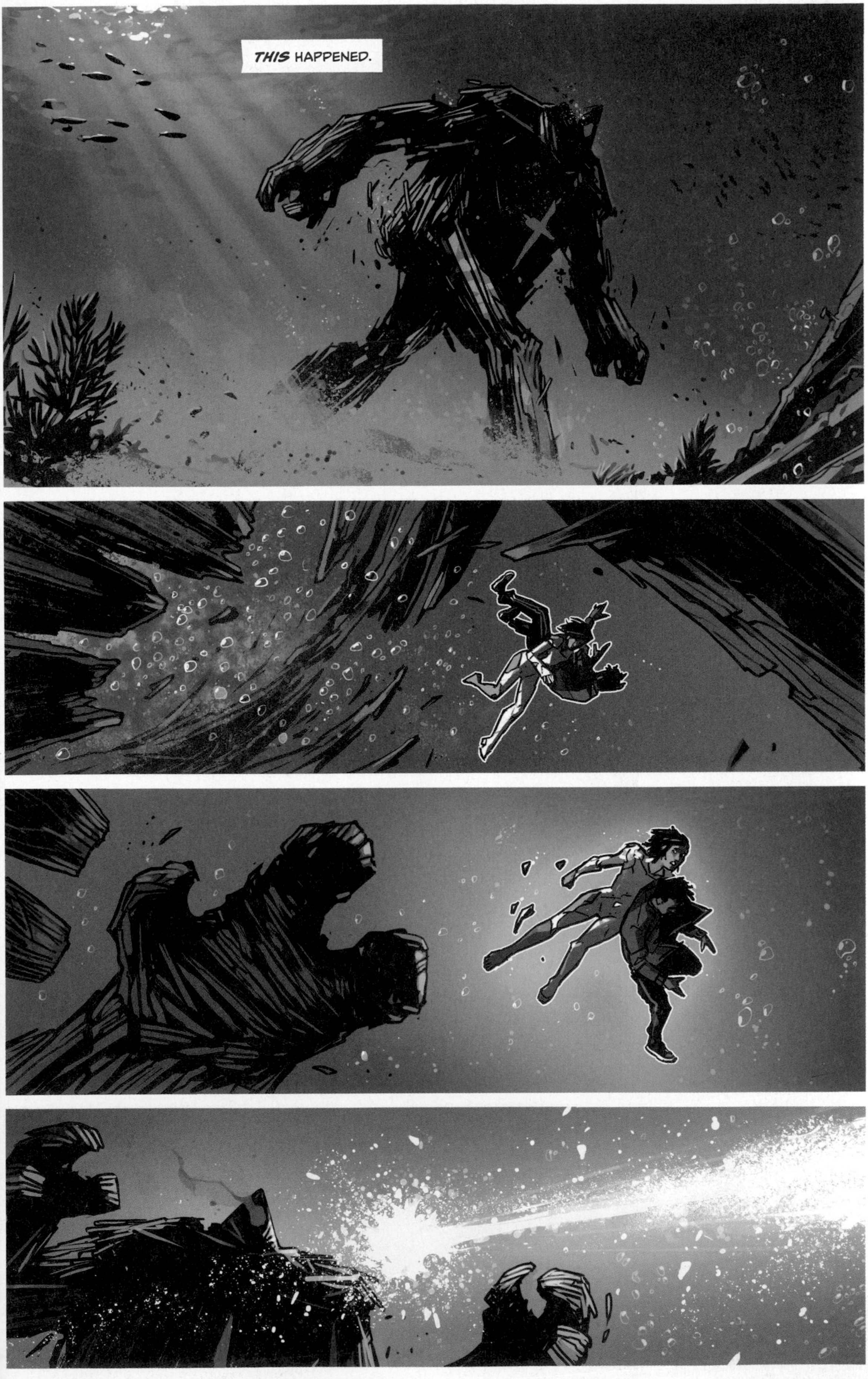
THIS HAPPENED.

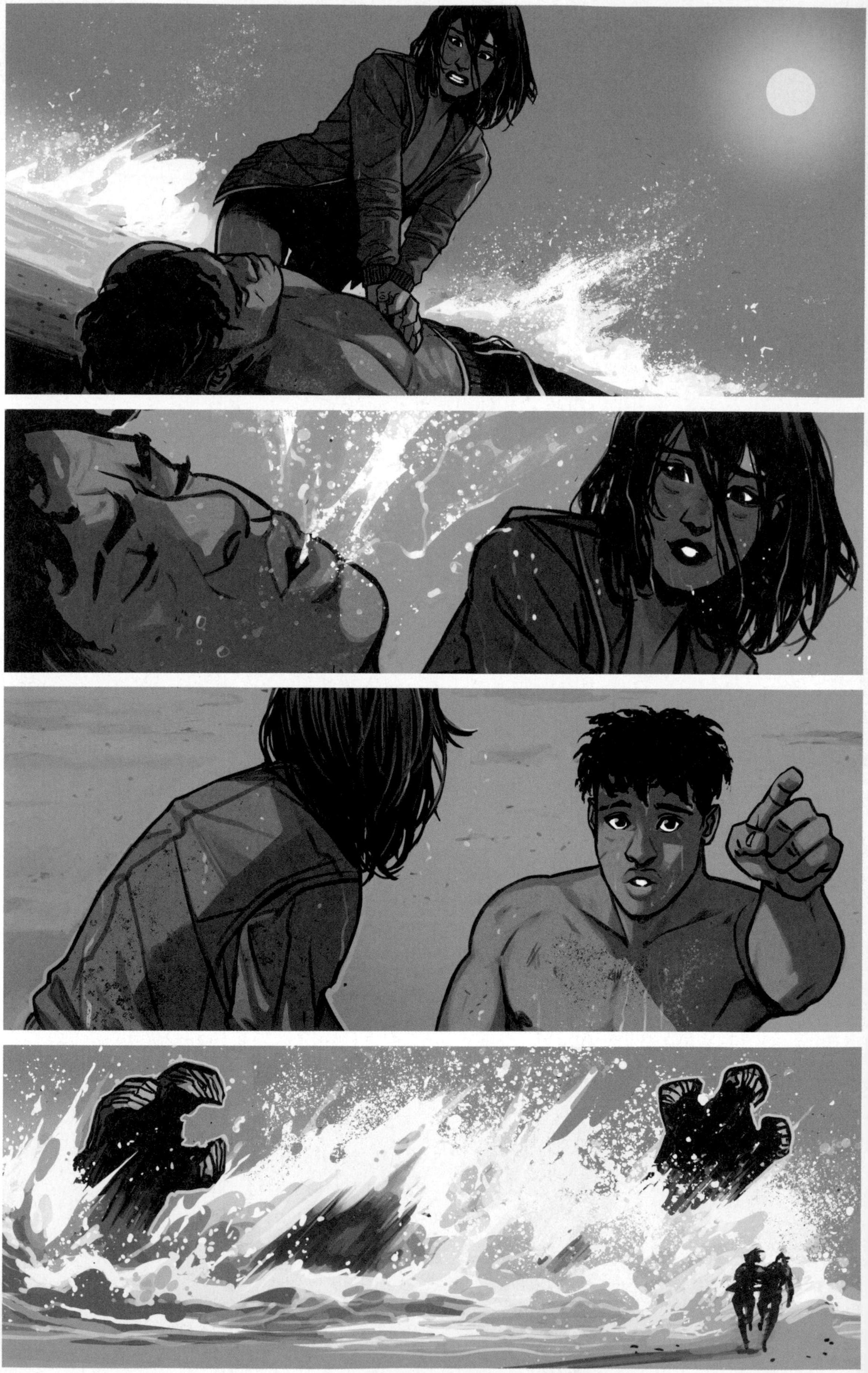

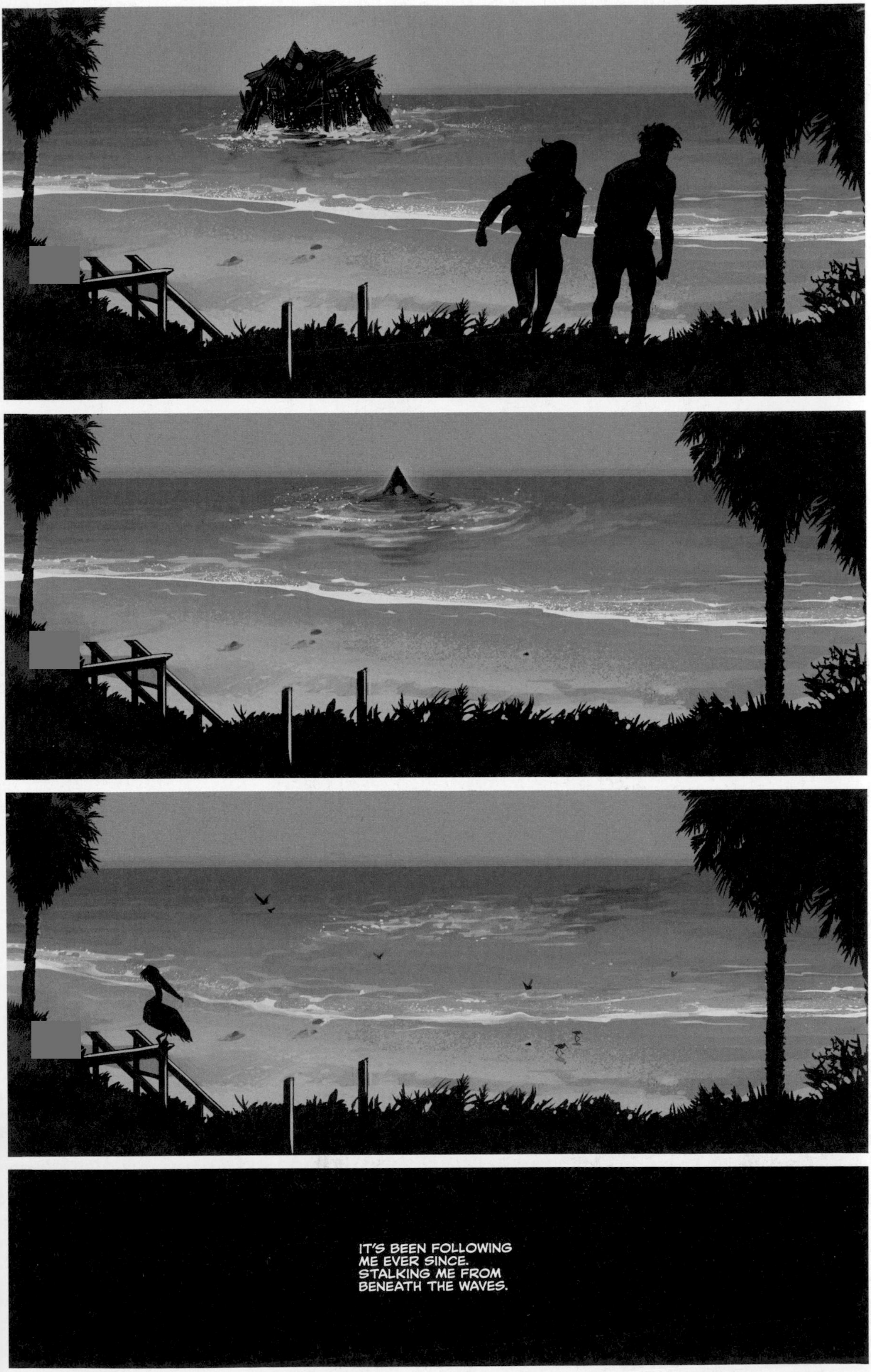
IT'S BEEN FOLLOWING ME EVER SINCE. STALKING ME FROM BENEATH THE WAVES.

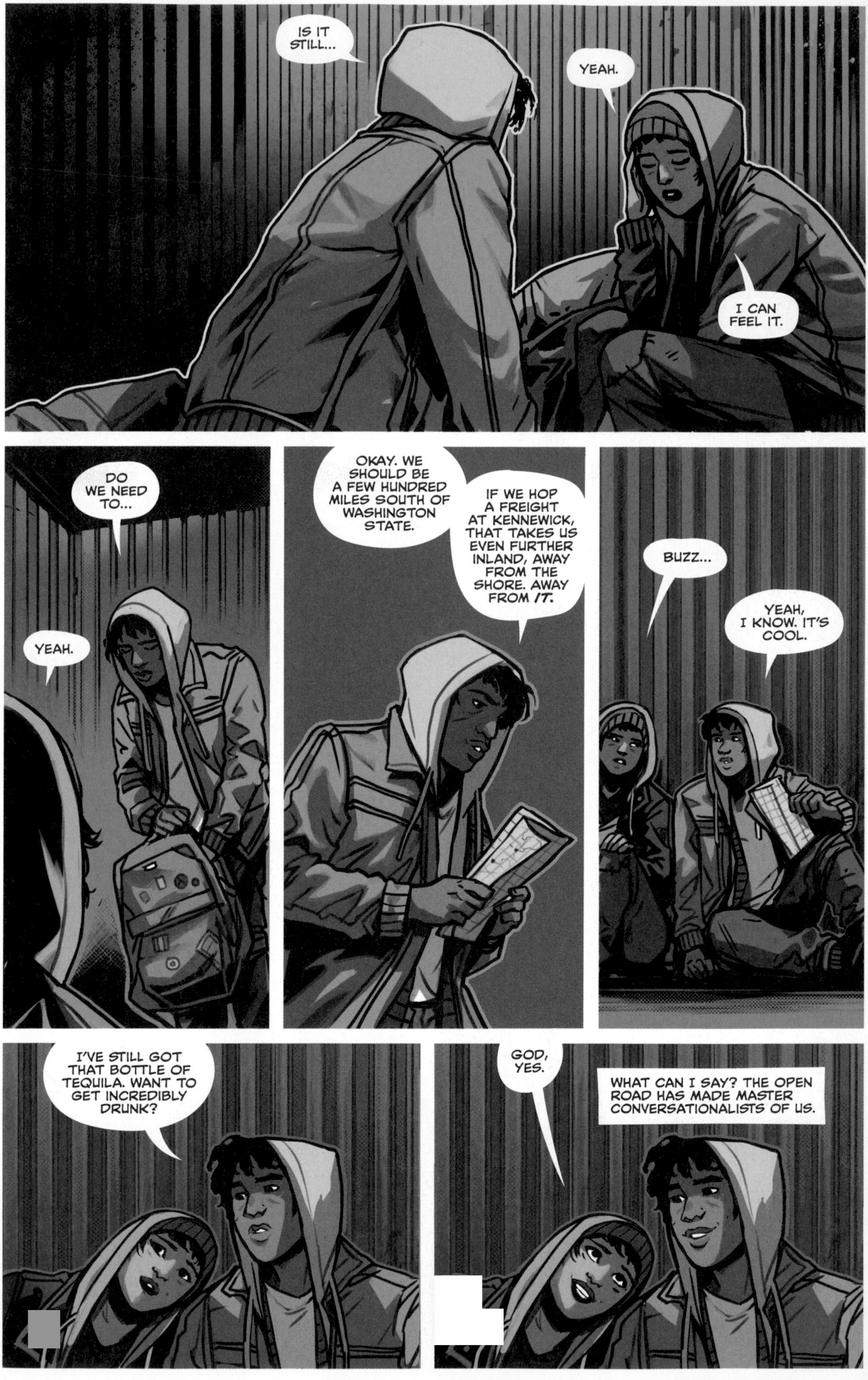
IS IT STILL...
YEAH.
I CAN FEEL IT.
DO WE NEED TO...
YEAH.
OKAY. WE SHOULD BE A FEW HUNDRED MILES SOUTH OF WASHINGTON STATE.
IF WE HOP A FREIGHT AT KENNEWICK, THAT TAKES US EVEN FURTHER INLAND, AWAY FROM THE SHORE. AWAY FROM IT.
BUZZ...
YEAH, I KNOW. IT'S COOL.
I'VE STILL GOT THAT BOTTLE OF TEQUILA. WANT TO GET INCREDIBLY DRUNK?
GOD, YES.
WHAT CAN I SAY? THE OPEN ROAD HAS MADE MASTER CONVERSATIONALISTS OF US.

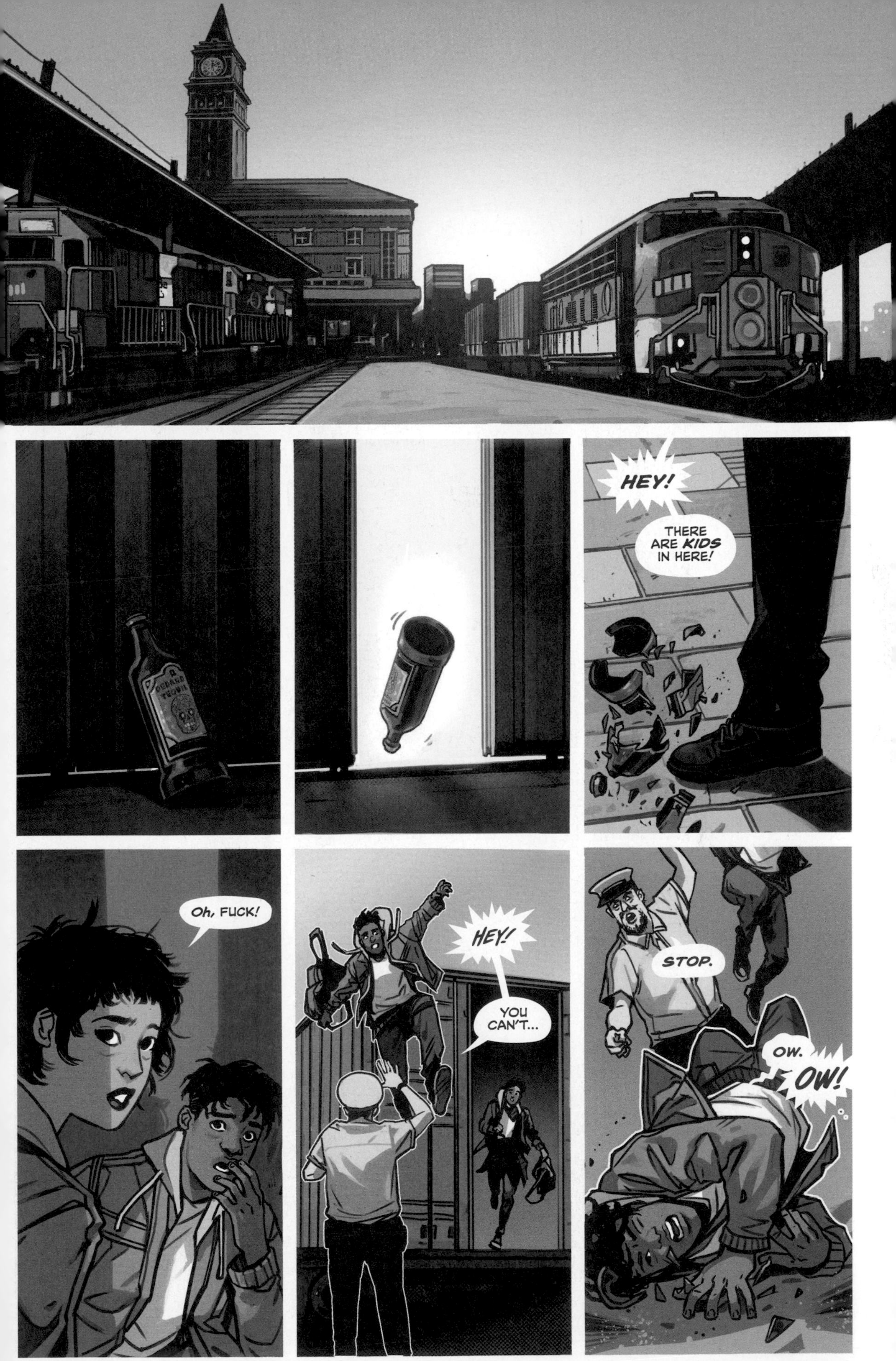
HEY!
THERE ARE KIDS IN HERE!
Oh, FUCK!
HEY!
YOU CAN'T...
STOP.
OW.
OW!

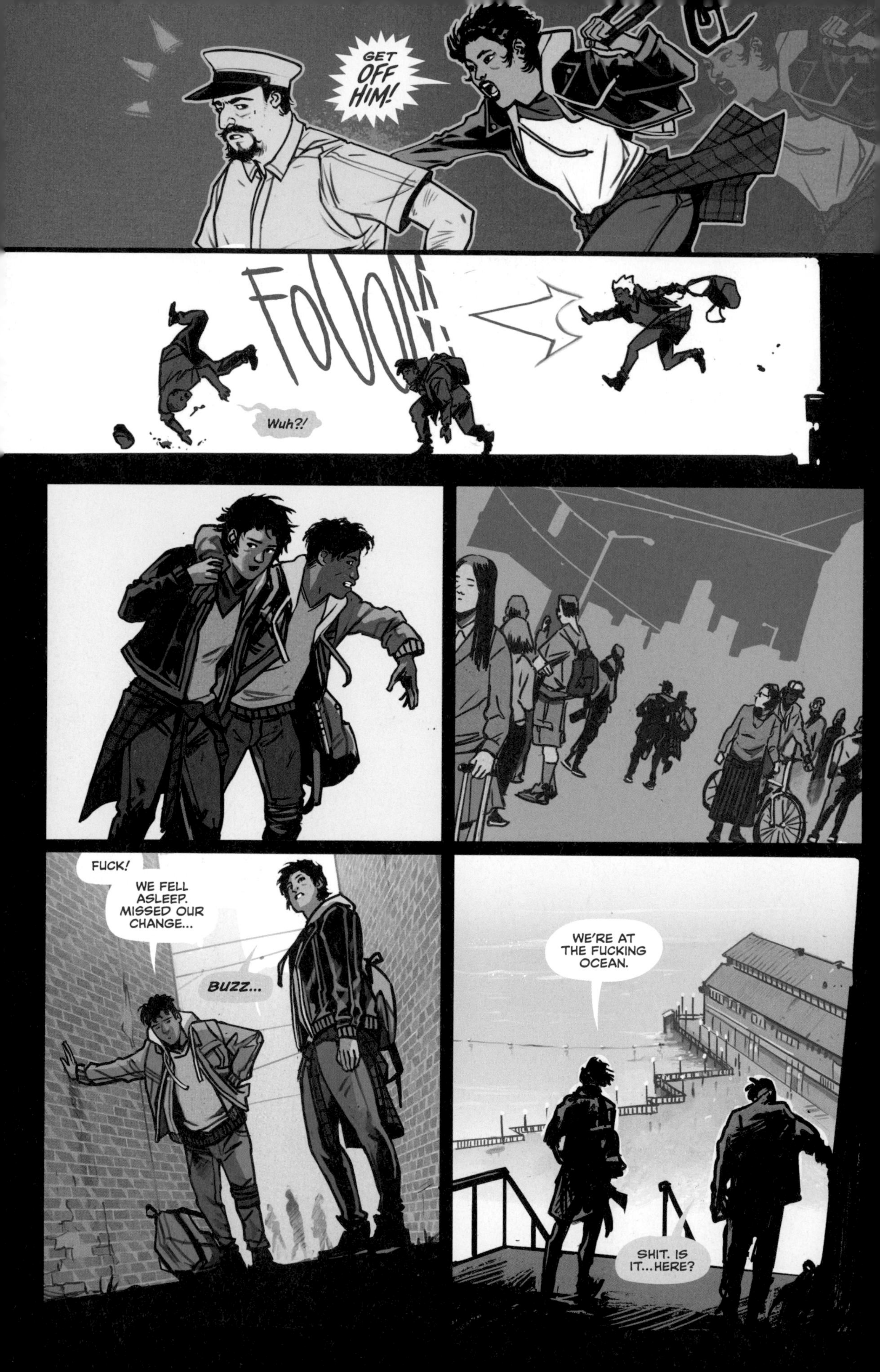
GET OFF HIM!
FOOOM!
Wuh?!
FUCK!
WE FELL ASLEEP. MISSED OUR CHANGE...
BUZZ...
WE'RE AT THE FUCKING OCEAN.
SHIT. IS IT...HERE?

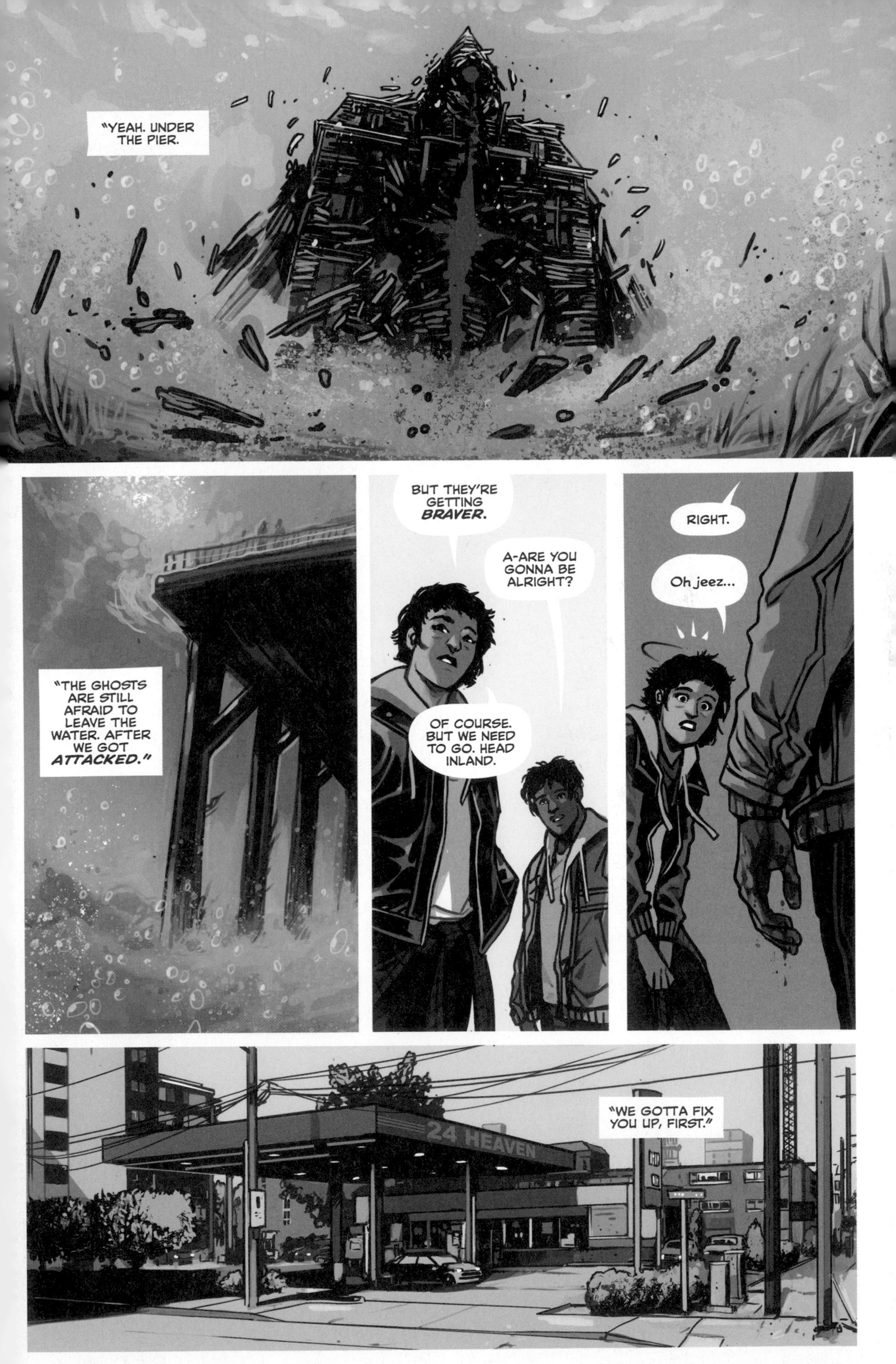
"YEAH. UNDER THE PIER.
"THE GHOSTS ARE STILL AFRAID TO LEAVE THE WATER. AFTER WE GOT ATTACKED."
BUT THEY'RE GETTING BRAVER.
A-ARE YOU GONNA BE ALRIGHT?
OF COURSE. BUT WE NEED TO GO. HEAD INLAND.
RIGHT.
Oh jeez...
24 HEAVEN
"WE GOTTA FIX YOU UP, FIRST."

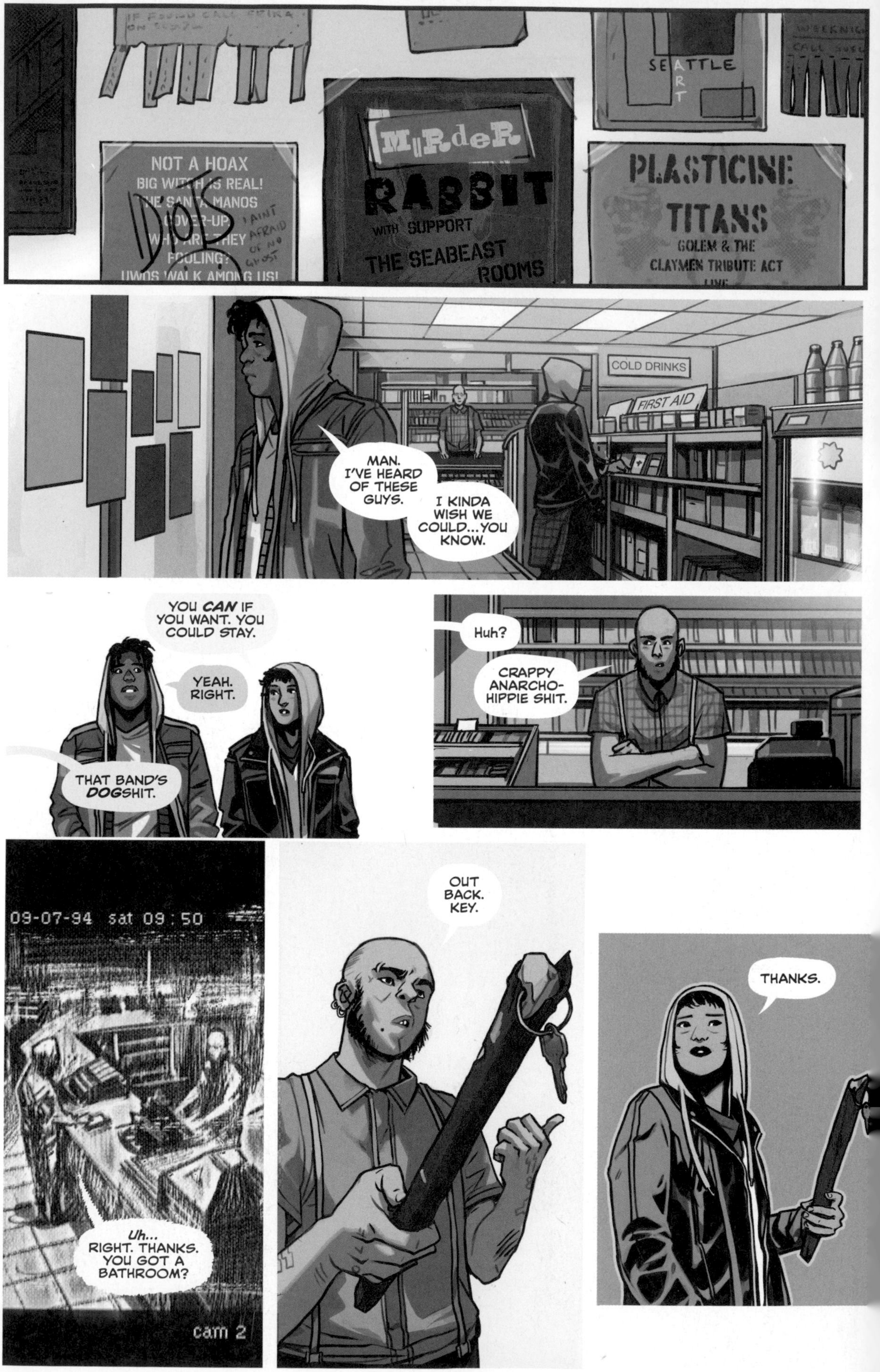
IF FOUND CALL ERIKA
NOT A HOAX
BIG WITCH IS REAL!
THE SANTA MANOS
COVER-UP
WHO ARE THEY
FOOLING?
UWOS WALK AMONG US!
IDIOTS
I AINT AFRAID OF NO GHOST
MURDER
RABBIT
WITH SUPPORT
THE SEABEAST
ROOMS
SEATTLE
ART
PLASTICINE
TITANS
GOLEM & THE
CLAYMEN TRIBUTE ACT
COLD DRINKS
FIRST AID
MAN. I'VE HEARD OF THESE GUYS.
I KINDA WISH WE COULD...YOU KNOW.
YOU CAN IF YOU WANT. YOU COULD STAY.
YEAH. RIGHT.
THAT BAND'S DOGSHIT.
Huh?
CRAPPY ANARCHO-HIPPIE SHIT.
09-07-94 sat 09:50
Uh... RIGHT. THANKS. YOU GOT A BATHROOM?
cam 2
OUT BACK. KEY.
THANKS.

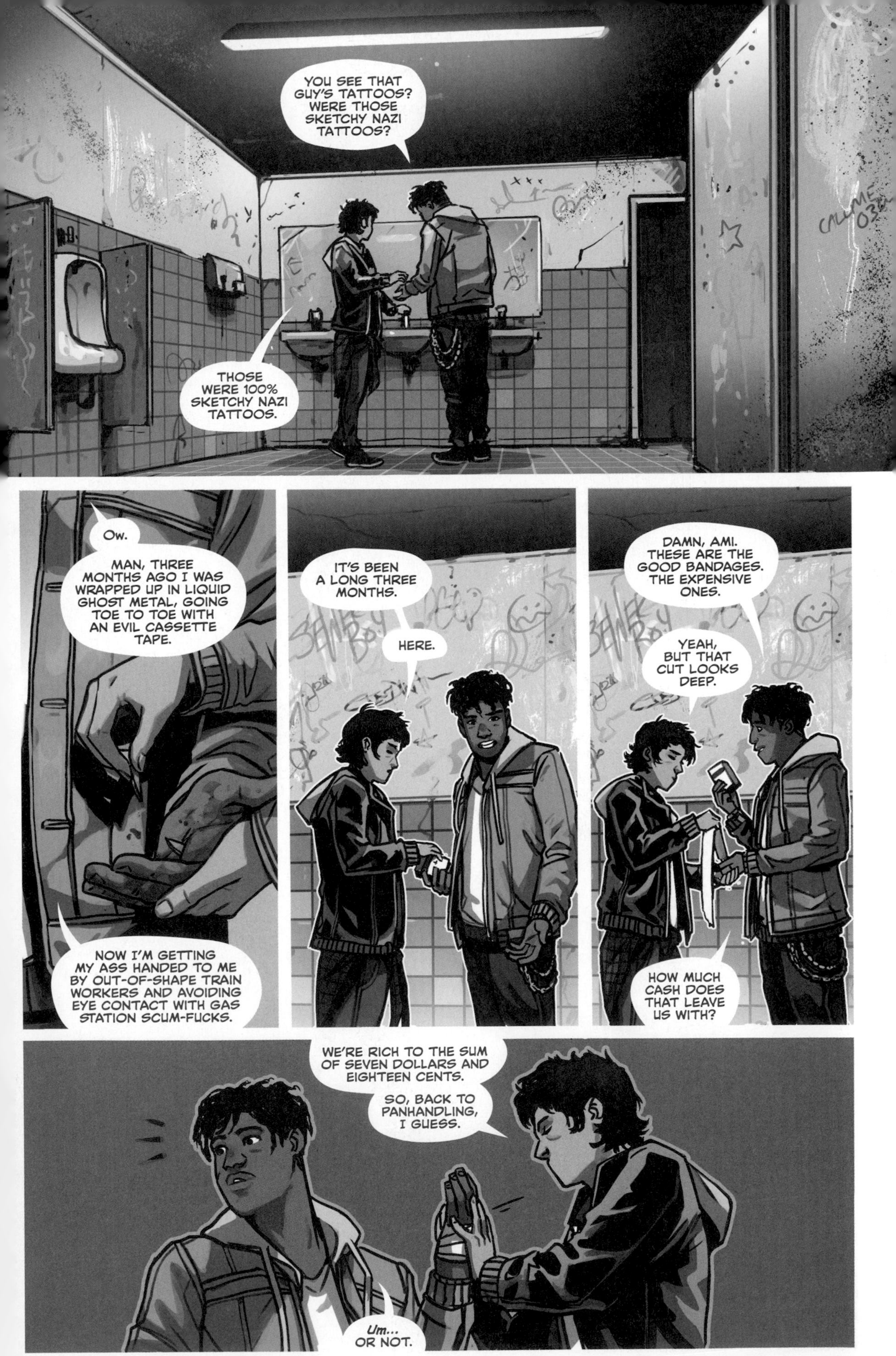
YOU SEE THAT GUY'S TATTOOS? WERE THOSE SKETCHY NAZI TATTOOS?
THOSE WERE 100% SKETCHY NAZI TATTOOS.
CALLME 03
OW.
MAN, THREE MONTHS AGO I WAS WRAPPED UP IN LIQUID GHOST METAL, GOING TOE TO TOE WITH AN EVIL CASSETTE TAPE.
NOW I'M GETTING MY ASS HANDED TO ME BY OUT-OF-SHAPE TRAIN WORKERS AND AVOIDING EYE CONTACT WITH GAS STATION SCUM-FUCKS.
IT'S BEEN A LONG THREE MONTHS.
HERE.
DAMN, AMI. THESE ARE THE GOOD BANDAGES. THE EXPENSIVE ONES.
YEAH, BUT THAT CUT LOOKS DEEP.
HOW MUCH CASH DOES THAT LEAVE US WITH?
WE'RE RICH TO THE SUM OF SEVEN DOLLARS AND EIGHTEEN CENTS.
SO, BACK TO PANHANDLING, I GUESS.
Um... OR NOT.

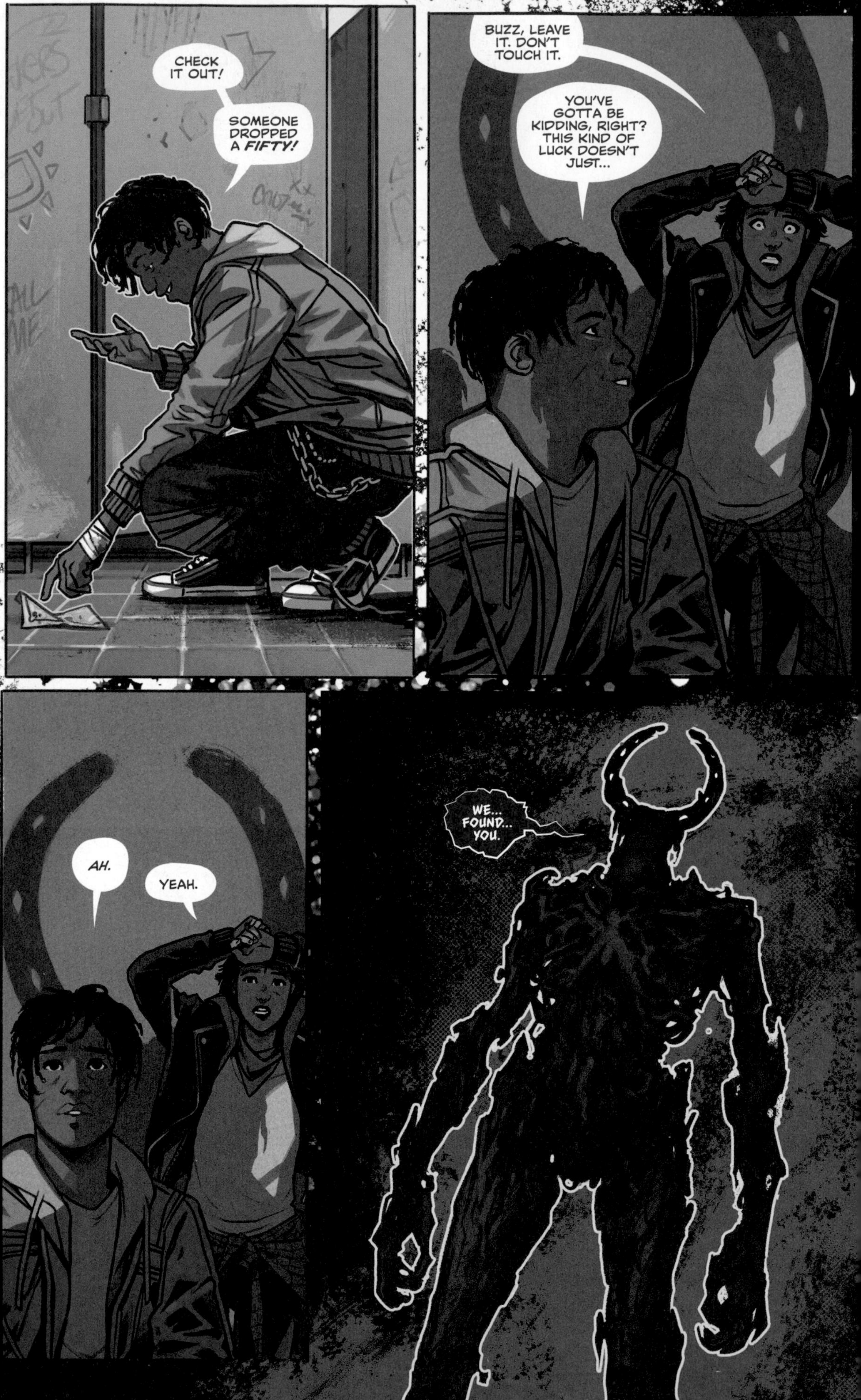
CHECK IT OUT!
SOMEONE DROPPED A *FIFTY!*
BUZZ, LEAVE IT. DON'T TOUCH IT.
YOU'VE GOTTA BE KIDDING, RIGHT? THIS KIND OF LUCK DOESN'T JUST...
AH.
YEAH.
WE... FOUND... YOU.

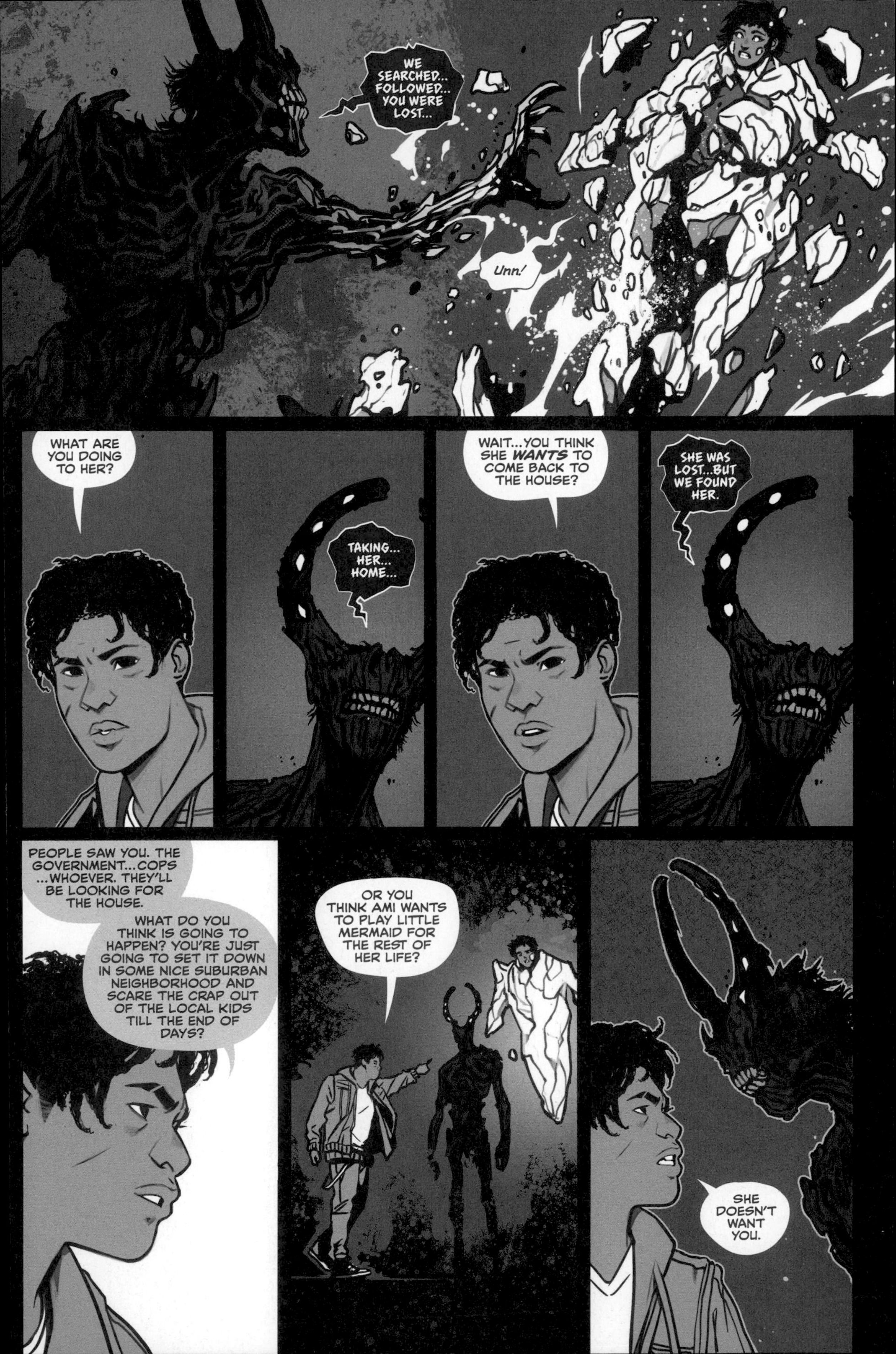
WE SEARCHED... FOLLOWED... YOU WERE LOST...
Unn!
WHAT ARE YOU DOING TO HER?
TAKING... HER... HOME...
WAIT...YOU THINK SHE WANTS TO COME BACK TO THE HOUSE?
SHE WAS LOST...BUT WE FOUND HER.
PEOPLE SAW YOU. THE GOVERNMENT...COPS ...WHOEVER. THEY'LL BE LOOKING FOR THE HOUSE.
WHAT DO YOU THINK IS GOING TO HAPPEN? YOU'RE JUST GOING TO SET IT DOWN IN SOME NICE SUBURBAN NEIGHBORHOOD AND SCARE THE CRAP OUT OF THE LOCAL KIDS TILL THE END OF DAYS?
OR YOU THINK AMI WANTS TO PLAY LITTLE MERMAID FOR THE REST OF HER LIFE?
SHE DOESN'T WANT YOU.

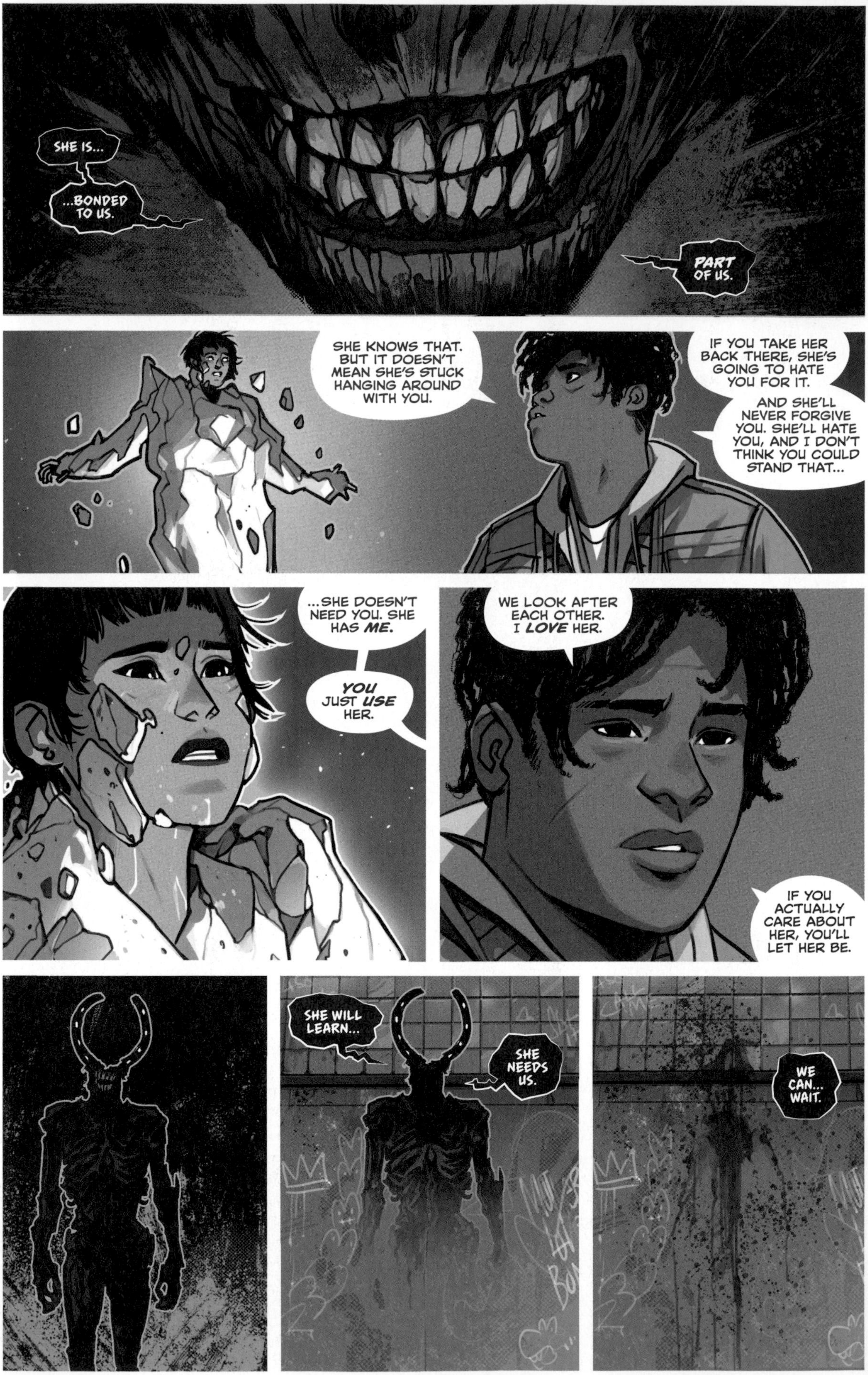
SHE IS...
...BONDED TO US.
PART OF US.
SHE KNOWS THAT. BUT IT DOESN'T MEAN SHE'S STUCK HANGING AROUND WITH YOU.
IF YOU TAKE HER BACK THERE, SHE'S GOING TO HATE YOU FOR IT.
AND SHE'LL NEVER FORGIVE YOU. SHE'LL HATE YOU, AND I DON'T THINK YOU COULD STAND THAT...
...SHE DOESN'T NEED YOU. SHE HAS ME.
YOU JUST USE HER.
WE LOOK AFTER EACH OTHER. I LOVE HER.
IF YOU ACTUALLY CARE ABOUT HER, YOU'LL LET HER BE.
SHE WILL LEARN...
SHE NEEDS US.
WE CAN... WAIT.

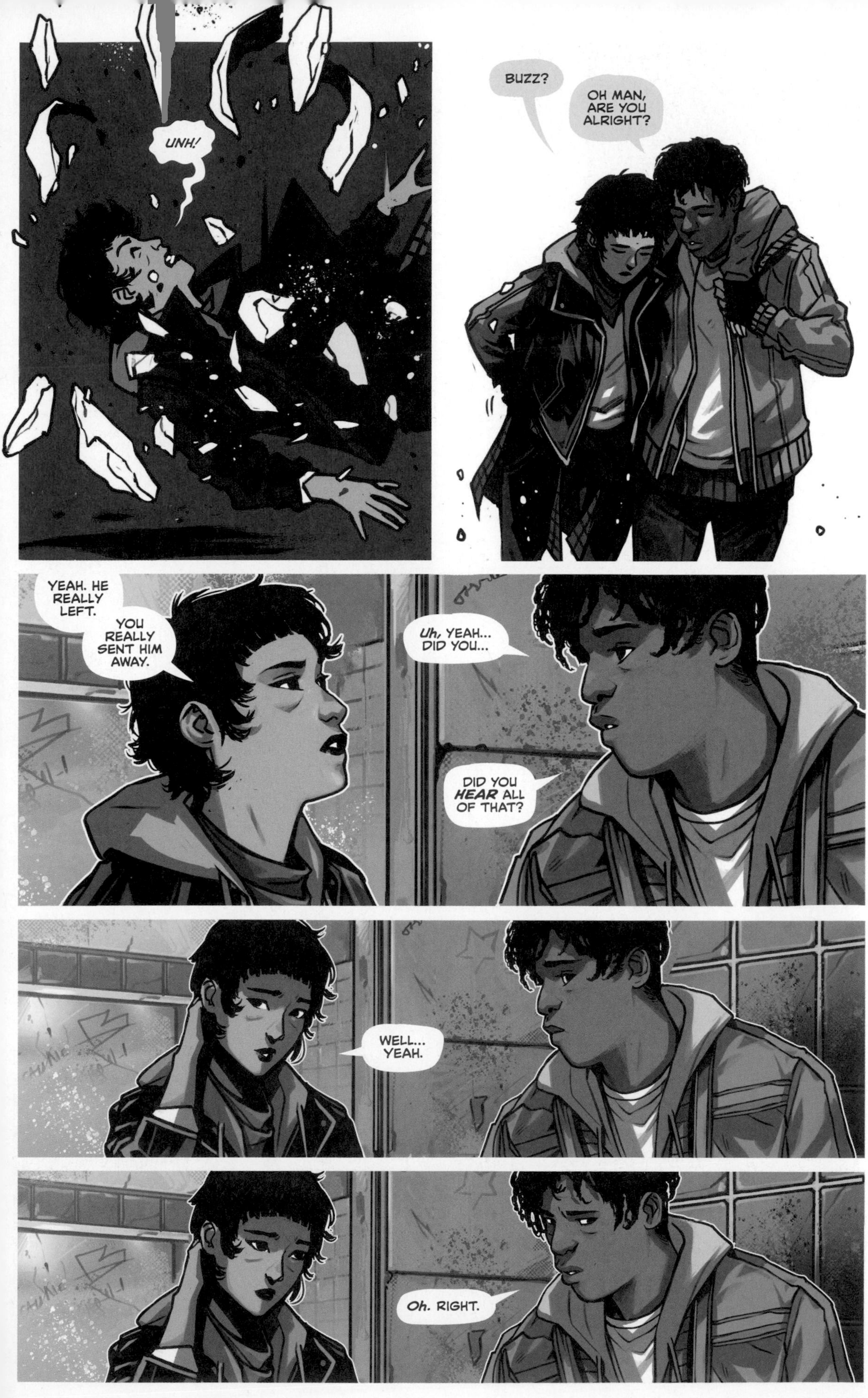
UNH!
BUZZ?
OH MAN, ARE YOU ALRIGHT?
YEAH. HE REALLY LEFT.
YOU REALLY SENT HIM AWAY.
Uh, YEAH... DID YOU...
DID YOU HEAR ALL OF THAT?
WELL... YEAH.
Oh. RIGHT.

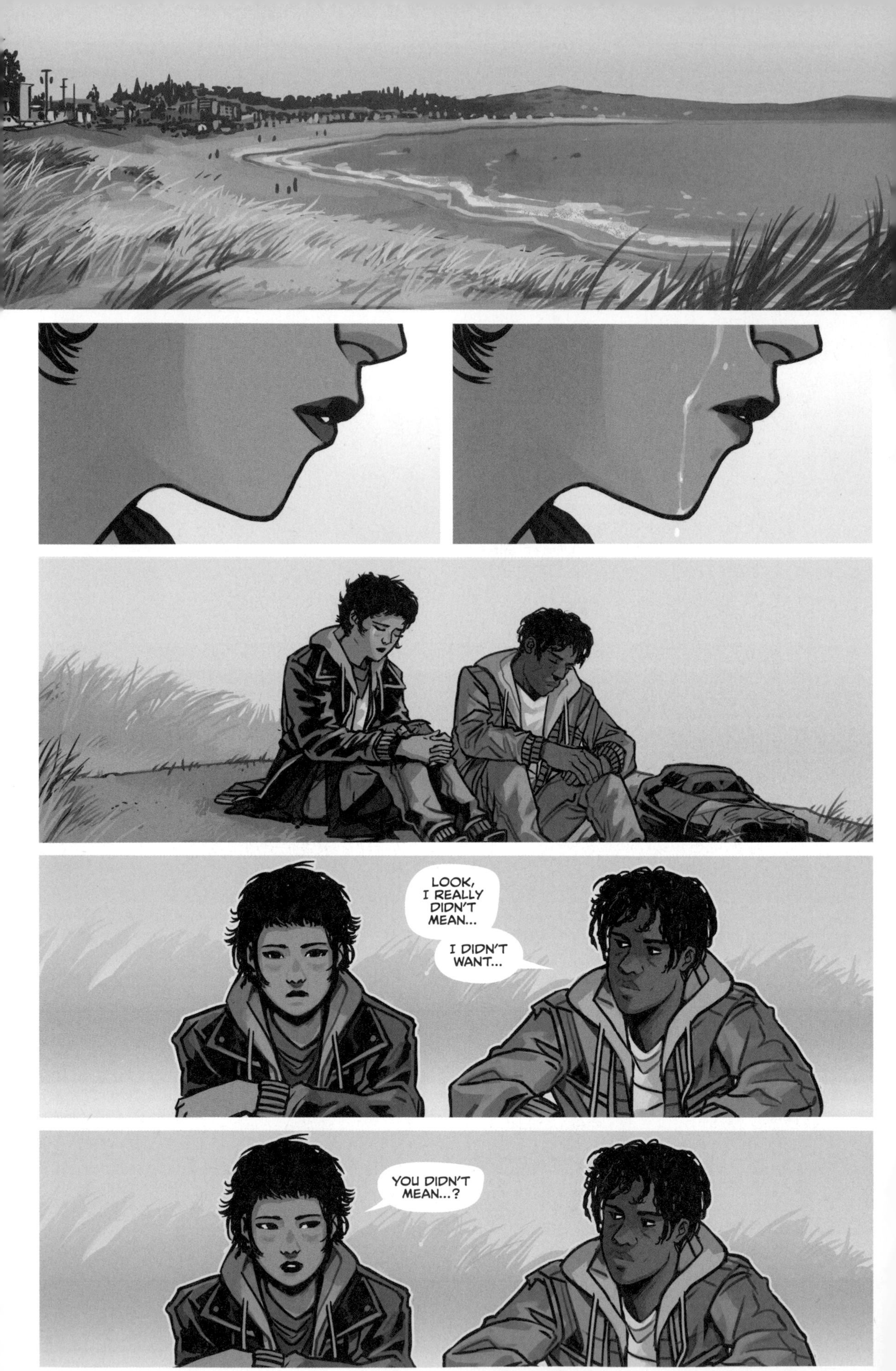
LOOK, I REALLY DIDN'T MEAN...
I DIDN'T WANT...
YOU DIDN'T MEAN...?

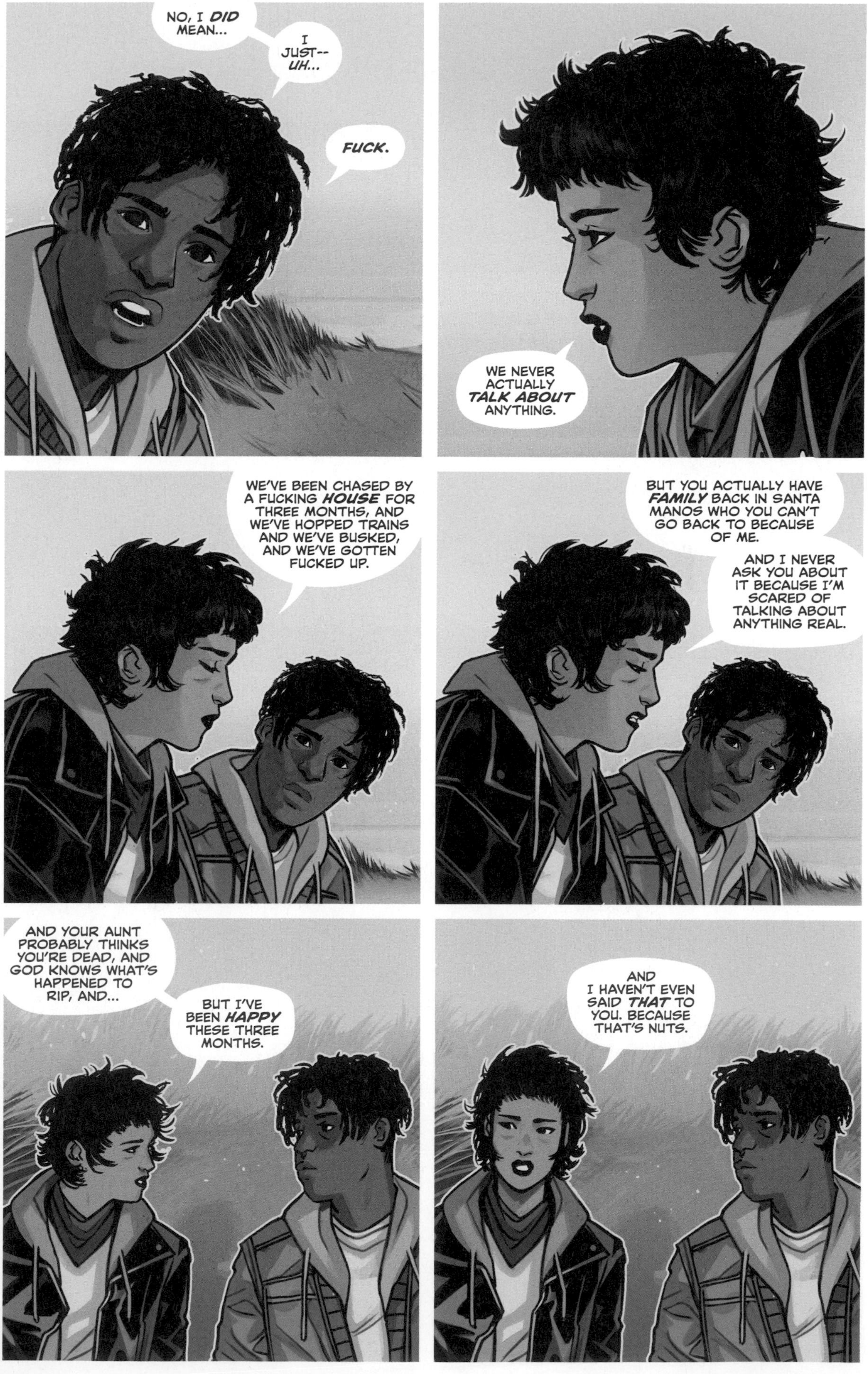
NO, I DID MEAN...
I JUST-- UH...
FUCK.
WE NEVER ACTUALLY TALK ABOUT ANYTHING.
WE'VE BEEN CHASED BY A FUCKING HOUSE FOR THREE MONTHS, AND WE'VE HOPPED TRAINS AND WE'VE BUSKED, AND WE'VE GOTTEN FUCKED UP.
BUT YOU ACTUALLY HAVE FAMILY BACK IN SANTA MANOS WHO YOU CAN'T GO BACK TO BECAUSE OF ME.
AND I NEVER ASK YOU ABOUT IT BECAUSE I'M SCARED OF TALKING ABOUT ANYTHING REAL.
AND YOUR AUNT PROBABLY THINKS YOU'RE DEAD, AND GOD KNOWS WHAT'S HAPPENED TO RIP, AND...
BUT I'VE BEEN HAPPY THESE THREE MONTHS.
AND I HAVEN'T EVEN SAID THAT TO YOU. BECAUSE THAT'S NUTS.

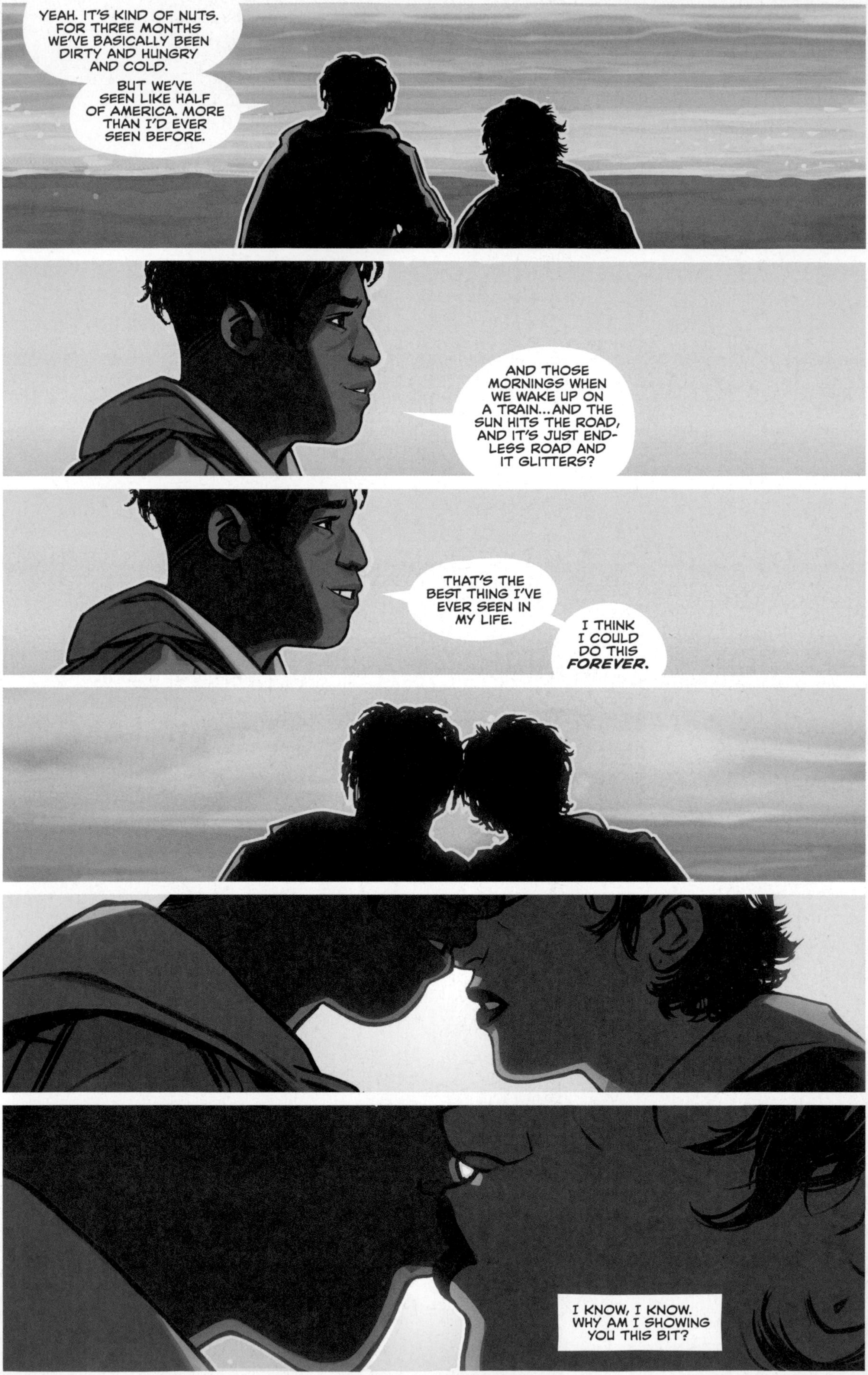
YEAH. IT'S KIND OF NUTS. FOR THREE MONTHS WE'VE BASICALLY BEEN DIRTY AND HUNGRY AND COLD.
BUT WE'VE SEEN LIKE HALF OF AMERICA. MORE THAN I'D EVER SEEN BEFORE.
AND THOSE MORNINGS WHEN WE WAKE UP ON A TRAIN...AND THE SUN HITS THE ROAD, AND IT'S JUST END-LESS ROAD AND IT GLITTERS?
THAT'S THE BEST THING I'VE EVER SEEN IN MY LIFE.
I THINK I COULD DO THIS ***FOREVER.***
I KNOW, I KNOW. WHY AM I SHOWING YOU THIS BIT?

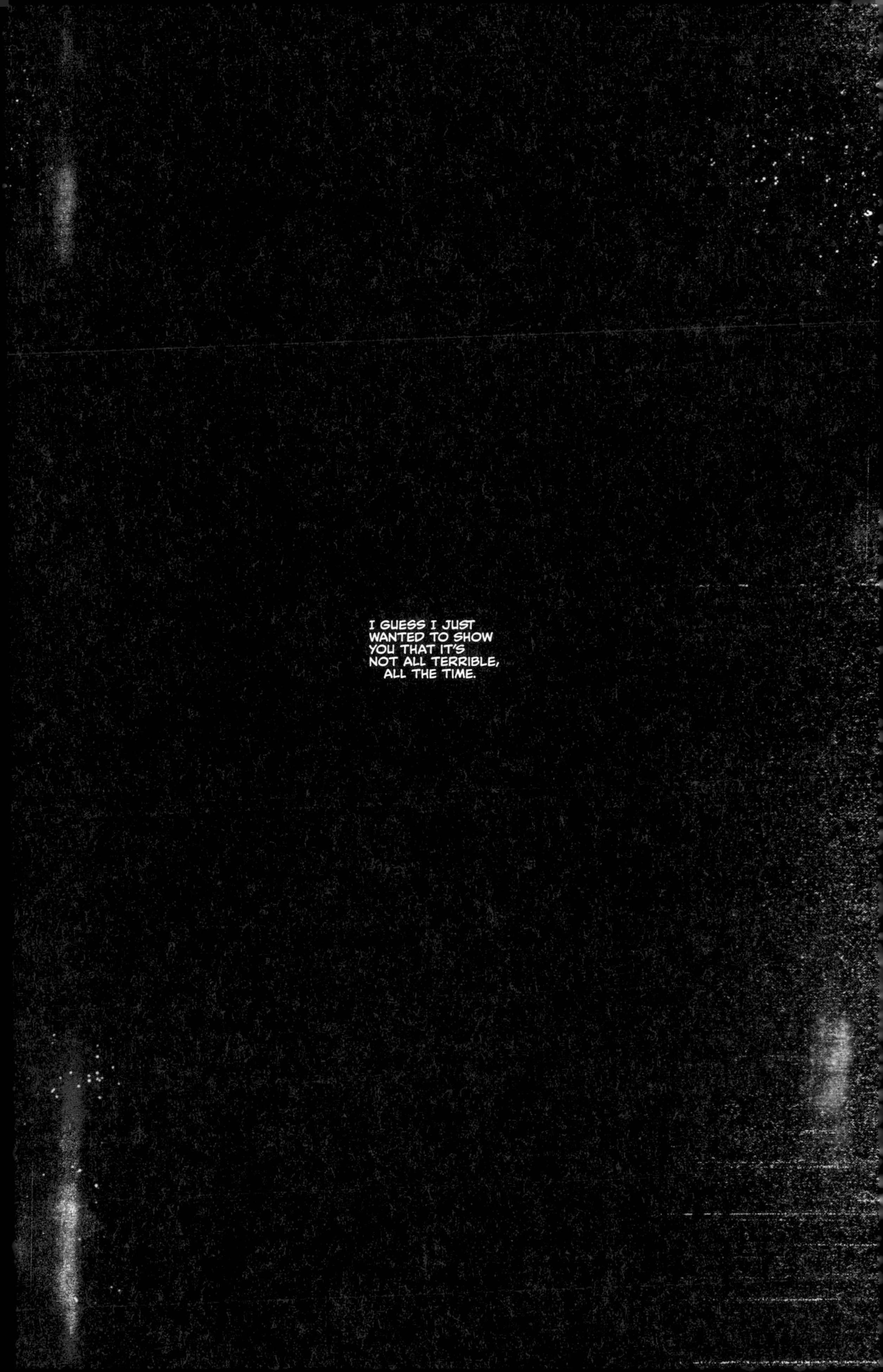
I GUESS I JUST WANTED TO SHOW YOU THAT IT'S NOT ALL TERRIBLE, ALL THE TIME.

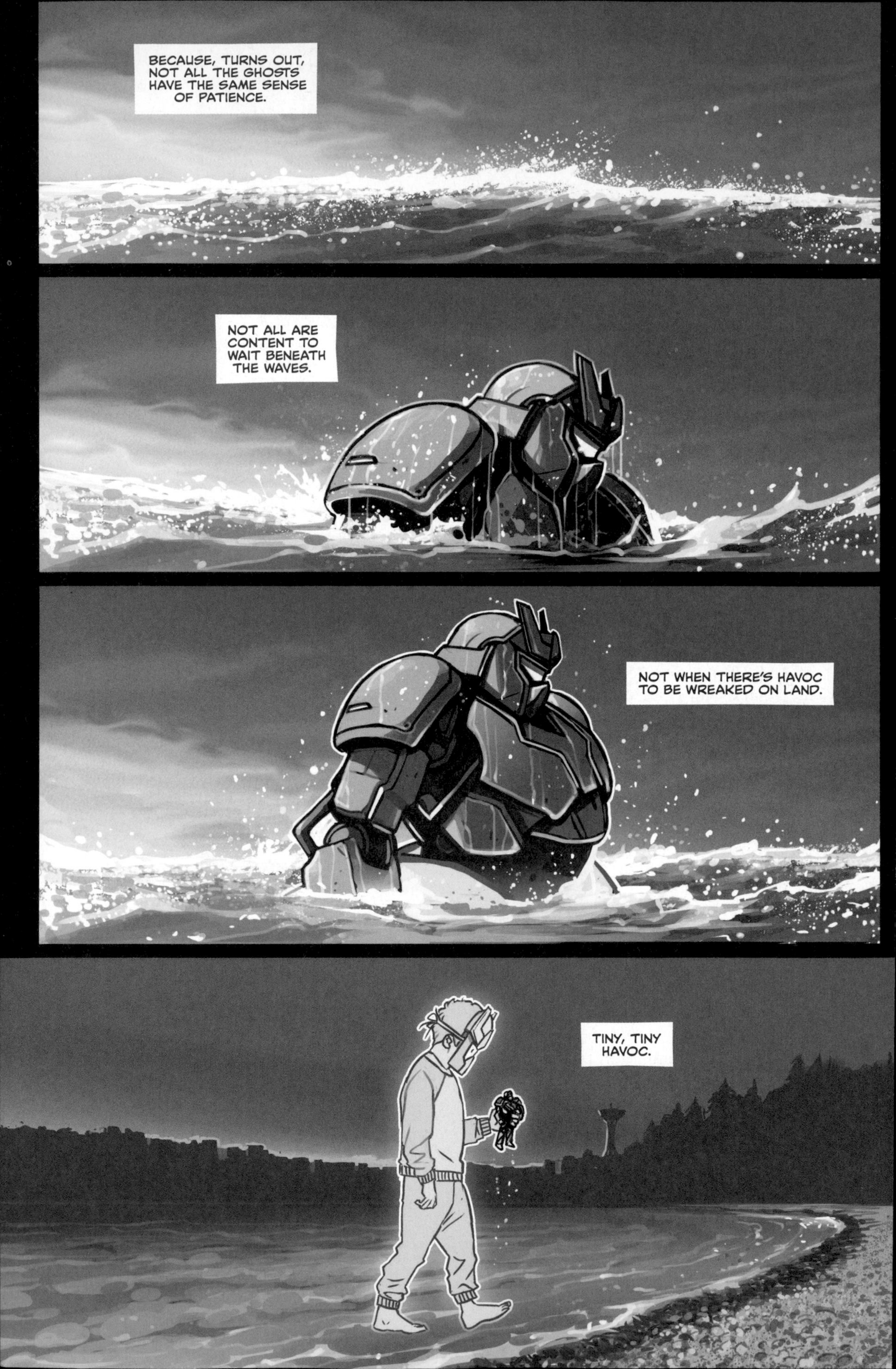
BECAUSE, TURNS OUT, NOT ALL THE GHOSTS HAVE THE SAME SENSE OF PATIENCE.
NOT ALL ARE CONTENT TO WAIT BENEATH THE WAVES.
NOT WHEN THERE'S HAVOC TO BE WREAKED ON LAND.
TINY, TINY HAVOC.

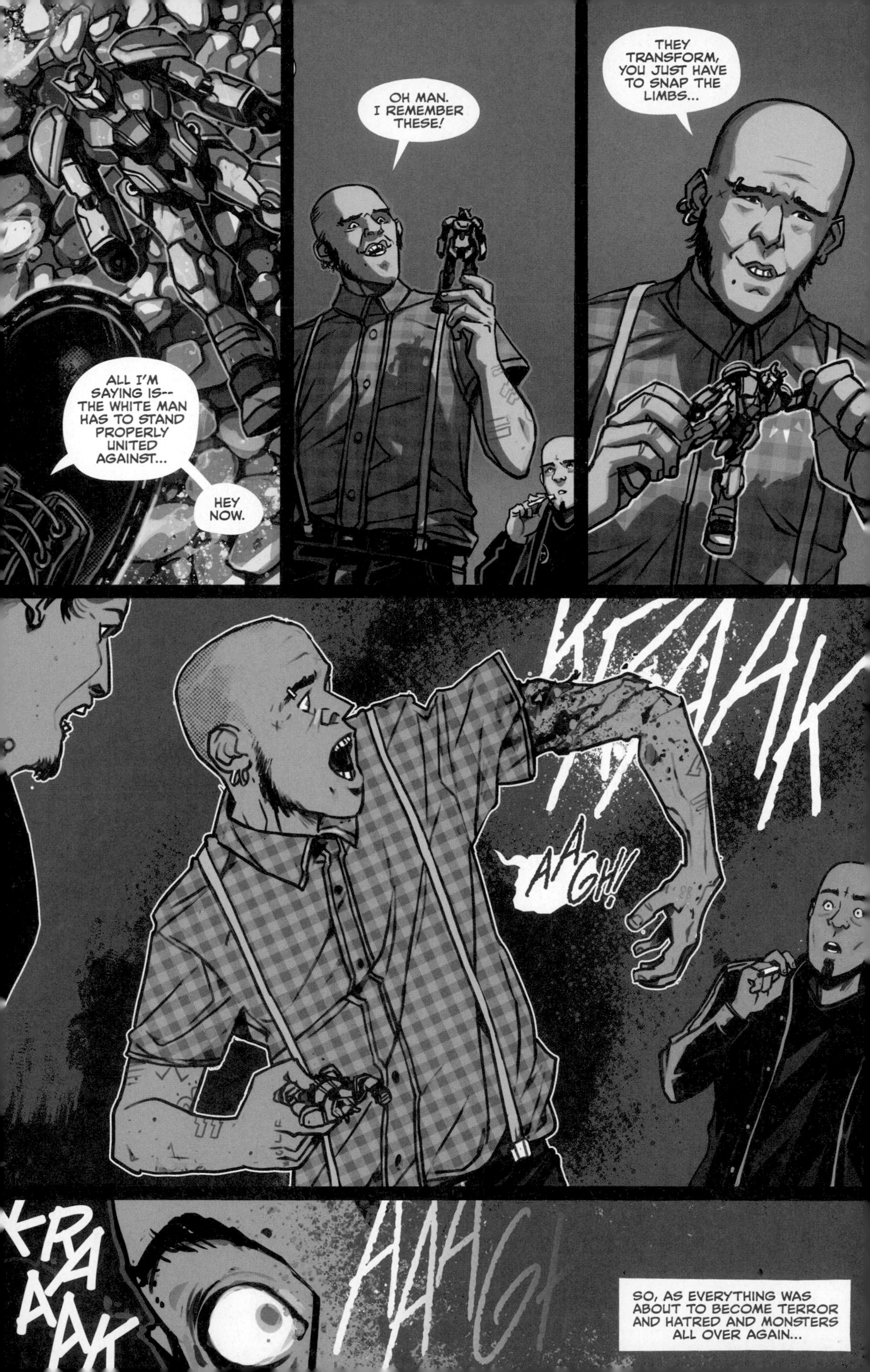
ALL I'M SAYING IS-- THE WHITE MAN HAS TO STAND PROPERLY UNITED AGAINST...
HEY NOW.
OH MAN. I REMEMBER THESE!
THEY TRANSFORM, YOU JUST HAVE TO SNAP THE LIMBS...
AAGH!
SO, AS EVERYTHING WAS ABOUT TO BECOME TERROR AND HATRED AND MONSTERS ALL OVER AGAIN...

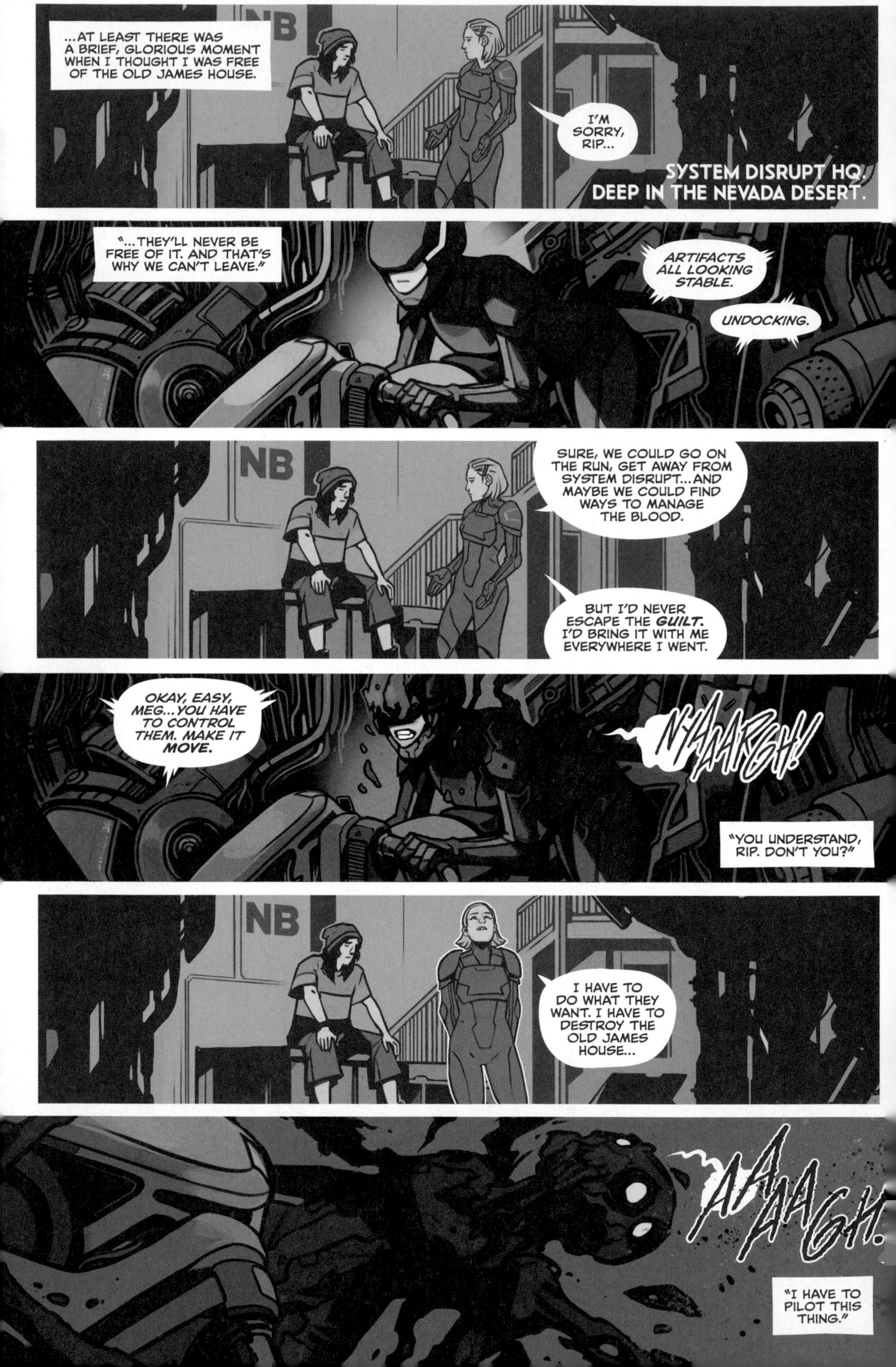
...AT LEAST THERE WAS A BRIEF, GLORIOUS MOMENT WHEN I THOUGHT I WAS FREE OF THE OLD JAMES HOUSE.
I'M SORRY, RIP...
SYSTEM DISRUPT HQ. DEEP IN THE NEVADA DESERT.
"...THEY'LL NEVER BE FREE OF IT. AND THAT'S WHY WE CAN'T LEAVE."
ARTIFACTS ALL LOOKING STABLE.
UNDOCKING.
SURE, WE COULD GO ON THE RUN, GET AWAY FROM SYSTEM DISRUPT...AND MAYBE WE COULD FIND WAYS TO MANAGE THE BLOOD.
BUT I'D NEVER ESCAPE THE GUILT. I'D BRING IT WITH ME EVERYWHERE I WENT.
OKAY, EASY, MEG...YOU HAVE TO CONTROL THEM. MAKE IT MOVE.
NYAARGH!
"YOU UNDERSTAND, RIP. DON'T YOU?"
I HAVE TO DO WHAT THEY WANT. I HAVE TO DESTROY THE OLD JAMES HOUSE...
AAAAAGH.
"I HAVE TO PILOT THIS THING."

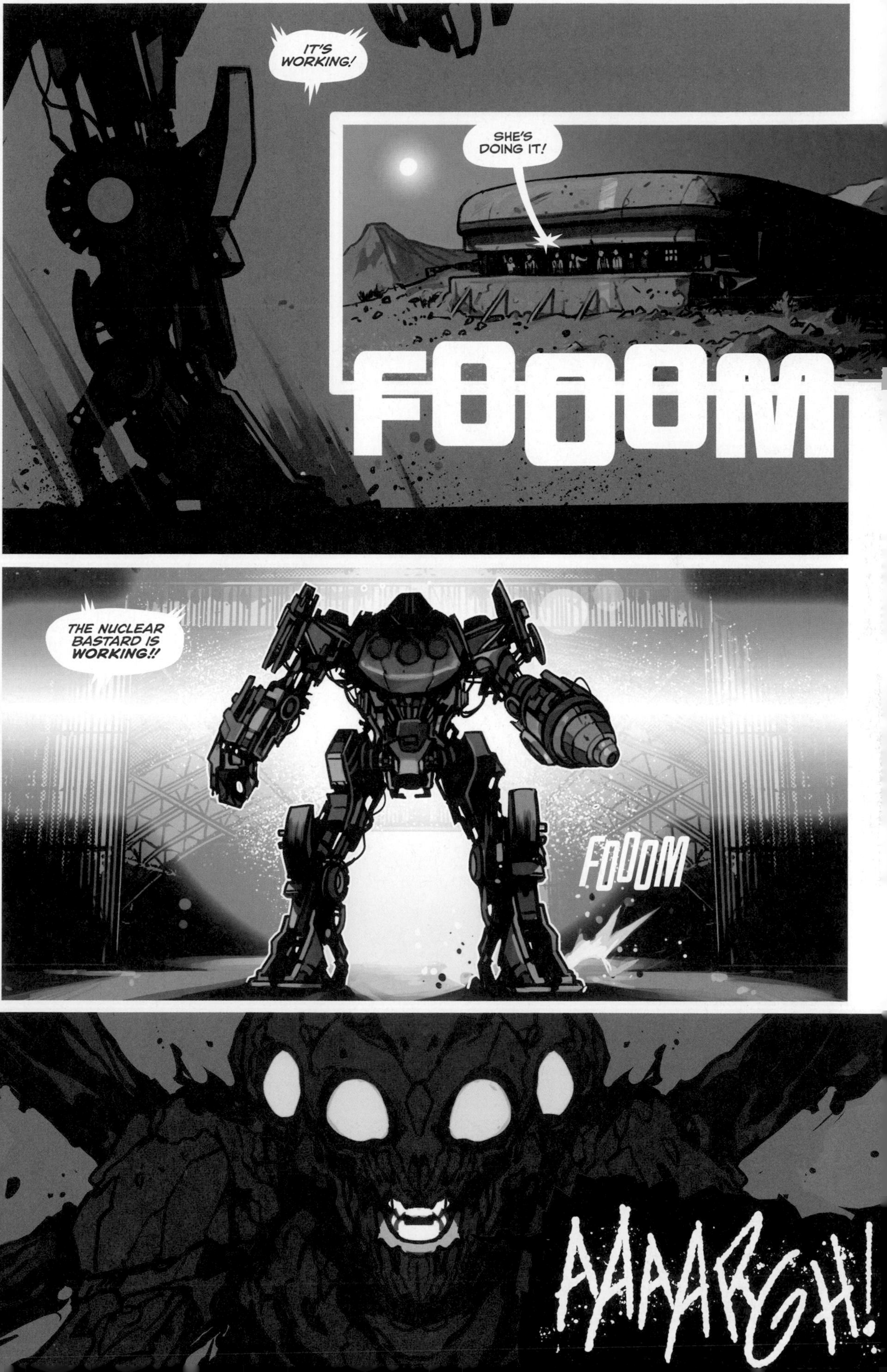
IT'S WORKING!
SHE'S DOING IT!
FOOOM
THE NUCLEAR BASTARD IS WORKING!!
FOOOM
AAAARGH!

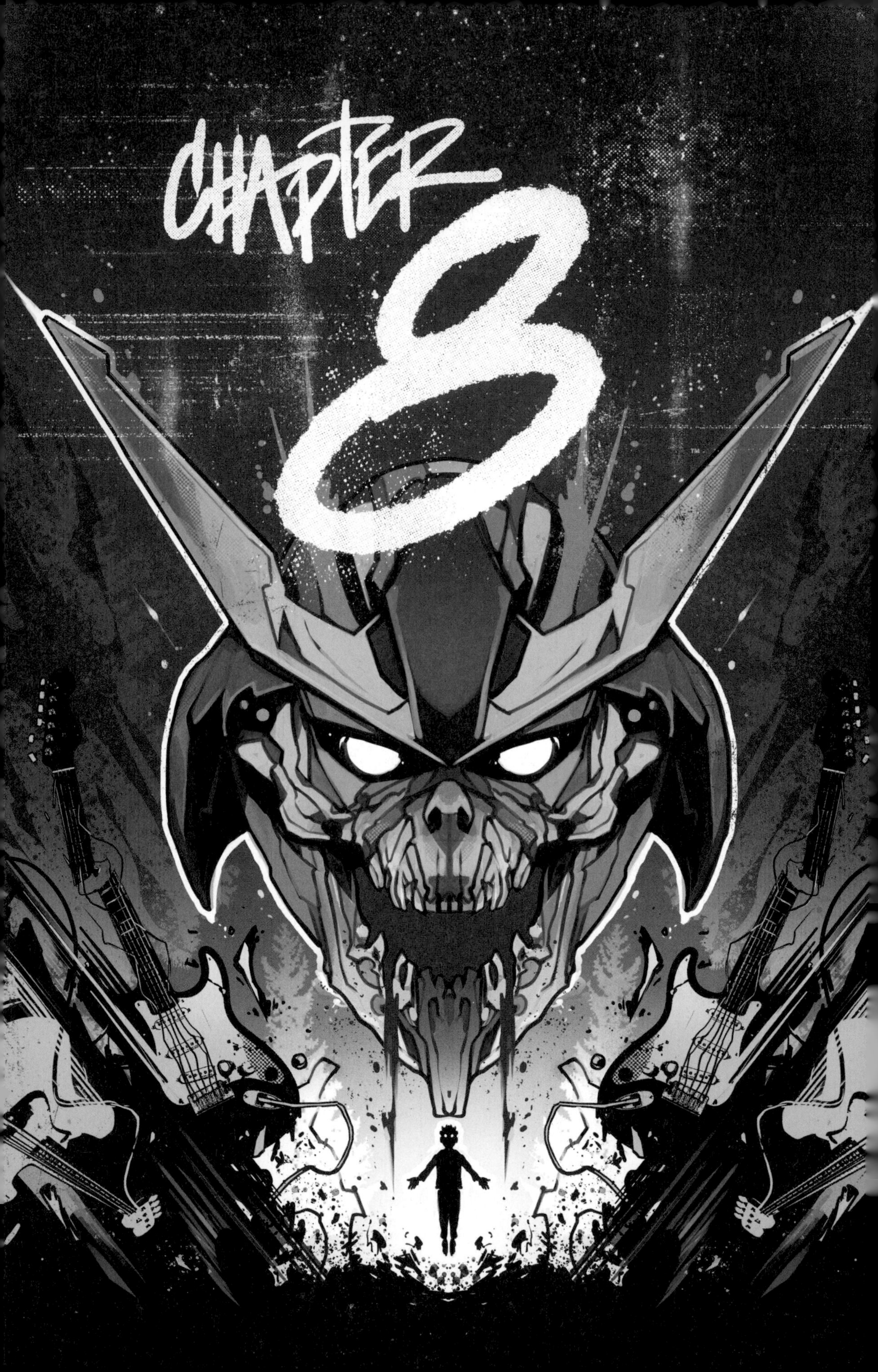
CHAPTER
8

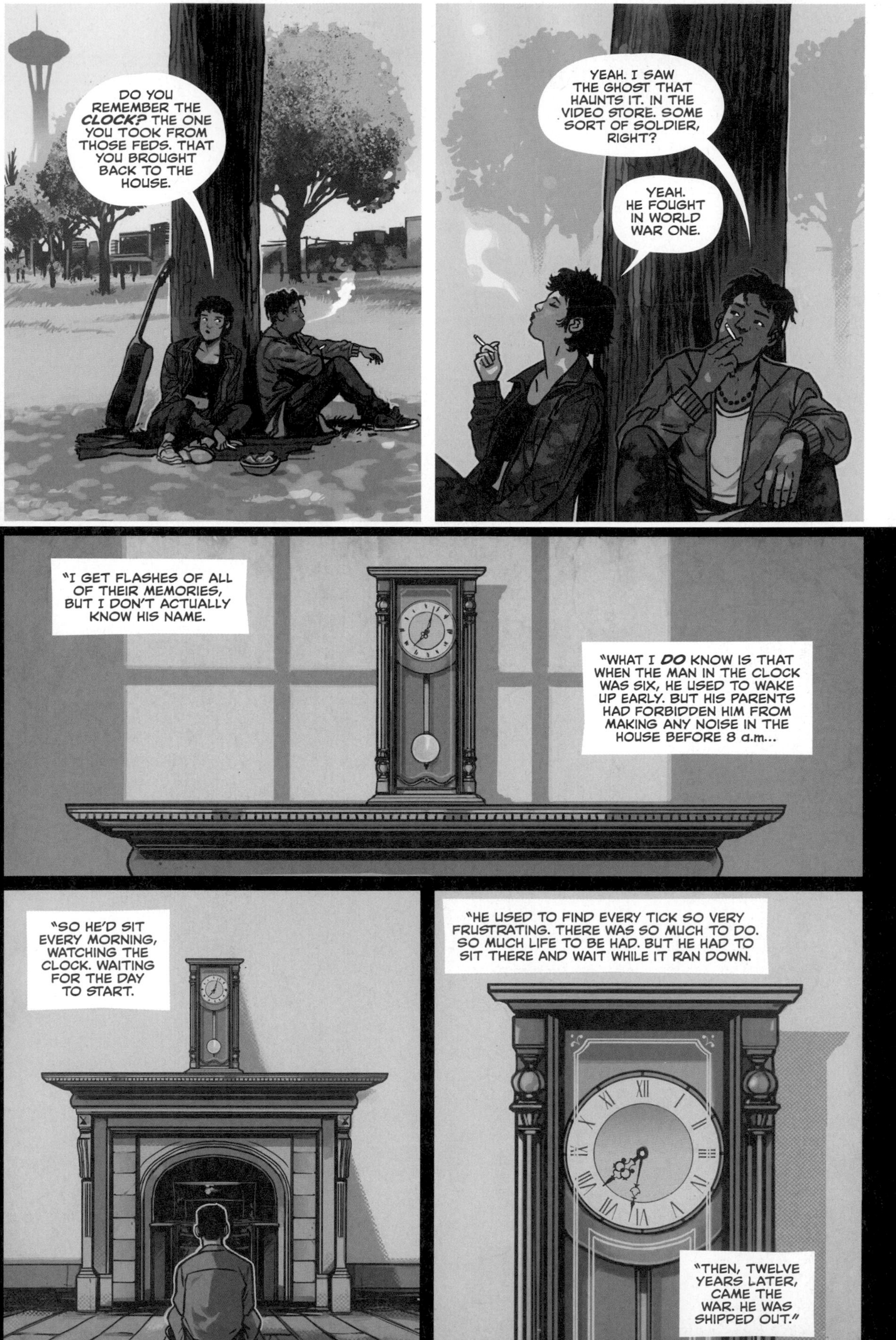
DO YOU REMEMBER THE CLOCK? THE ONE YOU TOOK FROM THOSE FEDS. THAT YOU BROUGHT BACK TO THE HOUSE.
YEAH. I SAW THE GHOST THAT HAUNTS IT. IN THE VIDEO STORE. SOME SORT OF SOLDIER, RIGHT?
YEAH. HE FOUGHT IN WORLD WAR ONE.
"I GET FLASHES OF ALL OF THEIR MEMORIES, BUT I DON'T ACTUALLY KNOW HIS NAME.
"WHAT I DO KNOW IS THAT WHEN THE MAN IN THE CLOCK WAS SIX, HE USED TO WAKE UP EARLY. BUT HIS PARENTS HAD FORBIDDEN HIM FROM MAKING ANY NOISE IN THE HOUSE BEFORE 8 a.m...
"SO HE'D SIT EVERY MORNING, WATCHING THE CLOCK. WAITING FOR THE DAY TO START.
"HE USED TO FIND EVERY TICK SO VERY FRUSTRATING. THERE WAS SO MUCH TO DO. SO MUCH LIFE TO BE HAD. BUT HE HAD TO SIT THERE AND WAIT WHILE IT RAN DOWN.
"THEN, TWELVE YEARS LATER, CAME THE WAR. HE WAS SHIPPED OUT."

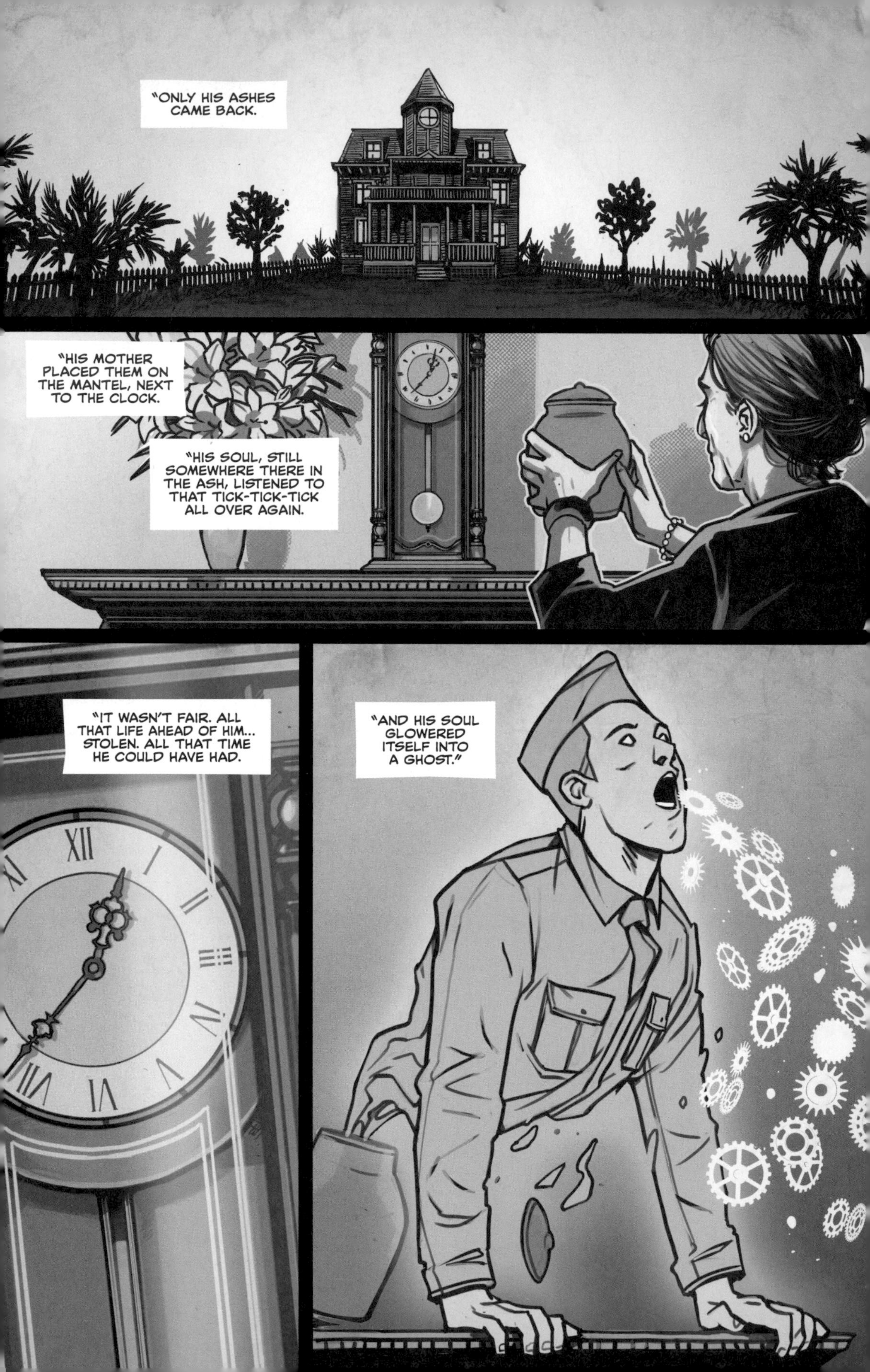
"ONLY HIS ASHES CAME BACK.
"HIS MOTHER PLACED THEM ON THE MANTEL, NEXT TO THE CLOCK.
"HIS SOUL, STILL SOMEWHERE THERE IN THE ASH, LISTENED TO THAT TICK-TICK-TICK ALL OVER AGAIN.
"IT WASN'T FAIR. ALL THAT LIFE AHEAD OF HIM... STOLEN. ALL THAT TIME HE COULD HAVE HAD.
"AND HIS SOUL GLOWERED ITSELF INTO A GHOST."

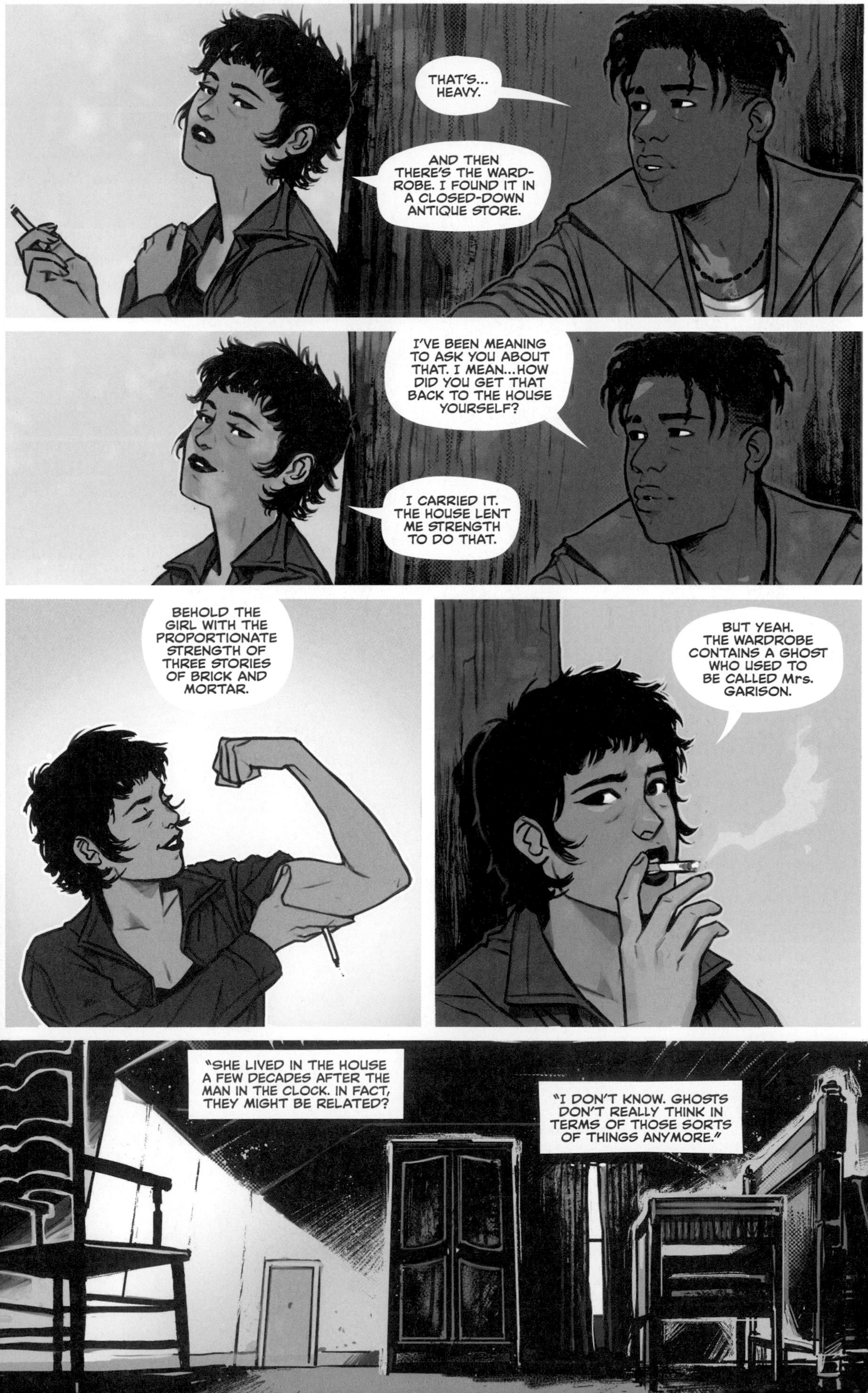
THAT'S... HEAVY.
AND THEN THERE'S THE WARD-ROBE. I FOUND IT IN A CLOSED-DOWN ANTIQUE STORE.
I'VE BEEN MEANING TO ASK YOU ABOUT THAT. I MEAN...HOW DID YOU GET THAT BACK TO THE HOUSE YOURSELF?
I CARRIED IT. THE HOUSE LENT ME STRENGTH TO DO THAT.
BEHOLD THE GIRL WITH THE PROPORTIONATE STRENGTH OF THREE STORIES OF BRICK AND MORTAR.
BUT YEAH. THE WARDROBE CONTAINS A GHOST WHO USED TO BE CALLED Mrs. GARISON.
"SHE LIVED IN THE HOUSE A FEW DECADES AFTER THE MAN IN THE CLOCK. IN FACT, THEY MIGHT BE RELATED?
"I DON'T KNOW. GHOSTS DON'T REALLY THINK IN TERMS OF THOSE SORTS OF THINGS ANYMORE."

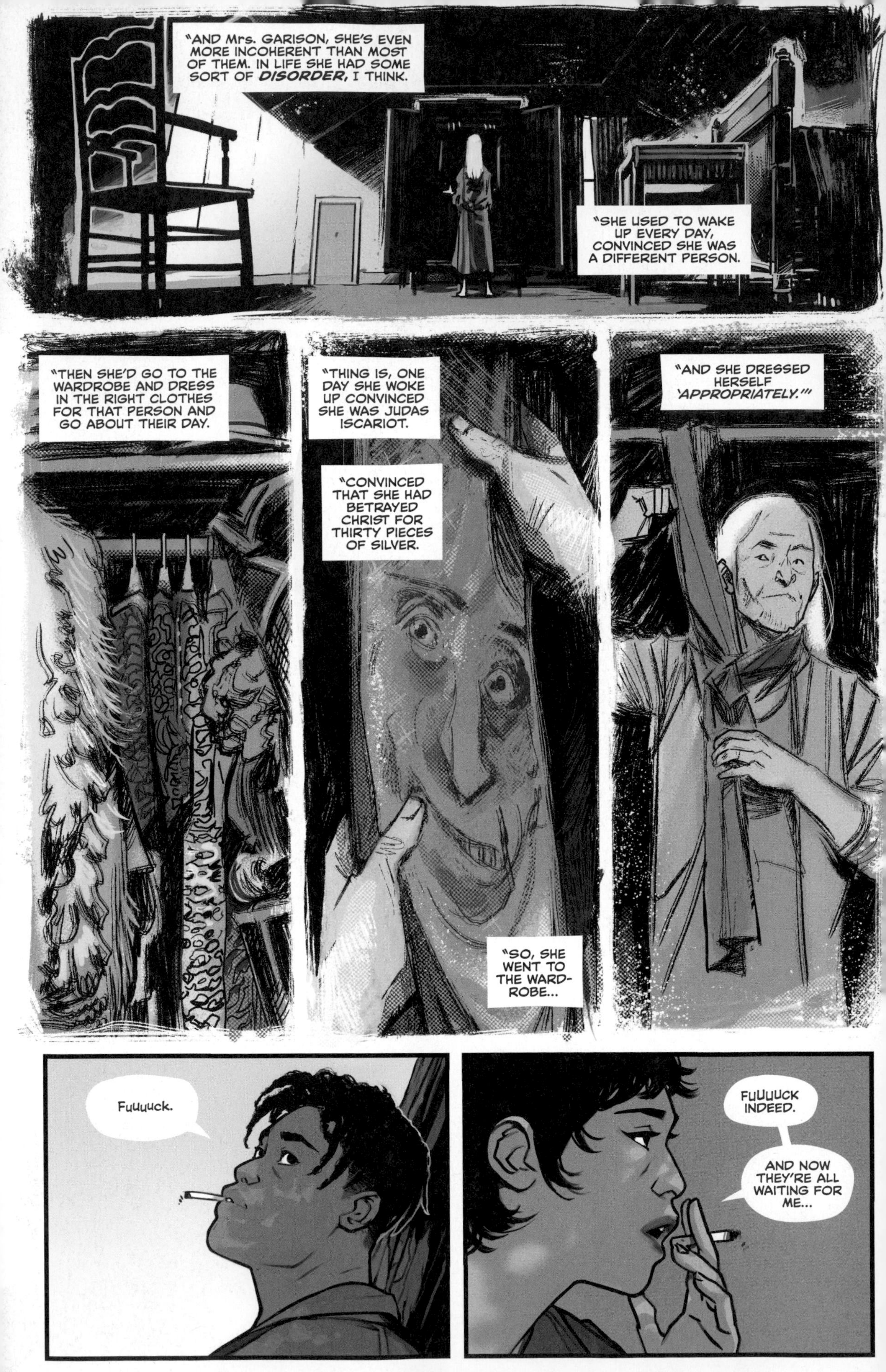
"AND Mrs. GARISON, SHE'S EVEN MORE INCOHERENT THAN MOST OF THEM. IN LIFE SHE HAD SOME SORT OF DISORDER, I THINK.
"SHE USED TO WAKE UP EVERY DAY, CONVINCED SHE WAS A DIFFERENT PERSON.
"THEN SHE'D GO TO THE WARDROBE AND DRESS IN THE RIGHT CLOTHES FOR THAT PERSON AND GO ABOUT THEIR DAY.
"THING IS, ONE DAY SHE WOKE UP CONVINCED SHE WAS JUDAS ISCARIOT.
"CONVINCED THAT SHE HAD BETRAYED CHRIST FOR THIRTY PIECES OF SILVER.
"SO, SHE WENT TO THE WARD-ROBE...
"AND SHE DRESSED HERSELF 'APPROPRIATELY.'"
Fuuuuck.
FUUUUCK INDEED.
AND NOW THEY'RE ALL WAITING FOR ME...

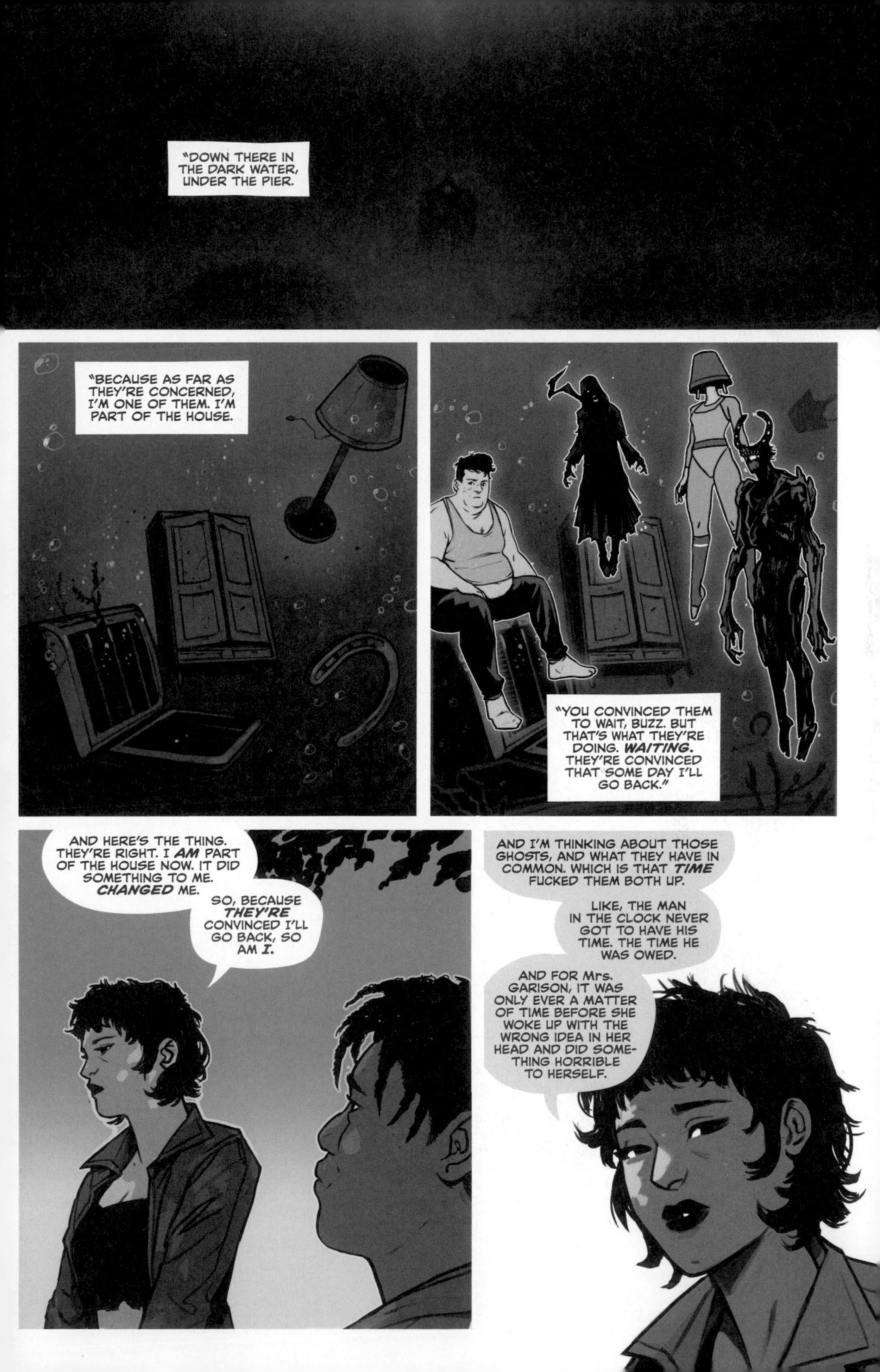
"DOWN THERE IN THE DARK WATER, UNDER THE PIER.
"BECAUSE AS FAR AS THEY'RE CONCERNED, I'M ONE OF THEM. I'M PART OF THE HOUSE.
"YOU CONVINCED THEM TO WAIT, BUZZ. BUT THAT'S WHAT THEY'RE DOING. WAITING. THEY'RE CONVINCED THAT SOME DAY I'LL GO BACK."
AND HERE'S THE THING. THEY'RE RIGHT. I AM PART OF THE HOUSE NOW. IT DID SOMETHING TO ME. CHANGED ME.
SO, BECAUSE THEY'RE CONVINCED I'LL GO BACK, SO AM I.
AND I'M THINKING ABOUT THOSE GHOSTS, AND WHAT THEY HAVE IN COMMON. WHICH IS THAT TIME FUCKED THEM BOTH UP.
LIKE, THE MAN IN THE CLOCK NEVER GOT TO HAVE HIS TIME. THE TIME HE WAS OWED.
AND FOR Mrs. GARISON, IT WAS ONLY EVER A MATTER OF TIME BEFORE SHE WOKE UP WITH THE WRONG IDEA IN HER HEAD AND DID SOMETHING HORRIBLE TO HERSELF.

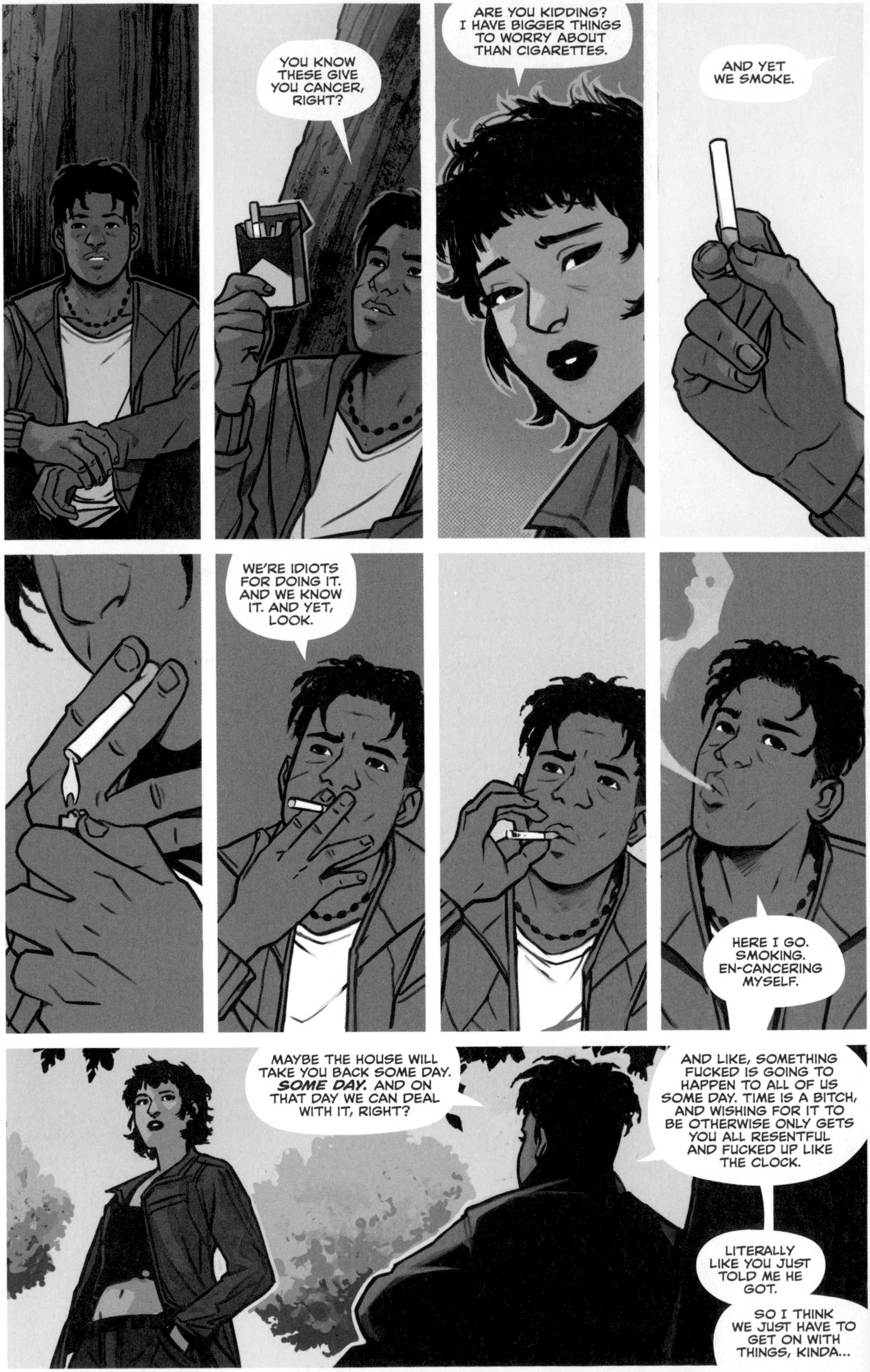
YOU KNOW THESE GIVE YOU CANCER, RIGHT?
ARE YOU KIDDING? I HAVE BIGGER THINGS TO WORRY ABOUT THAN CIGARETTES.
AND YET WE SMOKE.
WE'RE IDIOTS FOR DOING IT. AND WE KNOW IT. AND YET, LOOK.
HERE I GO. SMOKING. EN-CANCERING MYSELF.
MAYBE THE HOUSE WILL TAKE YOU BACK SOME DAY. *SOME DAY.* AND ON THAT DAY WE CAN DEAL WITH IT, RIGHT?
AND LIKE, SOMETHING FUCKED IS GOING TO HAPPEN TO ALL OF US SOME DAY. TIME IS A BITCH, AND WISHING FOR IT TO BE OTHERWISE ONLY GETS YOU ALL RESENTFUL AND FUCKED UP LIKE THE CLOCK.
LITERALLY LIKE YOU JUST TOLD ME HE GOT.
SO I THINK WE JUST HAVE TO GET ON WITH THINGS, KINDA...

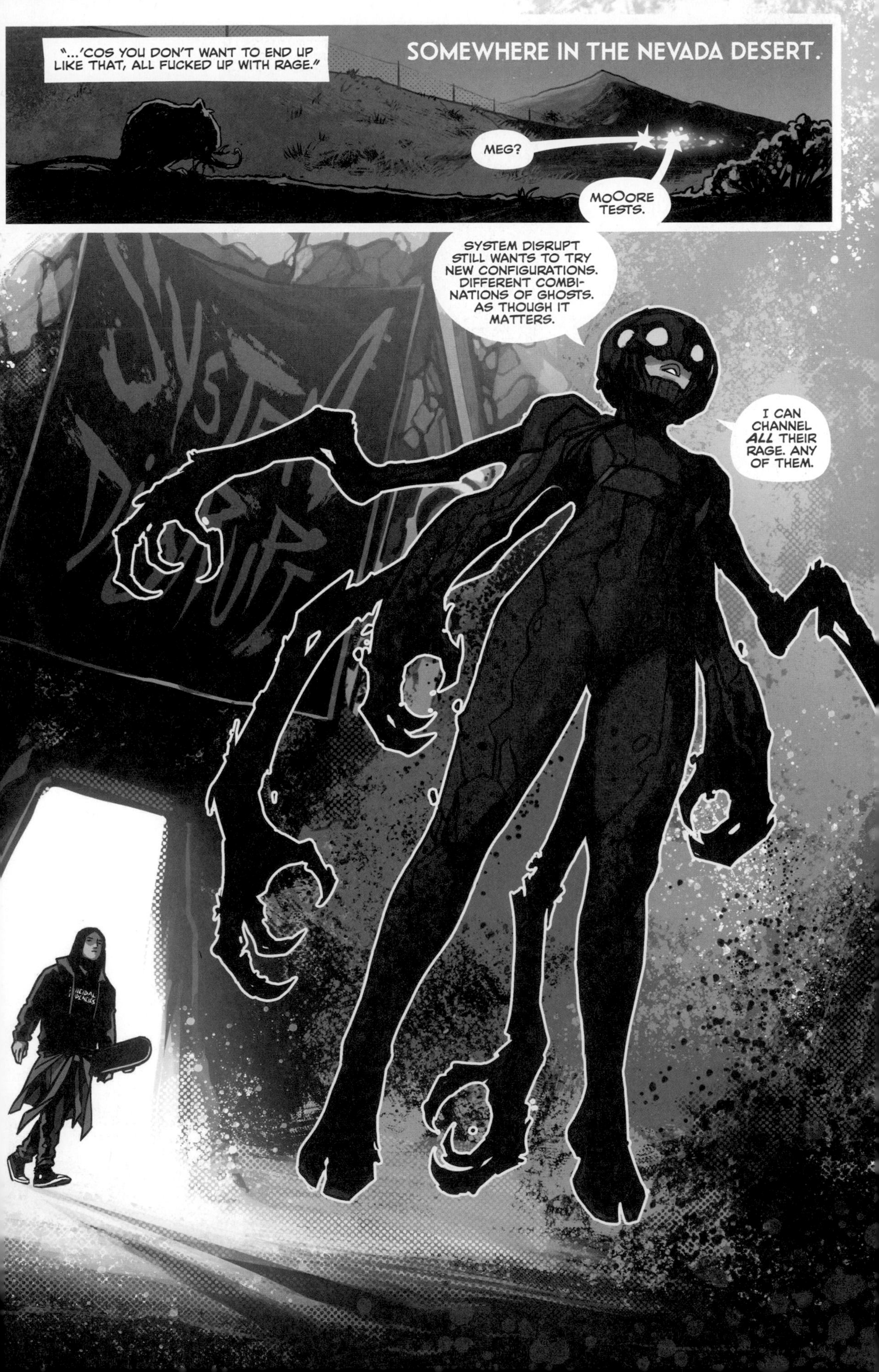
"...'COS YOU DON'T WANT TO END UP LIKE THAT, ALL FUCKED UP WITH RAGE."
SOMEWHERE IN THE NEVADA DESERT.
MEG?
MOOORE TESTS.
SYSTEM DISRUPT STILL WANTS TO TRY NEW CONFIGURATIONS. DIFFERENT COMBI- NATIONS OF GHOSTS. AS THOUGH IT MATTERS.
I CAN CHANNEL ALL THEIR RAGE. ANY OF THEM.

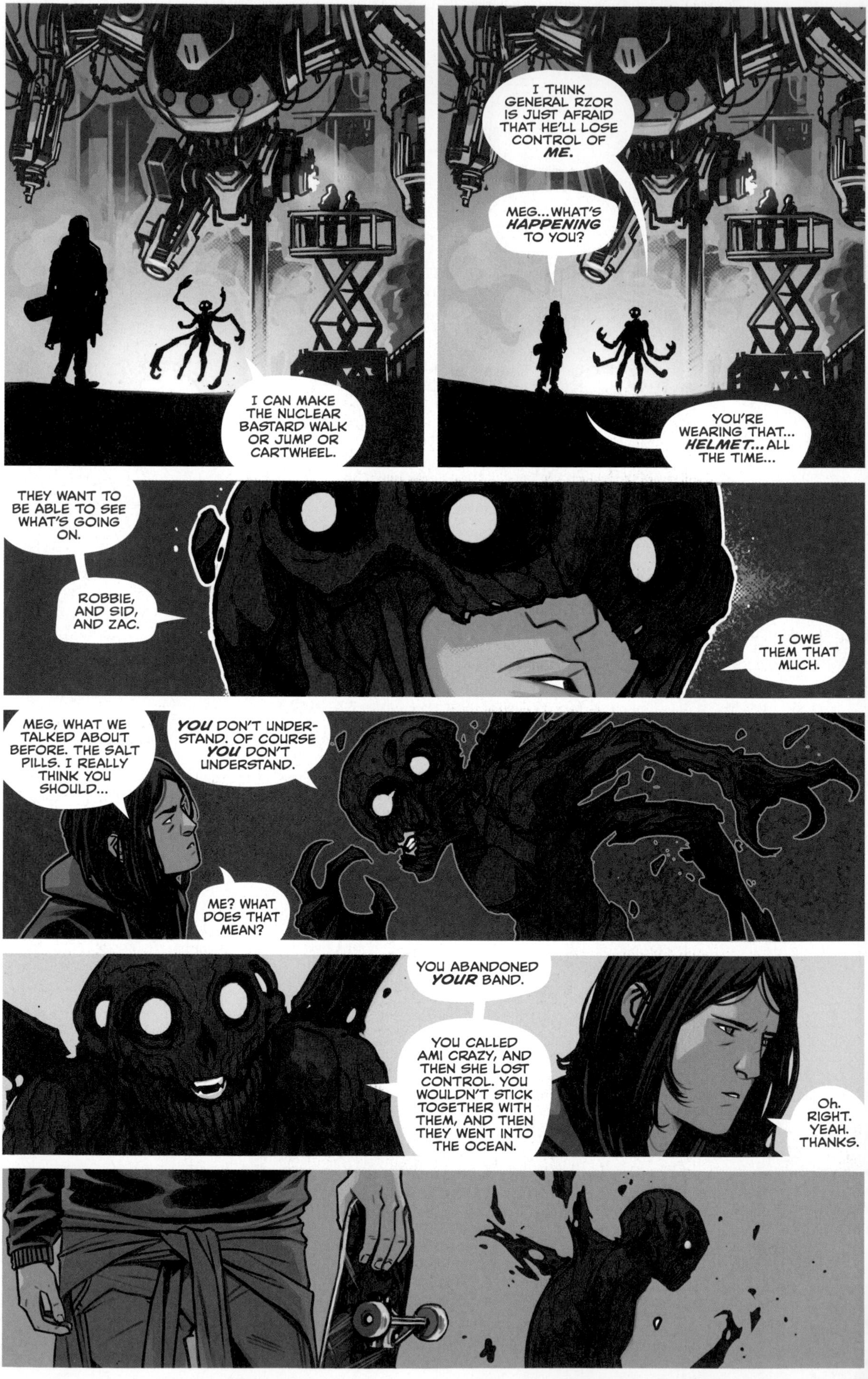
I CAN MAKE THE NUCLEAR BASTARD WALK OR JUMP OR CARTWHEEL.
I THINK GENERAL RZOR IS JUST AFRAID THAT HE'LL LOSE CONTROL OF *ME*.
MEG...WHAT'S *HAPPENING* TO YOU?
YOU'RE WEARING THAT... *HELMET*... ALL THE TIME...
THEY WANT TO BE ABLE TO SEE WHAT'S GOING ON.
ROBBIE, AND SID, AND ZAC.
I OWE THEM THAT MUCH.
MEG, WHAT WE TALKED ABOUT BEFORE. THE SALT PILLS. I REALLY THINK YOU SHOULD...
YOU DON'T UNDERSTAND. OF COURSE *YOU* DON'T UNDERSTAND.
ME? WHAT DOES THAT MEAN?
YOU ABANDONED *YOUR* BAND.
YOU CALLED AMI CRAZY, AND THEN SHE LOST CONTROL. YOU WOULDN'T STICK TOGETHER WITH THEM, AND THEN THEY WENT INTO THE OCEAN.
Oh. RIGHT. YEAH. THANKS.

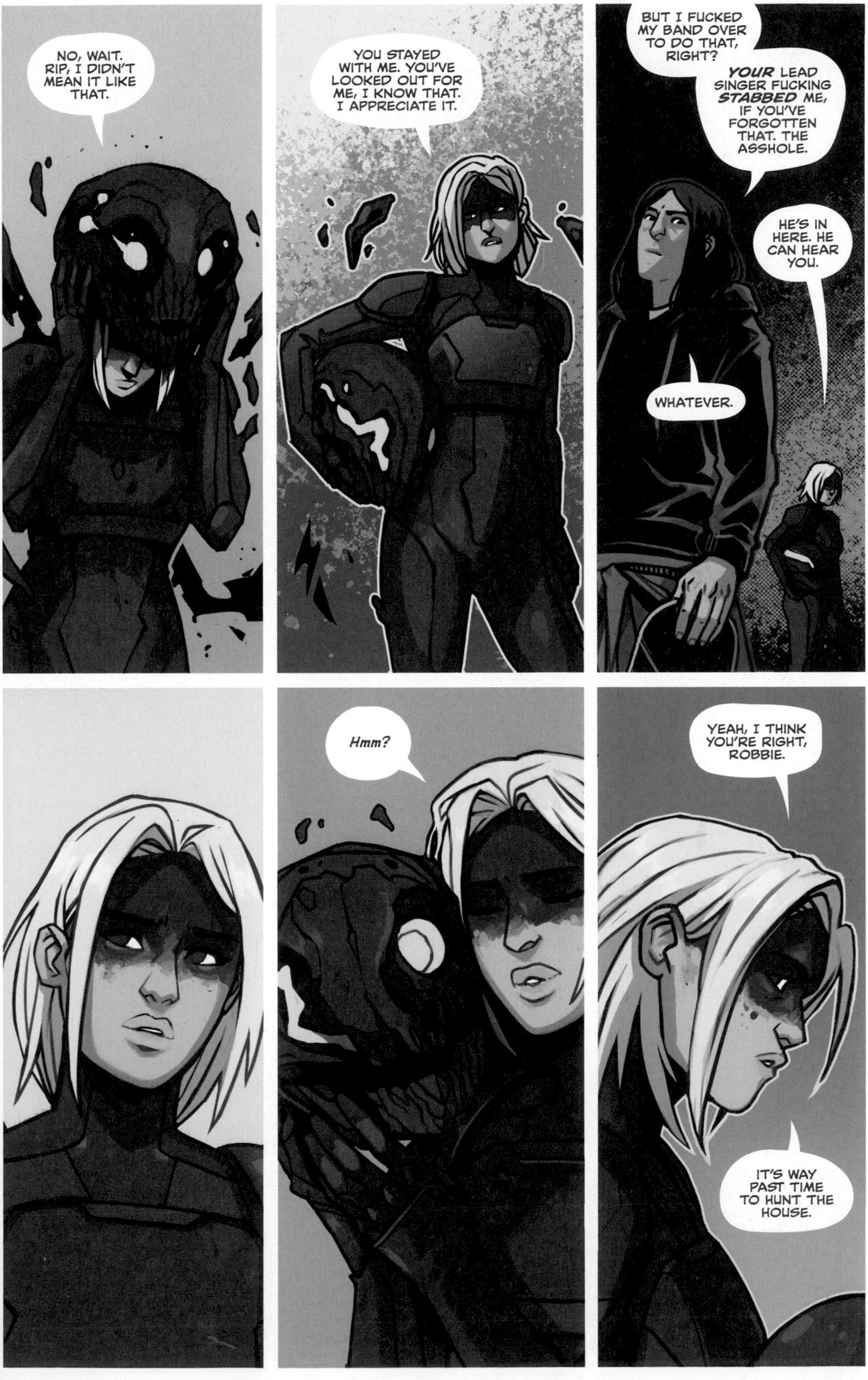
NO, WAIT. RIP, I DIDN'T MEAN IT LIKE THAT.
YOU STAYED WITH ME. YOU'VE LOOKED OUT FOR ME, I KNOW THAT. I APPRECIATE IT.
BUT I FUCKED MY BAND OVER TO DO THAT, RIGHT?
YOUR LEAD SINGER FUCKING *STABBED* ME, IF YOU'VE FORGOTTEN THAT. THE ASSHOLE.
HE'S IN HERE. HE CAN HEAR YOU.
WHATEVER.
Hmm?
YEAH, I THINK YOU'RE RIGHT, ROBBIE.
IT'S WAY PAST TIME TO HUNT THE HOUSE.

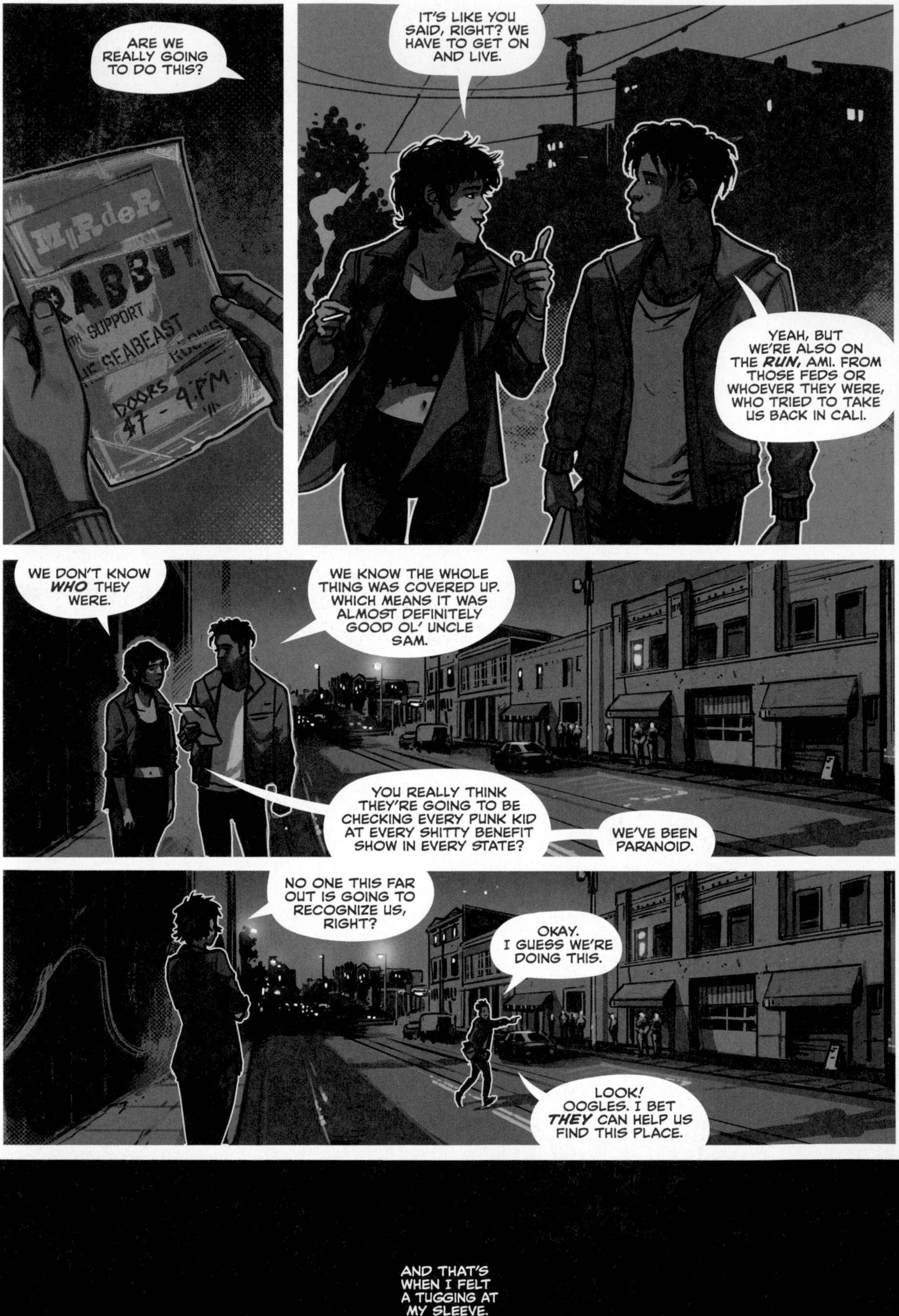

ARE WE REALLY GOING TO DO THIS?
RABBIT
SUPPORT
SEABEAST
DOORS
IT'S LIKE YOU SAID, RIGHT? WE HAVE TO GET ON AND LIVE.
YEAH, BUT WE'RE ALSO ON THE ***RUN,*** AMI. FROM THOSE FEDS OR WHOEVER THEY WERE, WHO TRIED TO TAKE US BACK IN CALI.
WE DON'T KNOW ***WHO*** THEY WERE.
WE KNOW THE WHOLE THING WAS COVERED UP. WHICH MEANS IT WAS ALMOST DEFINITELY GOOD OL' UNCLE SAM.
YOU REALLY THINK THEY'RE GOING TO BE CHECKING EVERY PUNK KID AT EVERY SHITTY BENEFIT SHOW IN EVERY STATE?
WE'VE BEEN PARANOID.
NO ONE THIS FAR OUT IS GOING TO RECOGNIZE US, RIGHT?
OKAY. I GUESS WE'RE DOING THIS.
LOOK! OOGLES. I BET ***THEY*** CAN HELP US FIND THIS PLACE.
AND THAT'S WHEN I FELT A TUGGING AT MY SLEEVE.

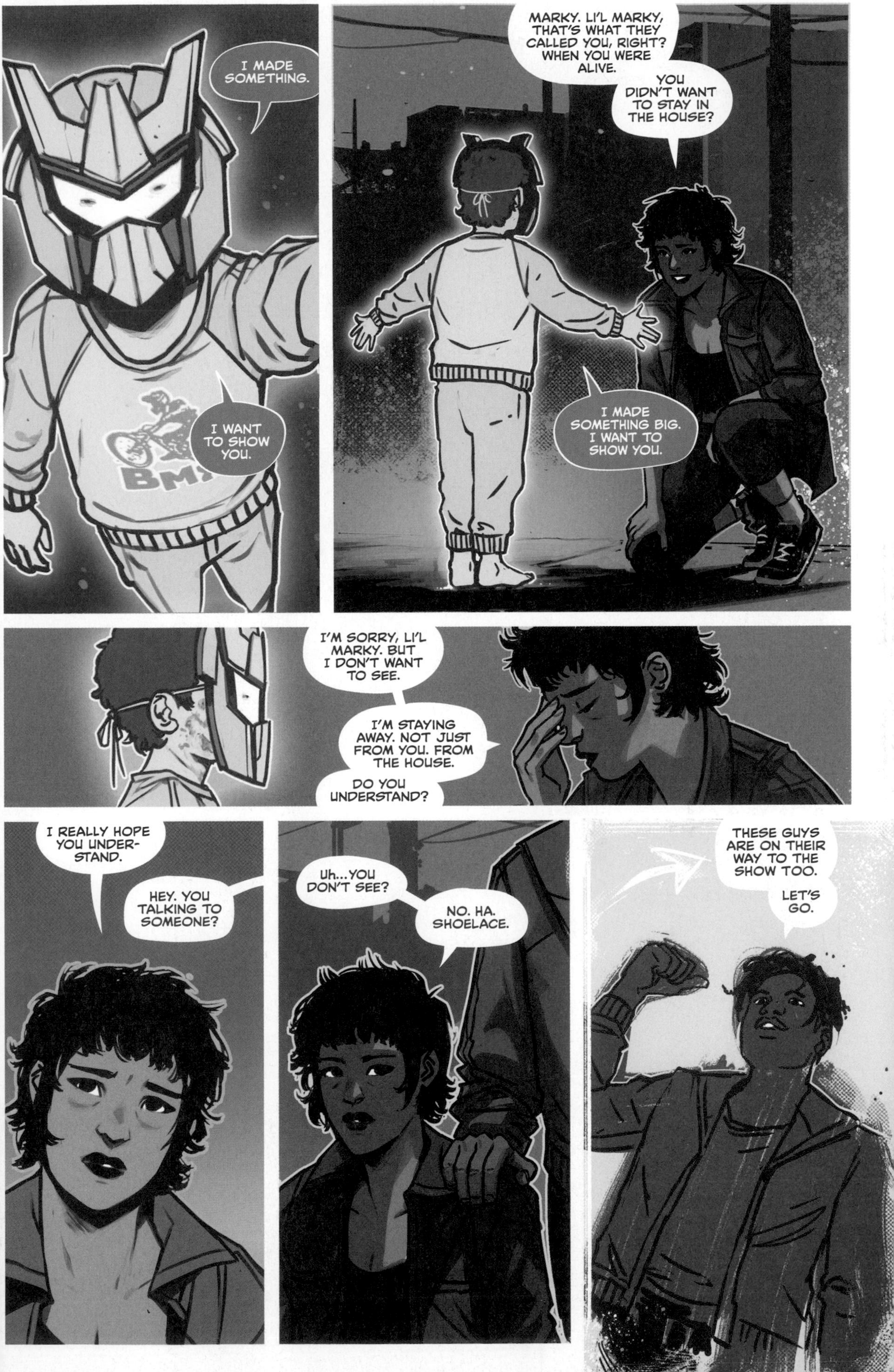
I MADE SOMETHING.
I WANT TO SHOW YOU.
MARKY. LI'L MARKY, THAT'S WHAT THEY CALLED YOU, RIGHT? WHEN YOU WERE ALIVE.
YOU DIDN'T WANT TO STAY IN THE HOUSE?
I MADE SOMETHING BIG. I WANT TO SHOW YOU.
I'M SORRY, LI'L MARKY. BUT I DON'T WANT TO SEE.
I'M STAYING AWAY. NOT JUST FROM YOU. FROM THE HOUSE.
DO YOU UNDERSTAND?
I REALLY HOPE YOU UNDER-STAND.
HEY. YOU TALKING TO SOMEONE?
Uh...YOU DON'T SEE?
NO. HA. SHOELACE.
THESE GUYS ARE ON THEIR WAY TO THE SHOW TOO.
LET'S GO.

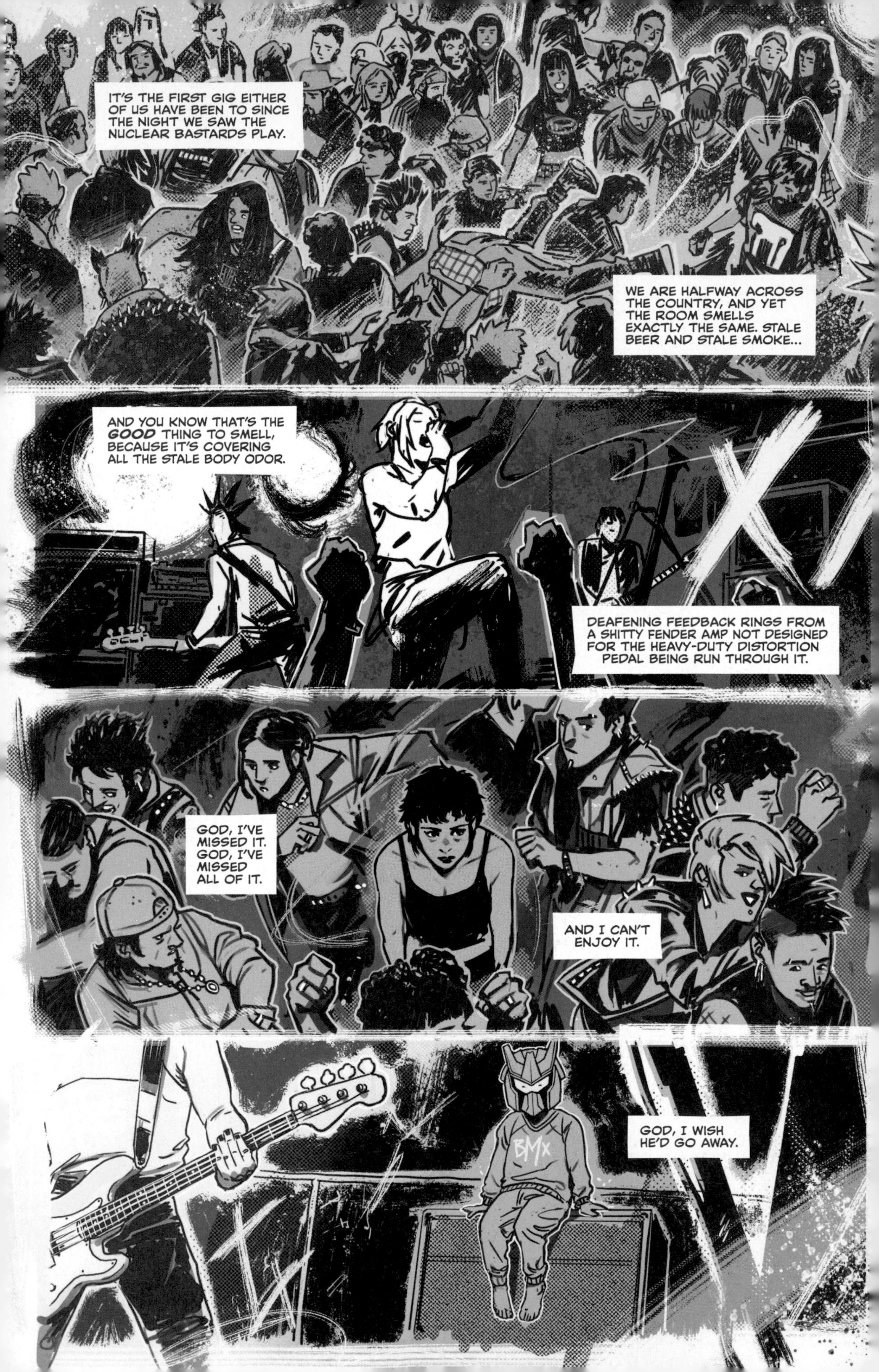
IT'S THE FIRST GIG EITHER OF US HAVE BEEN TO SINCE THE NIGHT WE SAW THE NUCLEAR BASTARDS PLAY.
WE ARE HALFWAY ACROSS THE COUNTRY, AND YET THE ROOM SMELLS EXACTLY THE SAME. STALE BEER AND STALE SMOKE...
AND YOU KNOW THAT'S THE GOOD THING TO SMELL, BECAUSE IT'S COVERING ALL THE STALE BODY ODOR.
DEAFENING FEEDBACK RINGS FROM A SHITTY FENDER AMP NOT DESIGNED FOR THE HEAVY-DUTY DISTORTION PEDAL BEING RUN THROUGH IT.
GOD, I'VE MISSED IT. GOD, I'VE MISSED ALL OF IT.
AND I CAN'T ENJOY IT.
BMX
GOD, I WISH HE'D GO AWAY.

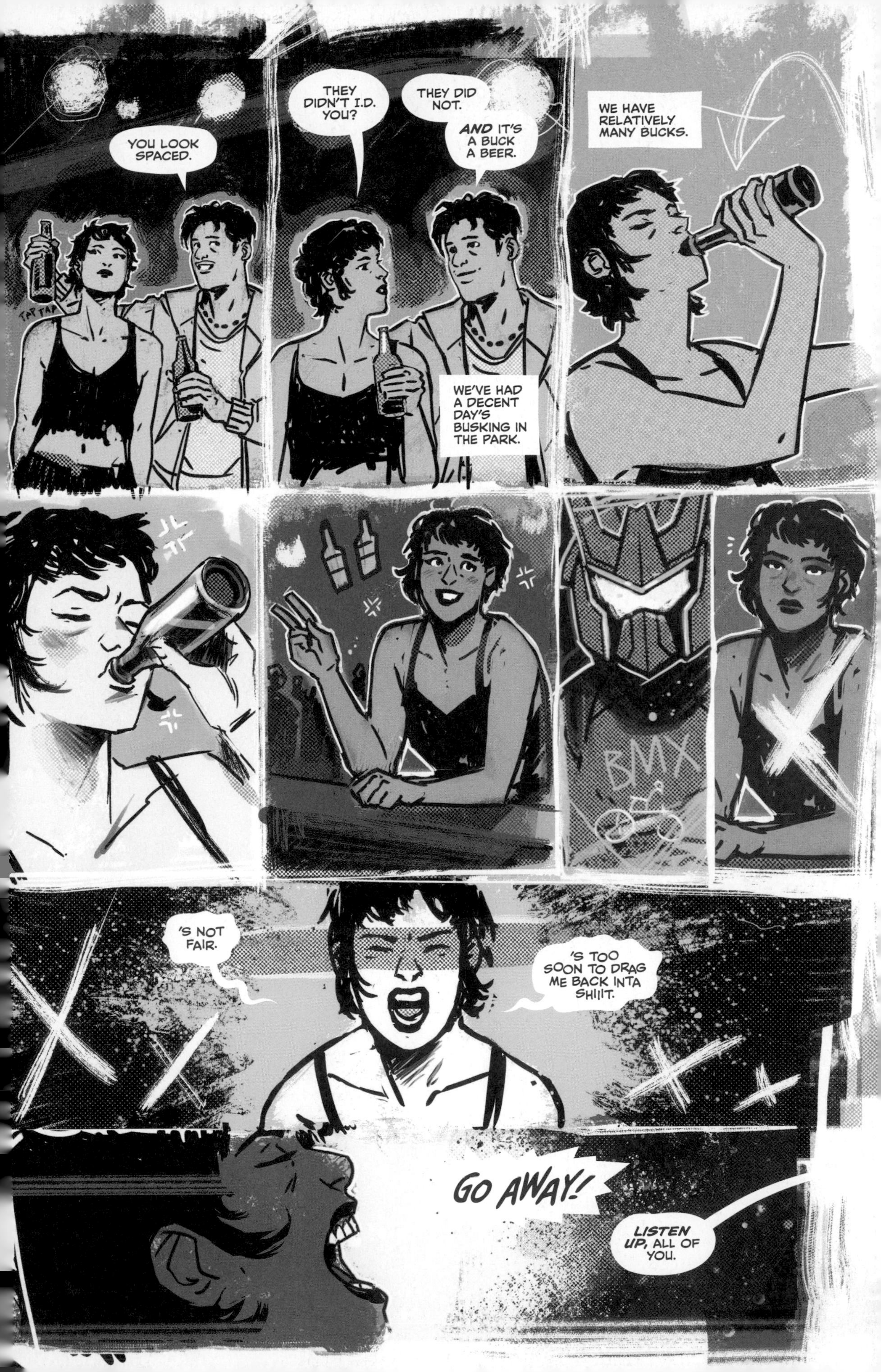
TAP TAP
YOU LOOK SPACED.
THEY DIDN'T I.D. YOU?
THEY DID NOT.
AND IT'S A BUCK A BEER.
WE'VE HAD A DECENT DAY'S BUSKING IN THE PARK.
WE HAVE RELATIVELY MANY BUCKS.
BMX
'S NOT FAIR.
'S TOO SOON TO DRAG ME BACK INTA SHIIIT.
GO AWAY!
LISTEN UP, ALL OF YOU.

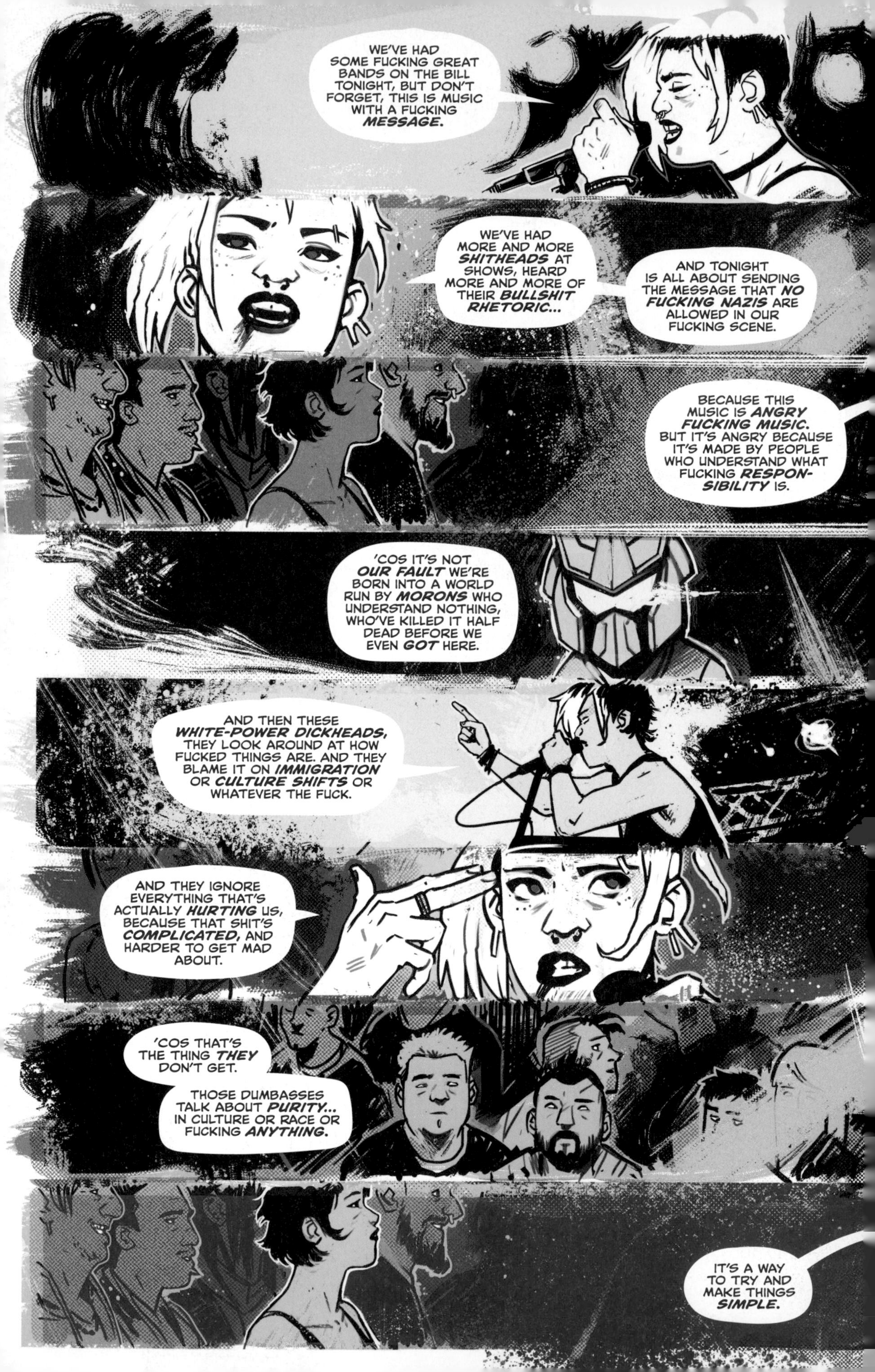

WE'VE HAD SOME FUCKING GREAT BANDS ON THE BILL TONIGHT, BUT DON'T FORGET, THIS IS MUSIC WITH A FUCKING MESSAGE.
WE'VE HAD MORE AND MORE SHITHEADS AT SHOWS, HEARD MORE AND MORE OF THEIR BULLSHIT RHETORIC...
AND TONIGHT IS ALL ABOUT SENDING THE MESSAGE THAT NO FUCKING NAZIS ARE ALLOWED IN OUR FUCKING SCENE.
BECAUSE THIS MUSIC IS ANGRY FUCKING MUSIC. BUT IT'S ANGRY BECAUSE IT'S MADE BY PEOPLE WHO UNDERSTAND WHAT FUCKING RESPON-SIBILITY IS.
'COS IT'S NOT OUR FAULT WE'RE BORN INTO A WORLD RUN BY MORONS WHO UNDERSTAND NOTHING, WHO'VE KILLED IT HALF DEAD BEFORE WE EVEN GOT HERE.
AND THEN THESE WHITE-POWER DICKHEADS, THEY LOOK AROUND AT HOW FUCKED THINGS ARE. AND THEY BLAME IT ON IMMIGRATION OR CULTURE SHIFTS OR WHATEVER THE FUCK.
AND THEY IGNORE EVERYTHING THAT'S ACTUALLY HURTING US, BECAUSE THAT SHIT'S COMPLICATED, AND HARDER TO GET MAD ABOUT.
'COS THAT'S THE THING THEY DON'T GET.
THOSE DUMBASSES TALK ABOUT PURITY... IN CULTURE OR RACE OR FUCKING ANYTHING.
IT'S A WAY TO TRY AND MAKE THINGS SIMPLE.

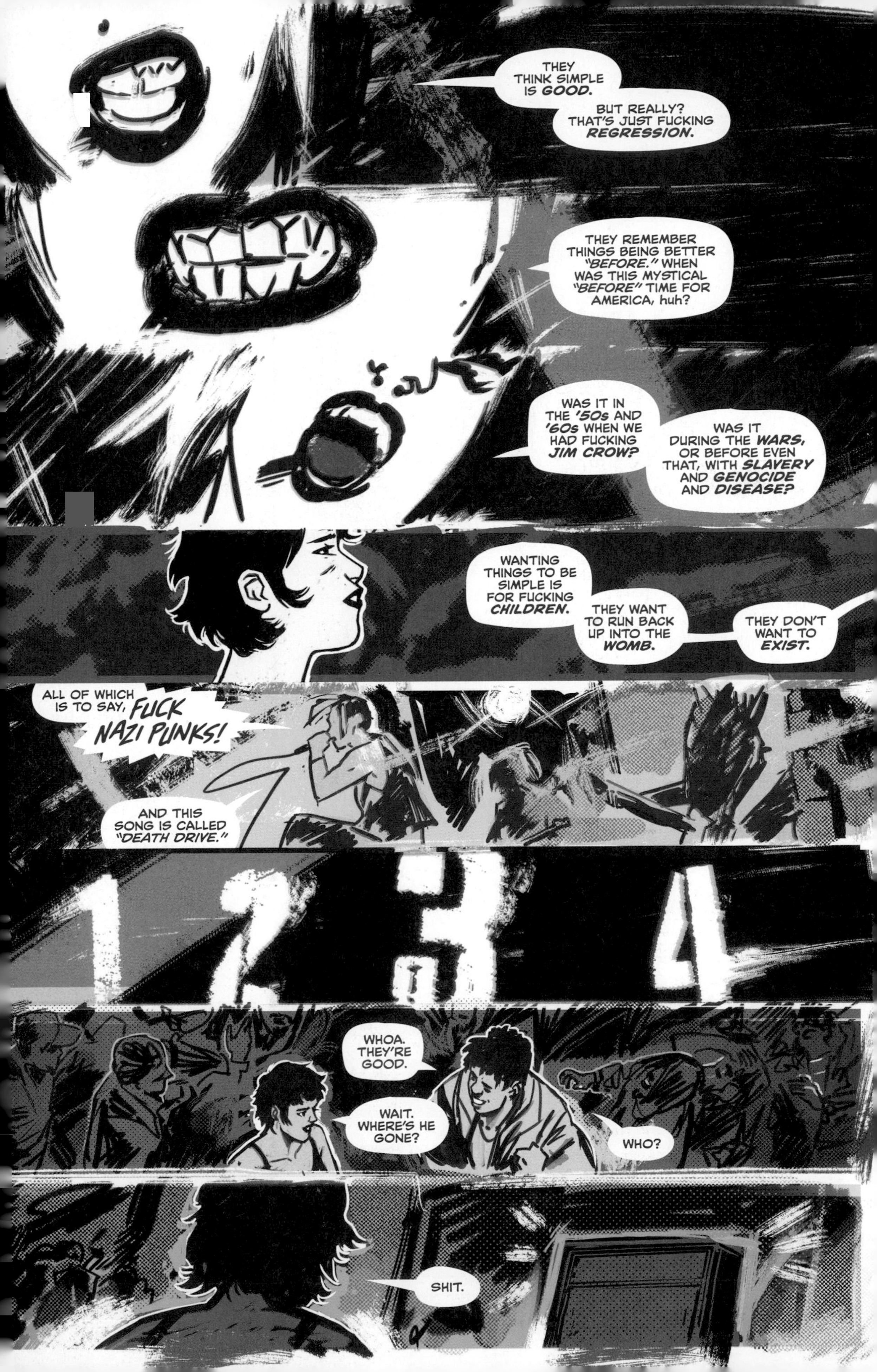
THEY THINK SIMPLE IS GOOD.
BUT REALLY? THAT'S JUST FUCKING REGRESSION.
THEY REMEMBER THINGS BEING BETTER "BEFORE." WHEN WAS THIS MYSTICAL "BEFORE" TIME FOR AMERICA, huh?
WAS IT IN THE '50s AND '60s WHEN WE HAD FUCKING JIM CROW?
WAS IT DURING THE WARS, OR BEFORE EVEN THAT, WITH SLAVERY AND GENOCIDE AND DISEASE?
WANTING THINGS TO BE SIMPLE IS FOR FUCKING CHILDREN.
THEY WANT TO RUN BACK UP INTO THE WOMB.
THEY DON'T WANT TO EXIST.
ALL OF WHICH IS TO SAY, FUCK NAZI PUNKS!
AND THIS SONG IS CALLED "DEATH DRIVE."
1 2 3 4
WHOA. THEY'RE GOOD.
WAIT. WHERE'S HE GONE?
WHO?
SHIT.

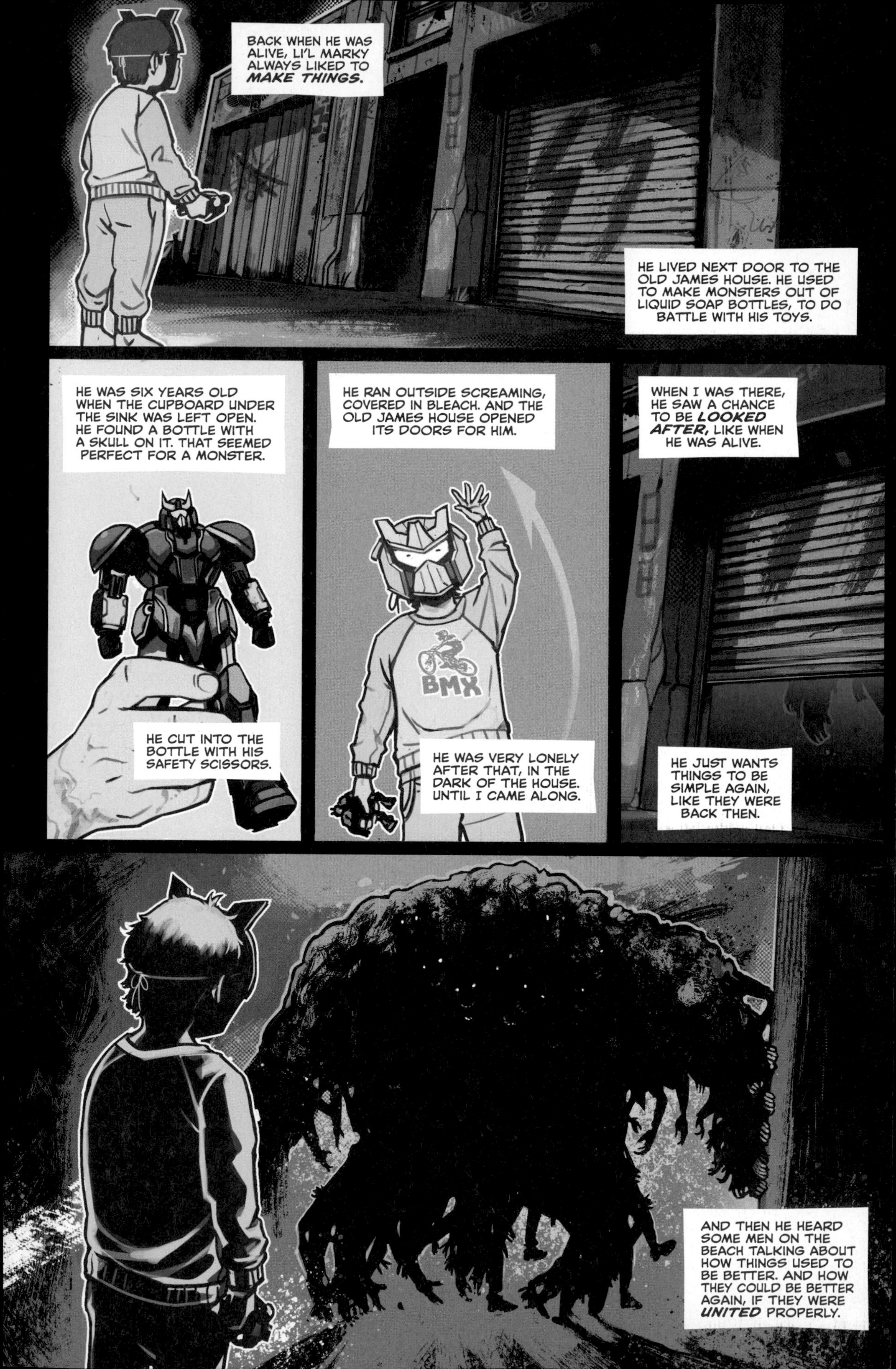
BACK WHEN HE WAS ALIVE, LI'L MARKY ALWAYS LIKED TO *MAKE THINGS.*
HE LIVED NEXT DOOR TO THE OLD JAMES HOUSE. HE USED TO MAKE MONSTERS OUT OF LIQUID SOAP BOTTLES, TO DO BATTLE WITH HIS TOYS.
HE WAS SIX YEARS OLD WHEN THE CUPBOARD UNDER THE SINK WAS LEFT OPEN. HE FOUND A BOTTLE WITH A SKULL ON IT. THAT SEEMED PERFECT FOR A MONSTER.
HE CUT INTO THE BOTTLE WITH HIS SAFETY SCISSORS.
HE RAN OUTSIDE SCREAMING, COVERED IN BLEACH. AND THE OLD JAMES HOUSE OPENED ITS DOORS FOR HIM.
BMX
HE WAS VERY LONELY AFTER THAT, IN THE DARK OF THE HOUSE. UNTIL I CAME ALONG.
WHEN I WAS THERE, HE SAW A CHANCE TO BE *LOOKED AFTER,* LIKE WHEN HE WAS ALIVE.
HE JUST WANTS THINGS TO BE SIMPLE AGAIN, LIKE THEY WERE BACK THEN.
AND THEN HE HEARD SOME MEN ON THE BEACH TALKING ABOUT HOW THINGS USED TO BE BETTER. AND HOW THEY COULD BE BETTER AGAIN, IF THEY WERE *UNITED* PROPERLY.

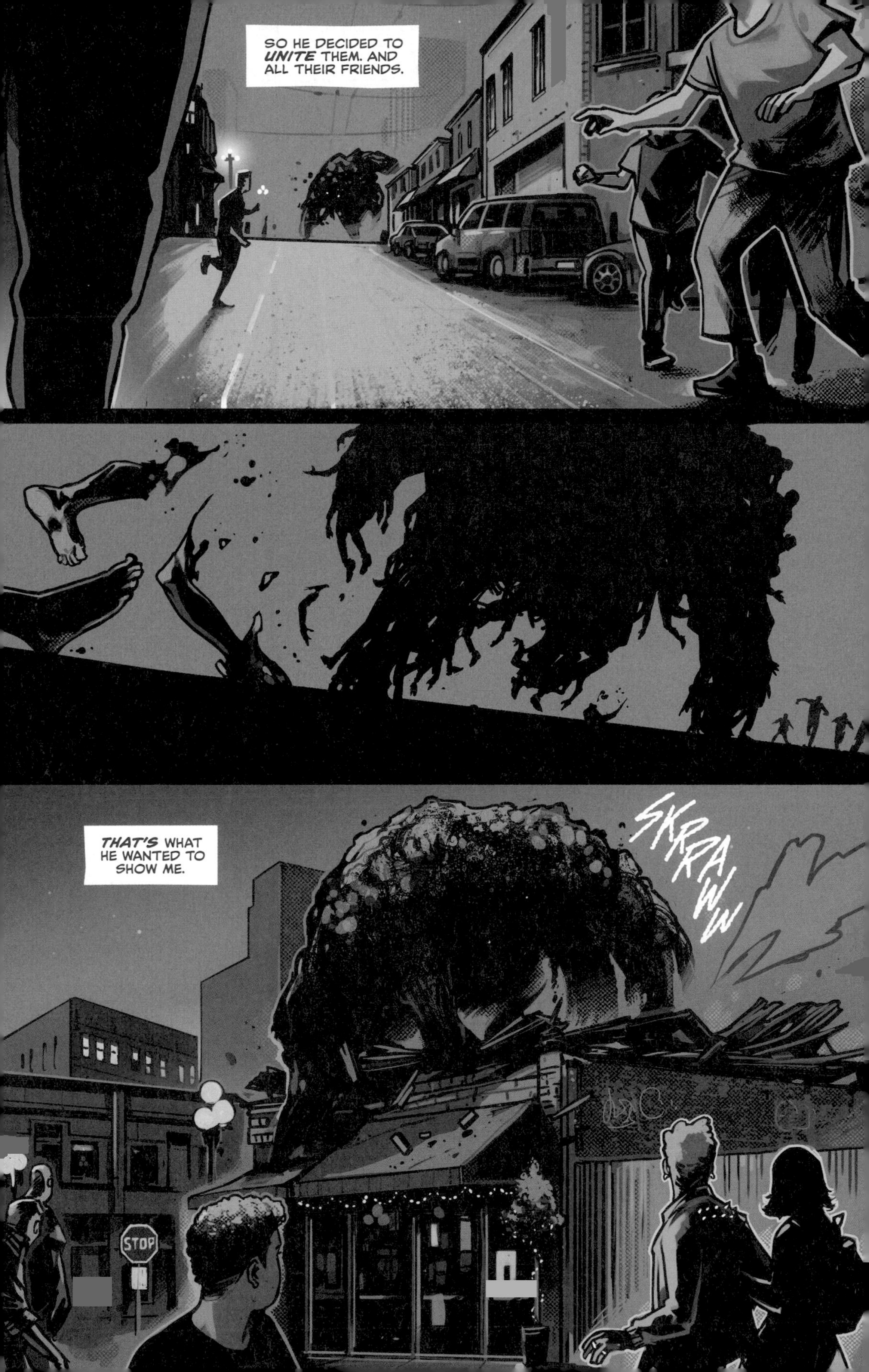
SO HE DECIDED TO *UNITE* THEM. AND ALL THEIR FRIENDS.
THAT'S WHAT HE WANTED TO SHOW ME.
SKRRAWW
STOP

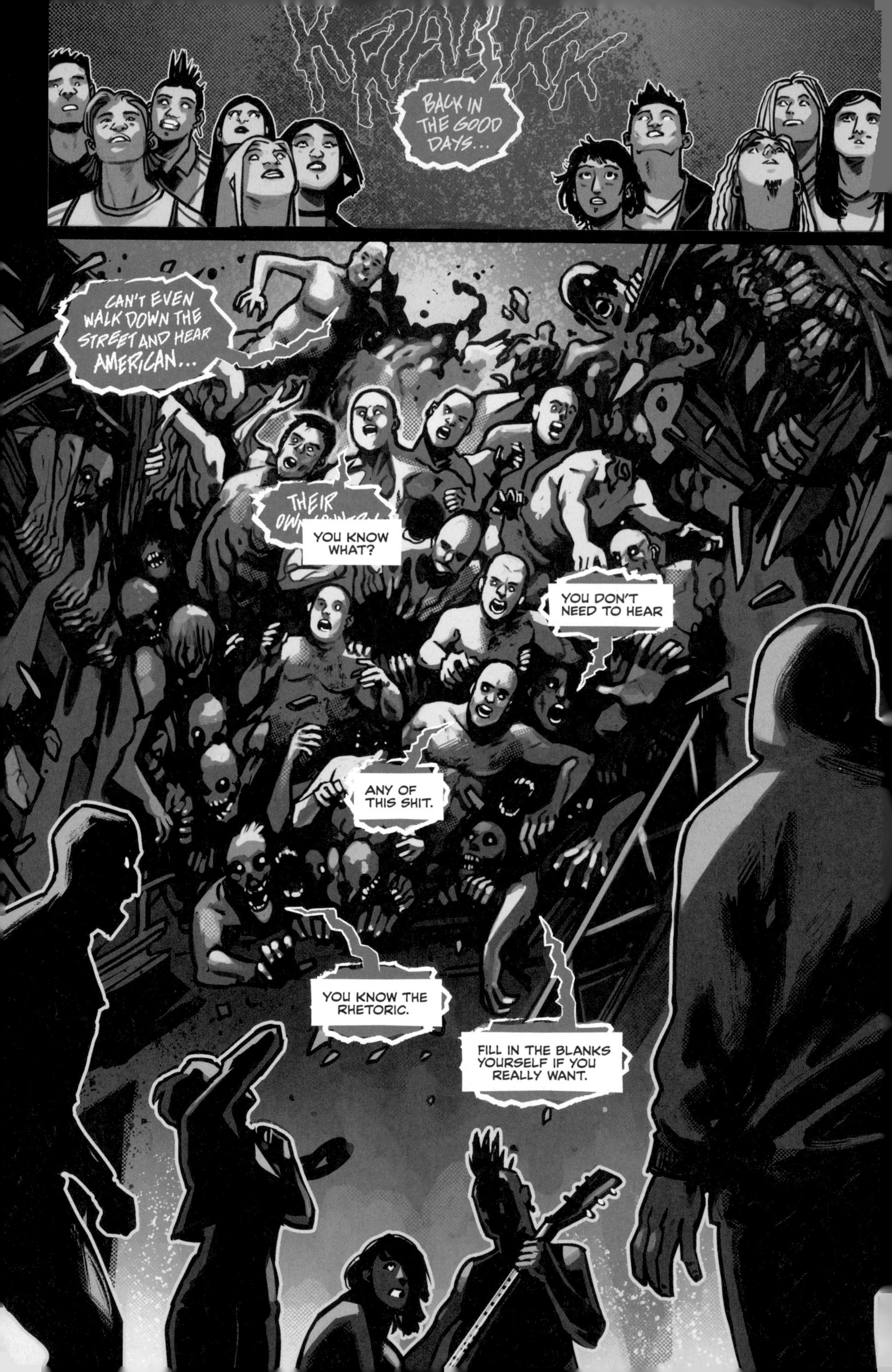
BACK IN THE GOOD DAYS...
CAN'T EVEN WALK DOWN THE STREET AND HEAR AMERICAN...
THEIR
YOU KNOW WHAT?
YOU DON'T NEED TO HEAR
ANY OF THIS SHIT.
YOU KNOW THE RHETORIC.
FILL IN THE BLANKS YOURSELF IF YOU REALLY WANT.

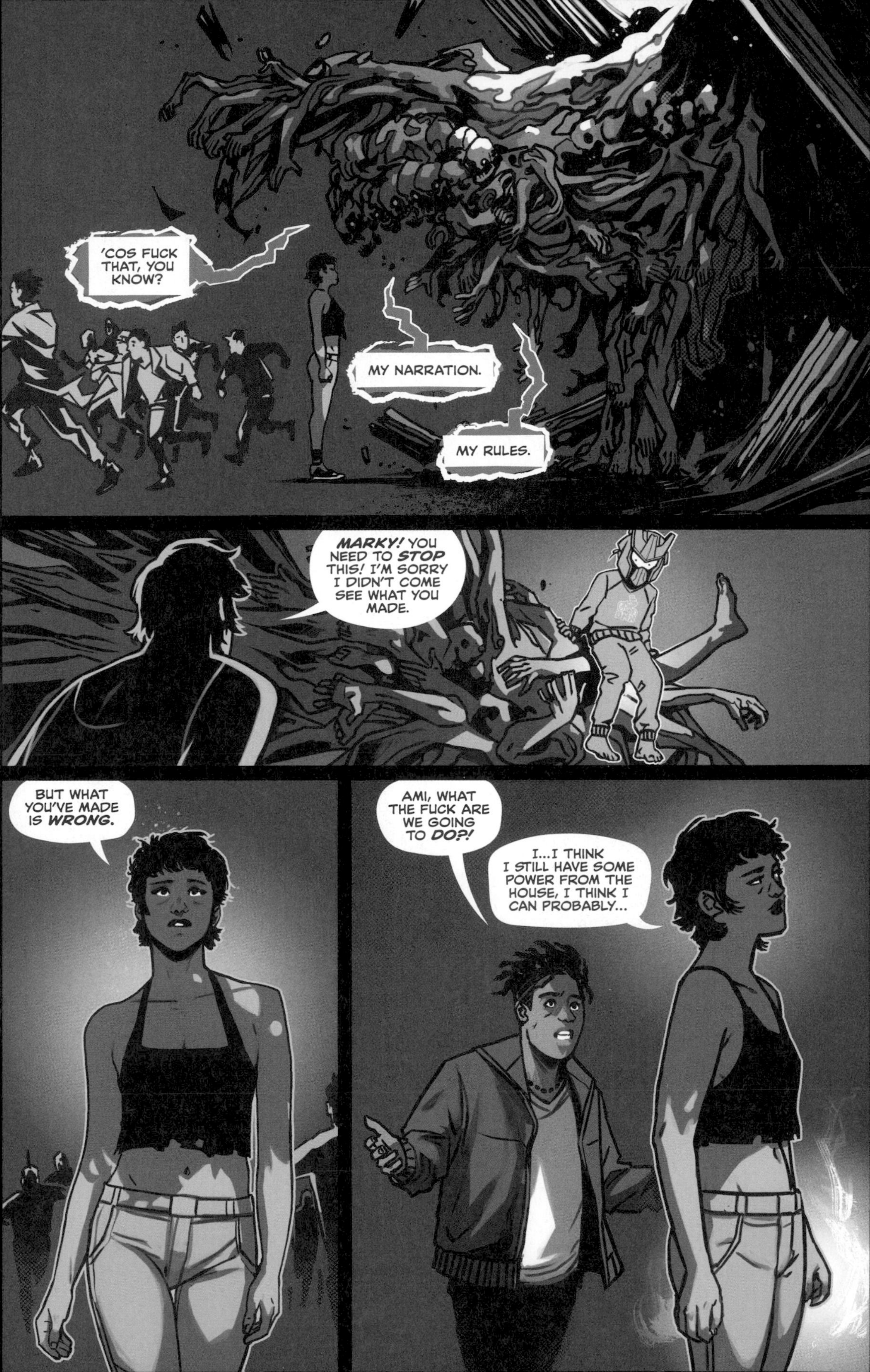
'COS FUCK THAT, YOU KNOW?
MY NARRATION.
MY RULES.
MARKY! YOU NEED TO STOP THIS! I'M SORRY I DIDN'T COME SEE WHAT YOU MADE.
BUT WHAT YOU'VE MADE IS WRONG.
AMI, WHAT THE FUCK ARE WE GOING TO DO?!
I...I THINK I STILL HAVE SOME POWER FROM THE HOUSE, I THINK I CAN PROBABLY...

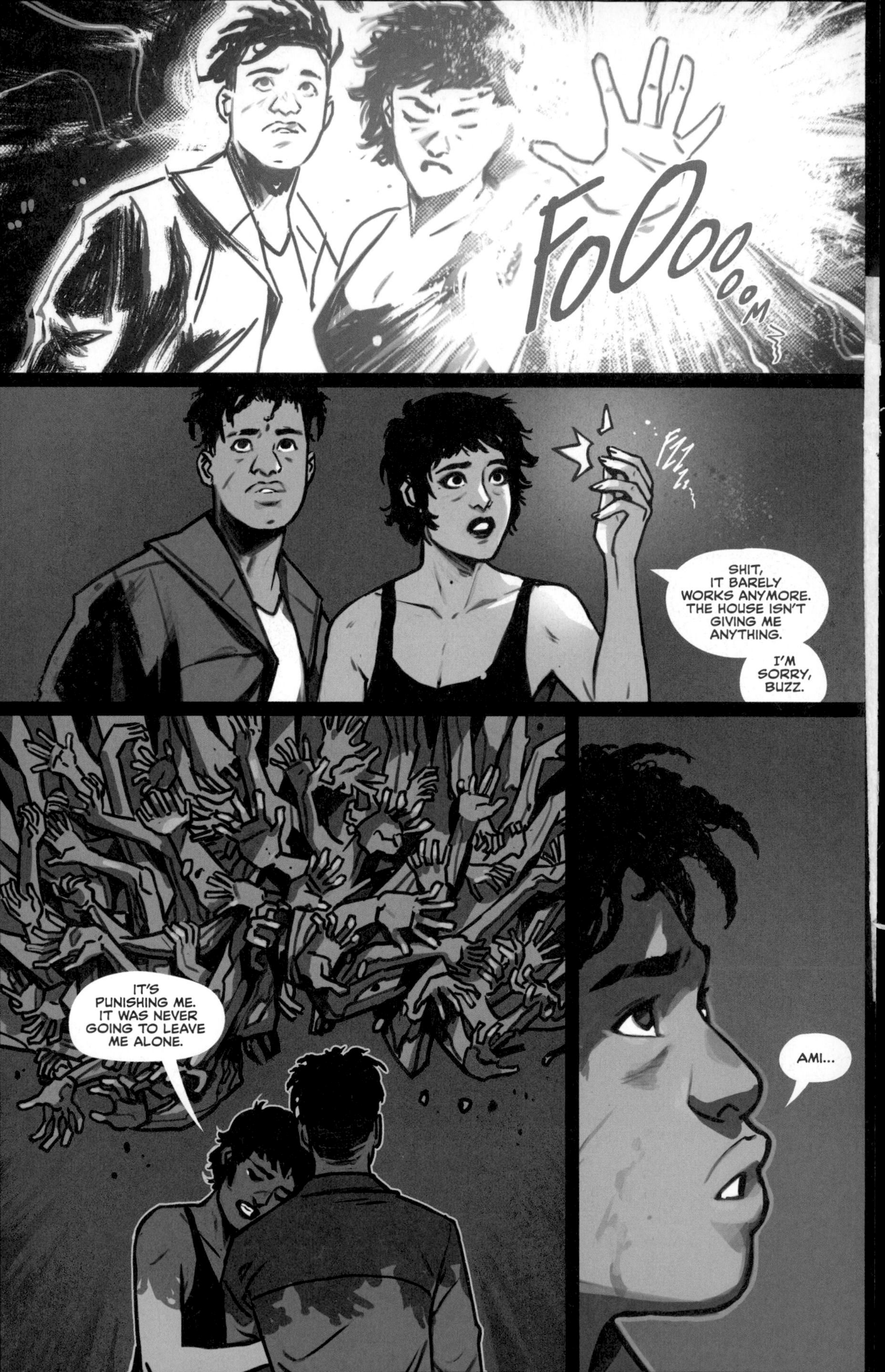
FOOOooomz
FZZZ
SHIT, IT BARELY WORKS ANYMORE. THE HOUSE ISN'T GIVING ME ANYTHING.
I'M SORRY, BUZZ.
IT'S PUNISHING ME. IT WAS NEVER GOING TO LEAVE ME ALONE.
AMI...

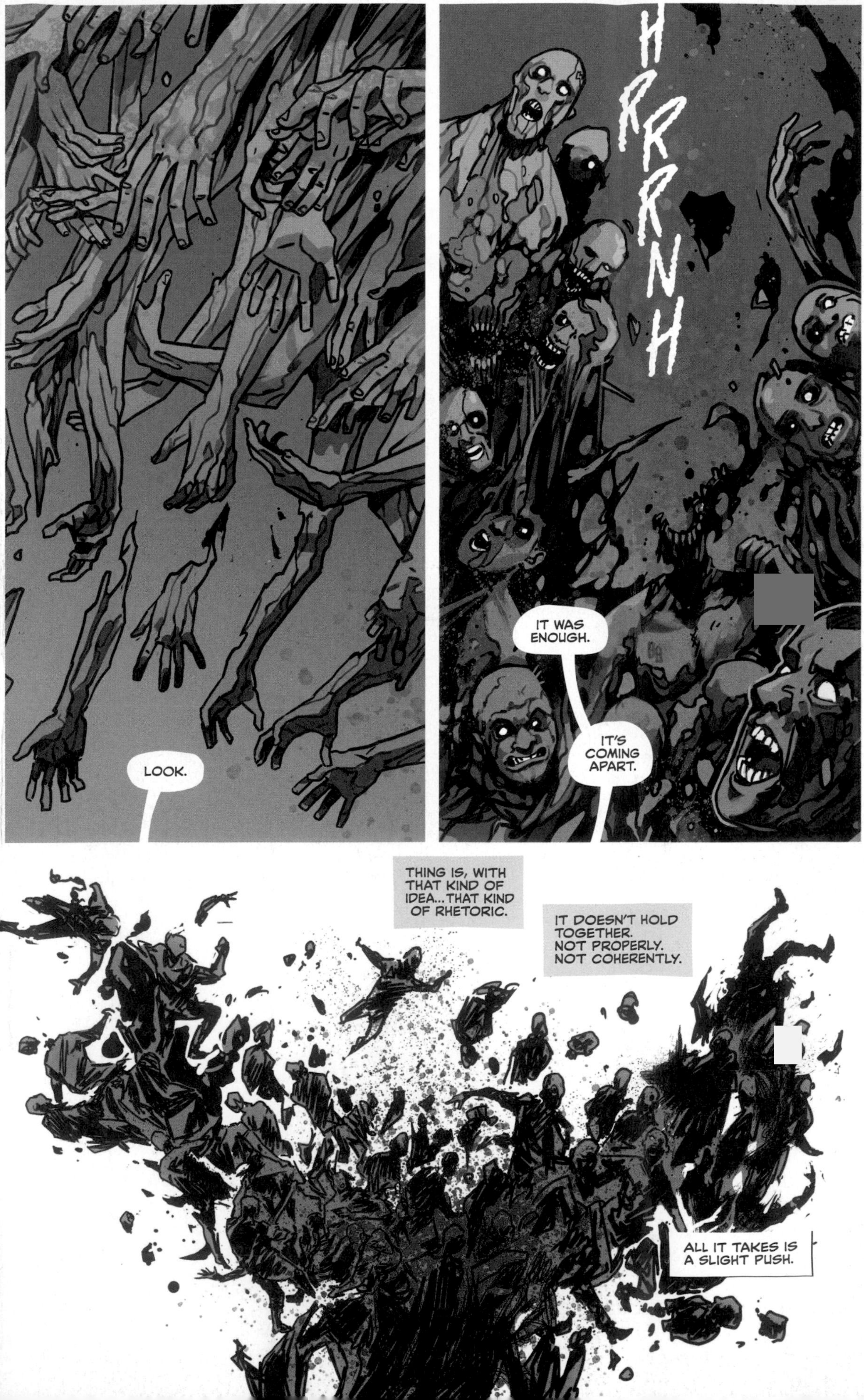
LOOK.
HRRRNH
IT WAS ENOUGH.
IT'S COMING APART.
THING IS, WITH THAT KIND OF IDEA...THAT KIND OF RHETORIC.
IT DOESN'T HOLD TOGETHER. NOT PROPERLY. NOT COHERENTLY.
ALL IT TAKES IS A SLIGHT PUSH.

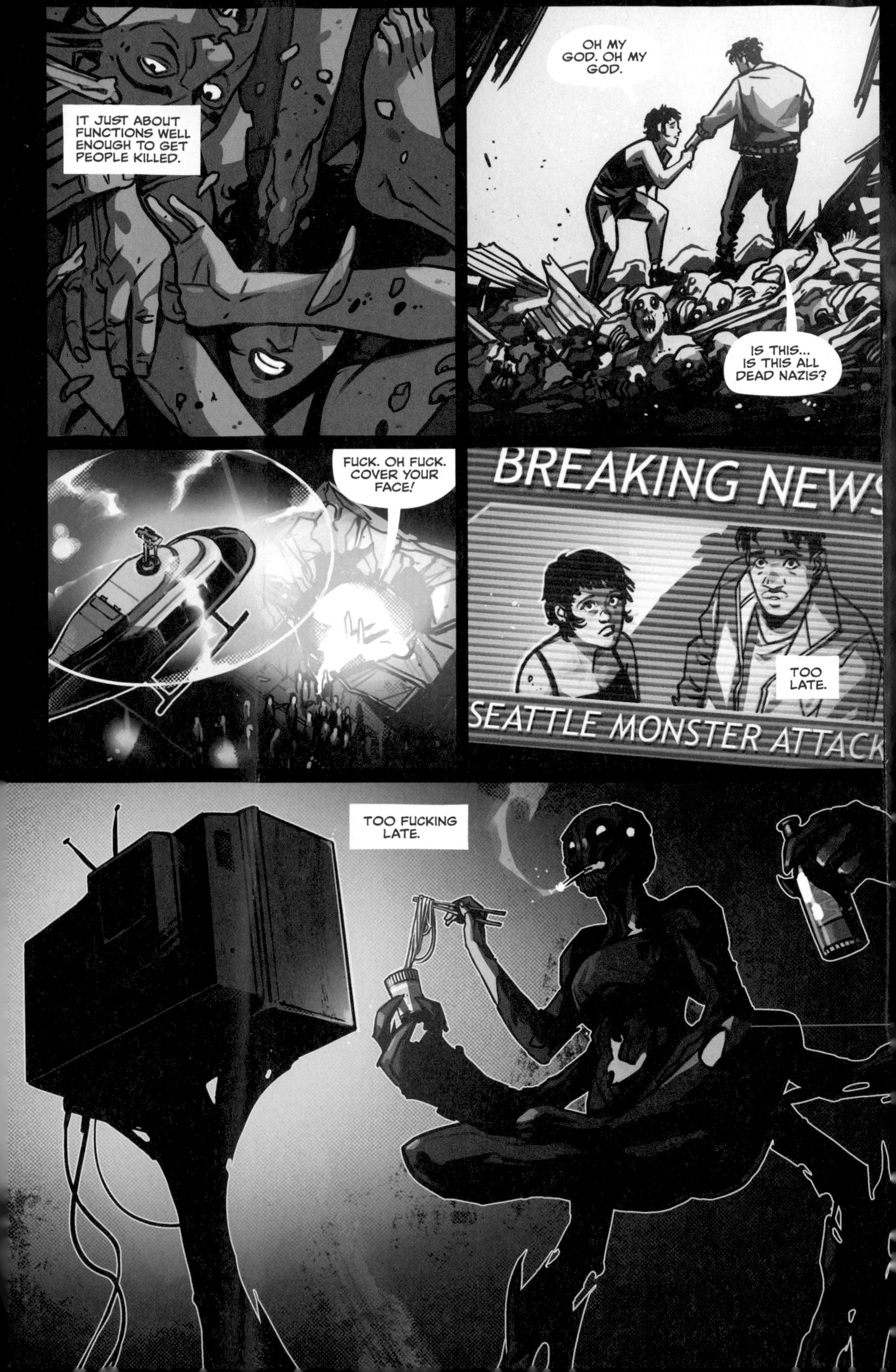
IT JUST ABOUT FUNCTIONS WELL ENOUGH TO GET PEOPLE KILLED.
OH MY GOD. OH MY GOD.
IS THIS... IS THIS ALL DEAD NAZIS?
FUCK. OH FUCK. COVER YOUR FACE!
BREAKING NEWS
TOO LATE.
SEATTLE MONSTER ATTACK
TOO FUCKING LATE.

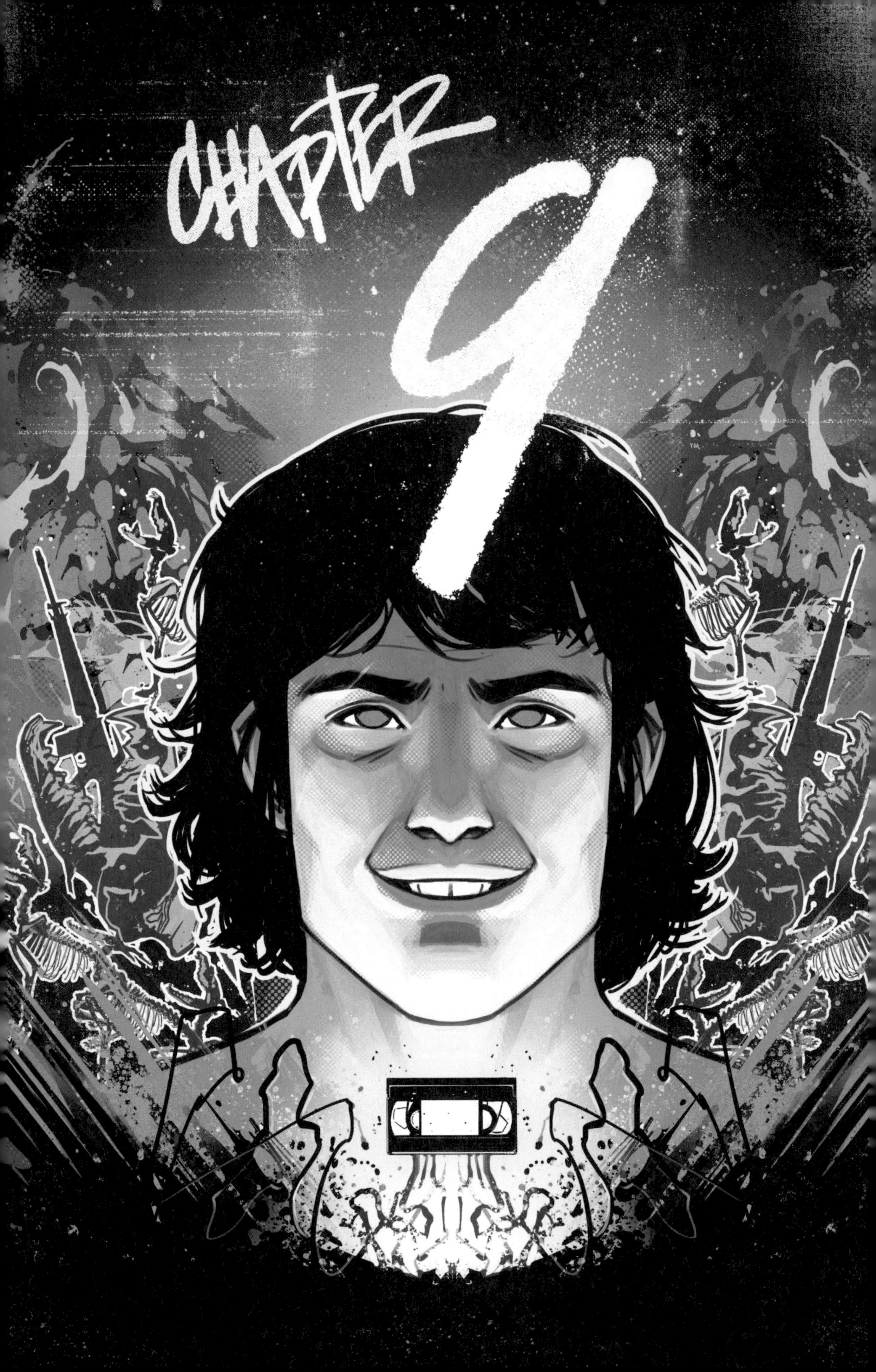
CHAPTER
9

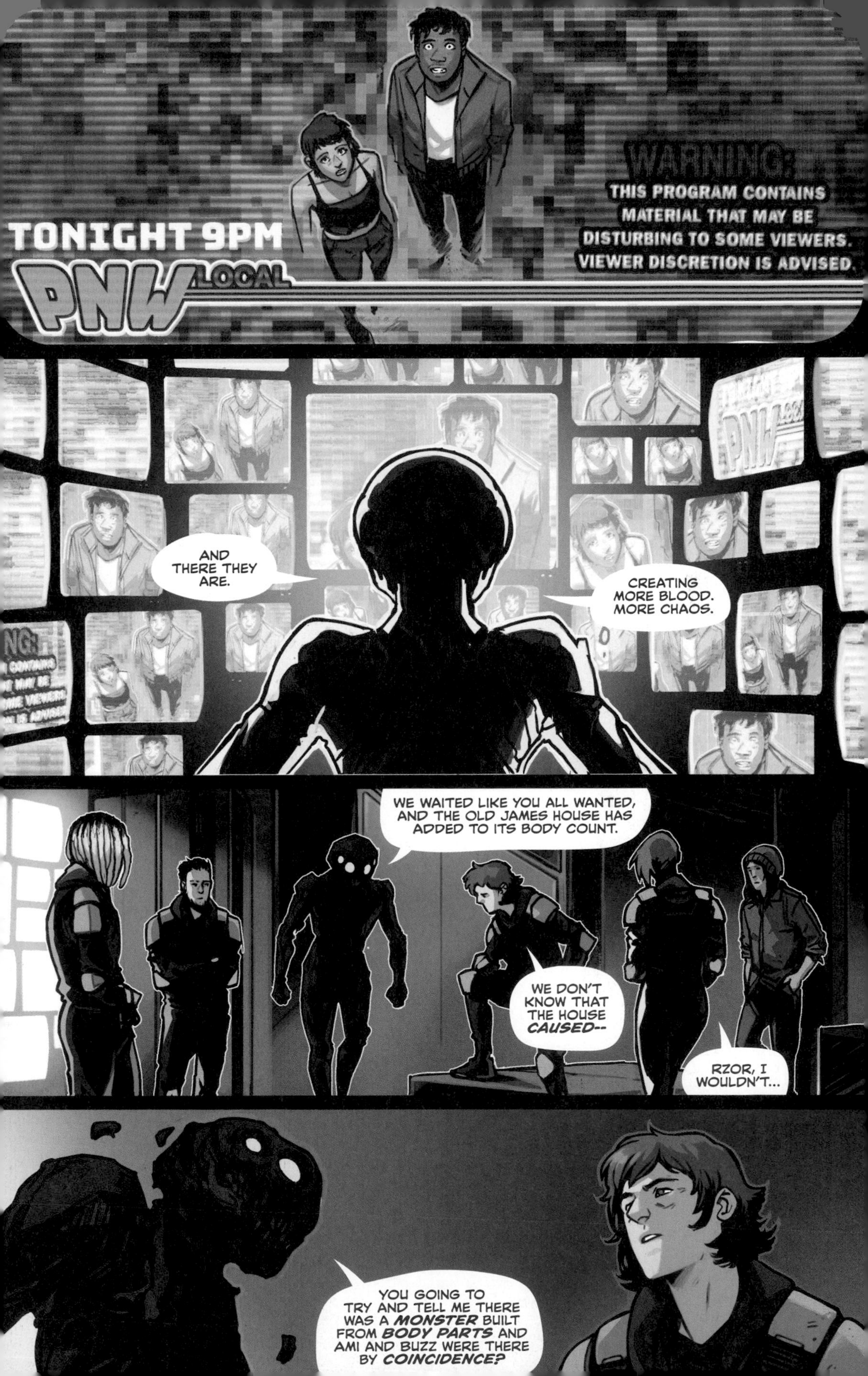
WARNING:
THIS PROGRAM CONTAINS MATERIAL THAT MAY BE DISTURBING TO SOME VIEWERS. VIEWER DISCRETION IS ADVISED.
TONIGHT 9PM
PNW LOCAL
AND THERE THEY ARE.
CREATING MORE BLOOD. MORE CHAOS.
WE WAITED LIKE YOU ALL WANTED, AND THE OLD JAMES HOUSE HAS ADDED TO ITS BODY COUNT.
WE DON'T KNOW THAT THE HOUSE CAUSED--
RZOR, I WOULDN'T...
YOU GOING TO TRY AND TELL ME THERE WAS A MONSTER BUILT FROM BODY PARTS AND AMI AND BUZZ WERE THERE BY COINCIDENCE?

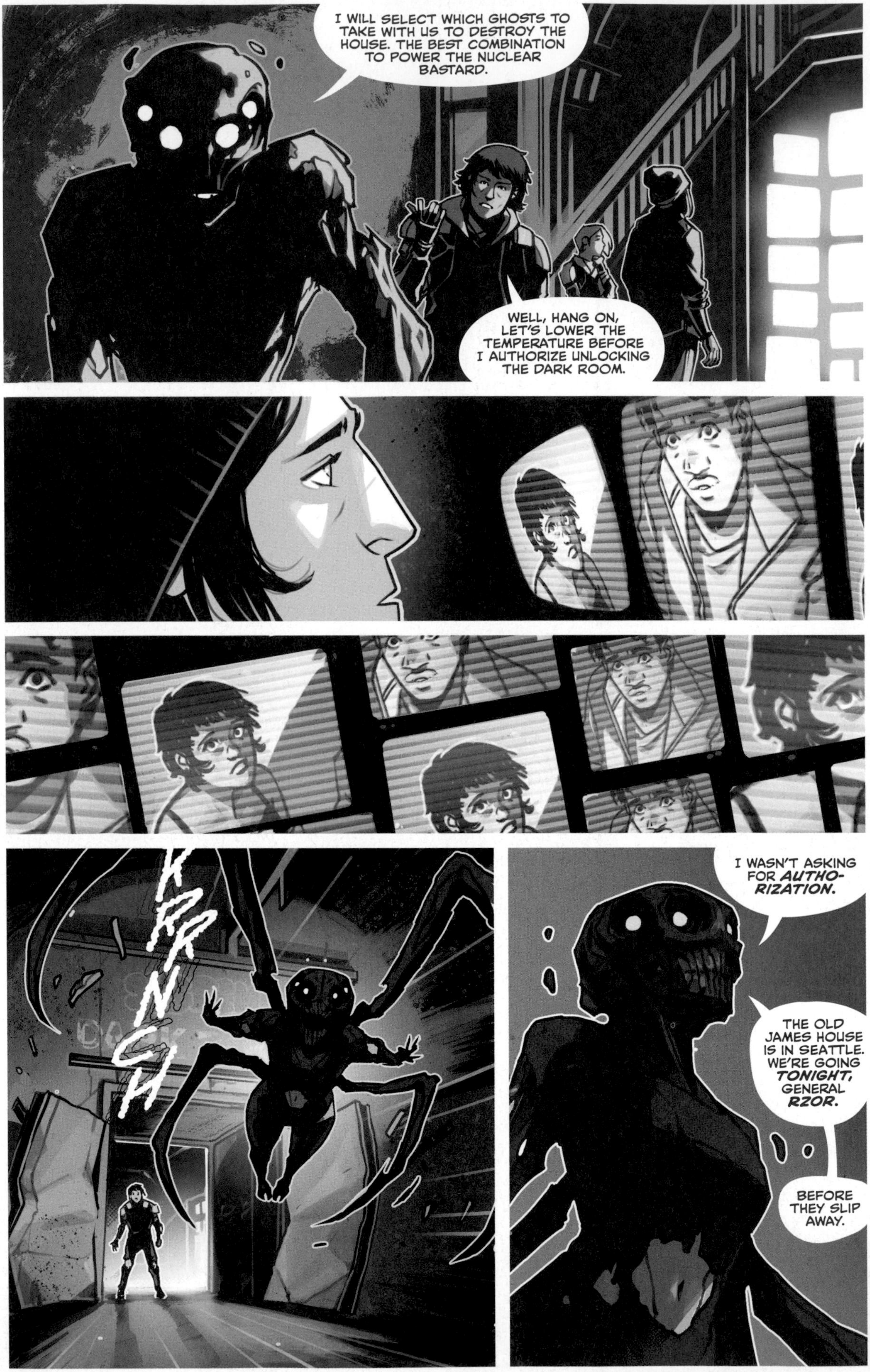
I WILL SELECT WHICH GHOSTS TO TAKE WITH US TO DESTROY THE HOUSE. THE BEST COMBINATION TO POWER THE NUCLEAR BASTARD.
WELL, HANG ON, LET'S LOWER THE TEMPERATURE BEFORE I AUTHORIZE UNLOCKING THE DARK ROOM.
KRRNCH
I WASN'T ASKING FOR AUTHO-RIZATION.
THE OLD JAMES HOUSE IS IN SEATTLE. WE'RE GOING TONIGHT, GENERAL RZOR.
BEFORE THEY SLIP AWAY.

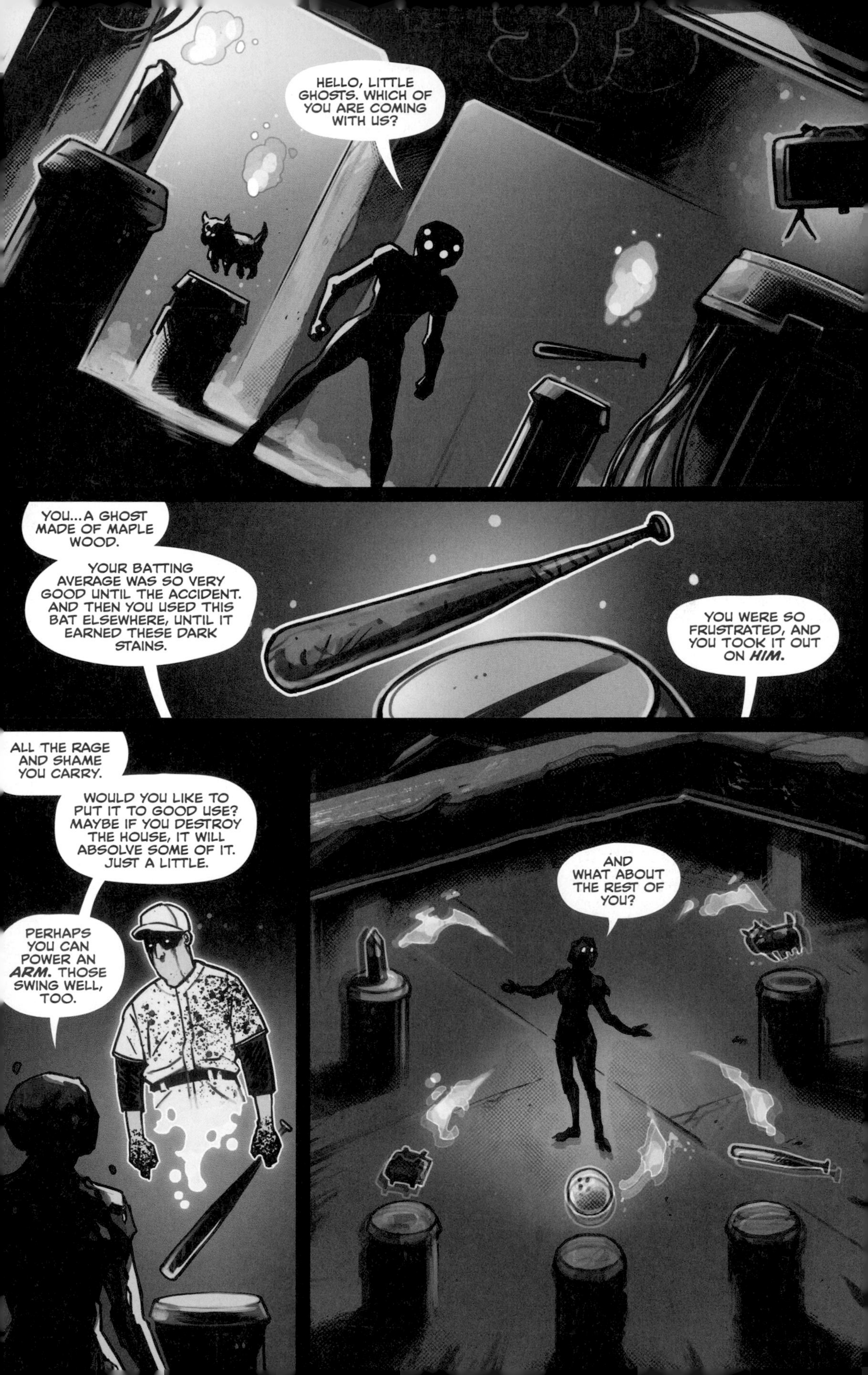
HELLO, LITTLE GHOSTS. WHICH OF YOU ARE COMING WITH US?
YOU...A GHOST MADE OF MAPLE WOOD.
YOUR BATTING AVERAGE WAS SO VERY GOOD UNTIL THE ACCIDENT. AND THEN YOU USED THIS BAT ELSEWHERE, UNTIL IT EARNED THESE DARK STAINS.
YOU WERE SO FRUSTRATED, AND YOU TOOK IT OUT ON ***HIM.***
ALL THE RAGE AND SHAME YOU CARRY.
WOULD YOU LIKE TO PUT IT TO GOOD USE? MAYBE IF YOU DESTROY THE HOUSE, IT WILL ABSOLVE SOME OF IT. JUST A LITTLE.
PERHAPS YOU CAN POWER AN ***ARM.*** THOSE SWING WELL, TOO.
AND WHAT ABOUT THE REST OF YOU?

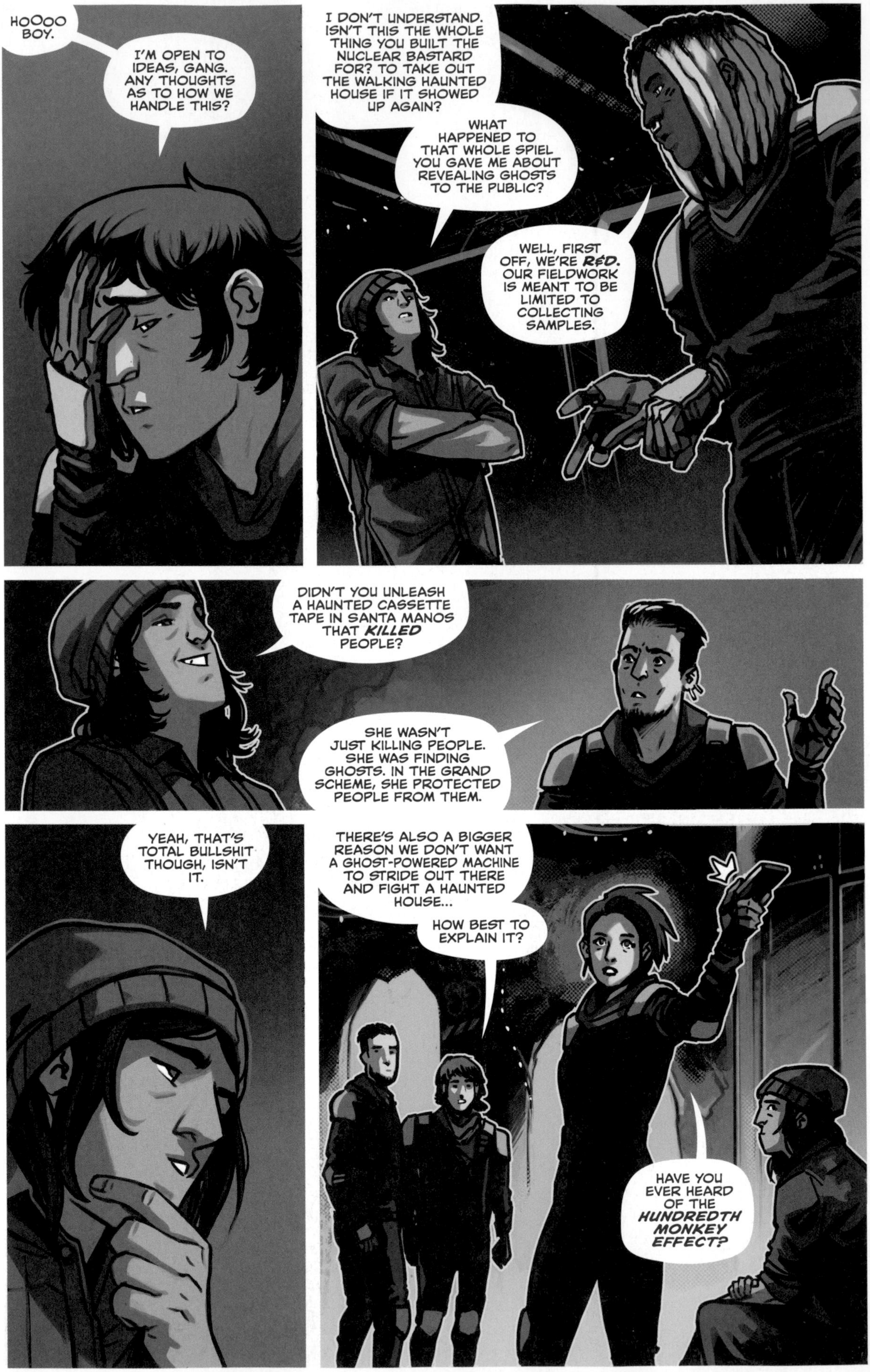
HOOOO BOY.
I'M OPEN TO IDEAS, GANG. ANY THOUGHTS AS TO HOW WE HANDLE THIS?
I DON'T UNDERSTAND. ISN'T THIS THE WHOLE THING YOU BUILT THE NUCLEAR BASTARD FOR? TO TAKE OUT THE WALKING HAUNTED HOUSE IF IT SHOWED UP AGAIN?
WHAT HAPPENED TO THAT WHOLE SPIEL YOU GAVE ME ABOUT REVEALING GHOSTS TO THE PUBLIC?
WELL, FIRST OFF, WE'RE R&D. OUR FIELDWORK IS MEANT TO BE LIMITED TO COLLECTING SAMPLES.
DIDN'T YOU UNLEASH A HAUNTED CASSETTE TAPE IN SANTA MANOS THAT KILLED PEOPLE?
SHE WASN'T JUST KILLING PEOPLE. SHE WAS FINDING GHOSTS. IN THE GRAND SCHEME, SHE PROTECTED PEOPLE FROM THEM.
YEAH, THAT'S TOTAL BULLSHIT THOUGH, ISN'T IT.
THERE'S ALSO A BIGGER REASON WE DON'T WANT A GHOST-POWERED MACHINE TO STRIDE OUT THERE AND FIGHT A HAUNTED HOUSE...
HOW BEST TO EXPLAIN IT?
HAVE YOU EVER HEARD OF THE HUNDREDTH MONKEY EFFECT?

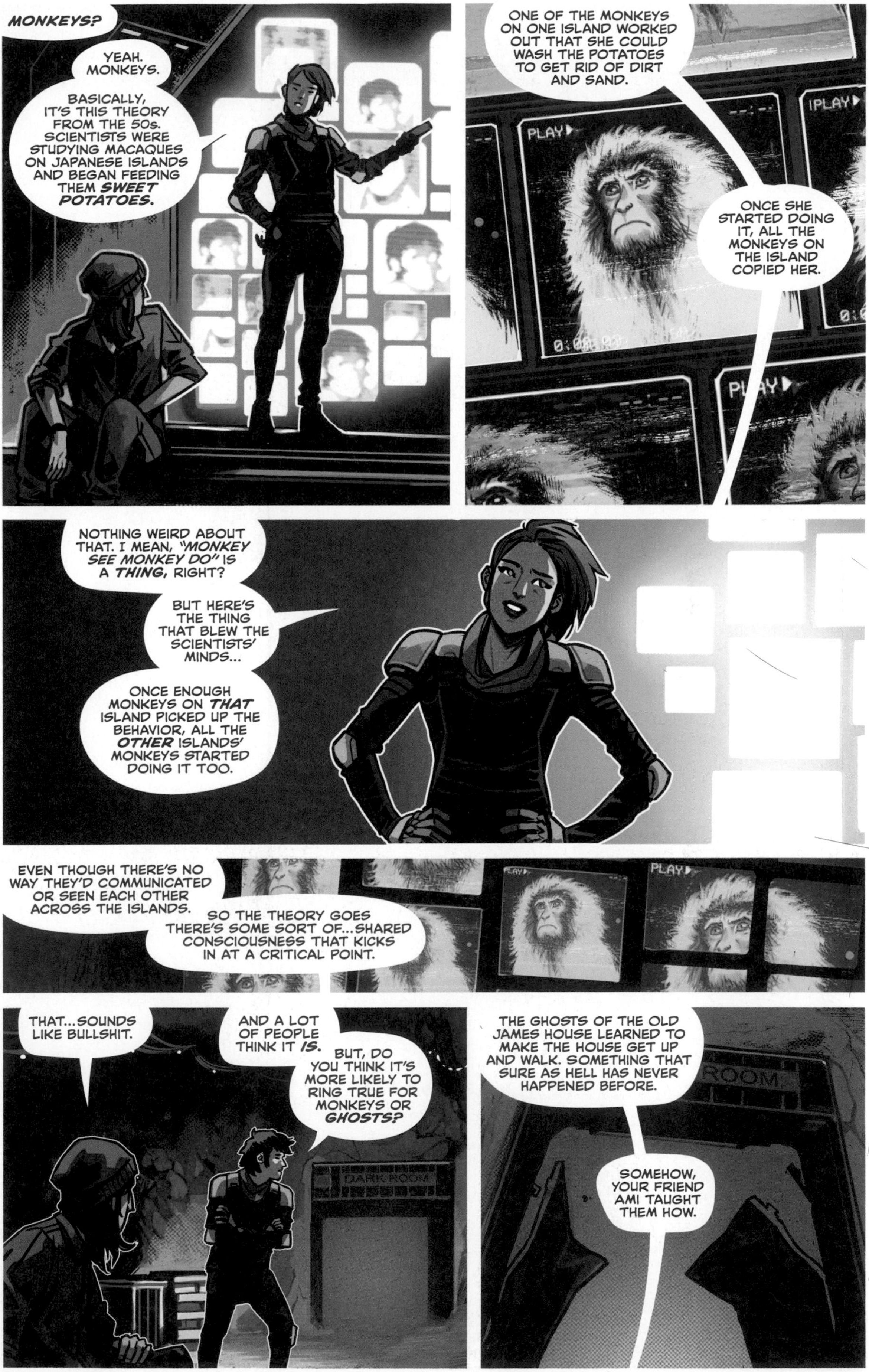
MONKEYS?
YEAH. MONKEYS.
BASICALLY, IT'S THIS THEORY FROM THE 50s. SCIENTISTS WERE STUDYING MACAQUES ON JAPANESE ISLANDS AND BEGAN FEEDING THEM SWEET POTATOES.
ONE OF THE MONKEYS ON ONE ISLAND WORKED OUT THAT SHE COULD WASH THE POTATOES TO GET RID OF DIRT AND SAND.
PLAY
PLAY
PLAY
ONCE SHE STARTED DOING IT, ALL THE MONKEYS ON THE ISLAND COPIED HER.
NOTHING WEIRD ABOUT THAT. I MEAN, "MONKEY SEE MONKEY DO" IS A THING, RIGHT?
BUT HERE'S THE THING THAT BLEW THE SCIENTISTS' MINDS...
ONCE ENOUGH MONKEYS ON THAT ISLAND PICKED UP THE BEHAVIOR, ALL THE OTHER ISLANDS' MONKEYS STARTED DOING IT TOO.
EVEN THOUGH THERE'S NO WAY THEY'D COMMUNICATED OR SEEN EACH OTHER ACROSS THE ISLANDS.
SO THE THEORY GOES THERE'S SOME SORT OF...SHARED CONSCIOUSNESS THAT KICKS IN AT A CRITICAL POINT.
PLAY
PLAY
THAT...SOUNDS LIKE BULLSHIT.
AND A LOT OF PEOPLE THINK IT IS.
BUT, DO YOU THINK IT'S MORE LIKELY TO RING TRUE FOR MONKEYS OR GHOSTS?
DARK ROOM
THE GHOSTS OF THE OLD JAMES HOUSE LEARNED TO MAKE THE HOUSE GET UP AND WALK. SOMETHING THAT SURE AS HELL HAS NEVER HAPPENED BEFORE.
ROOM
SOMEHOW, YOUR FRIEND AMI TAUGHT THEM HOW.

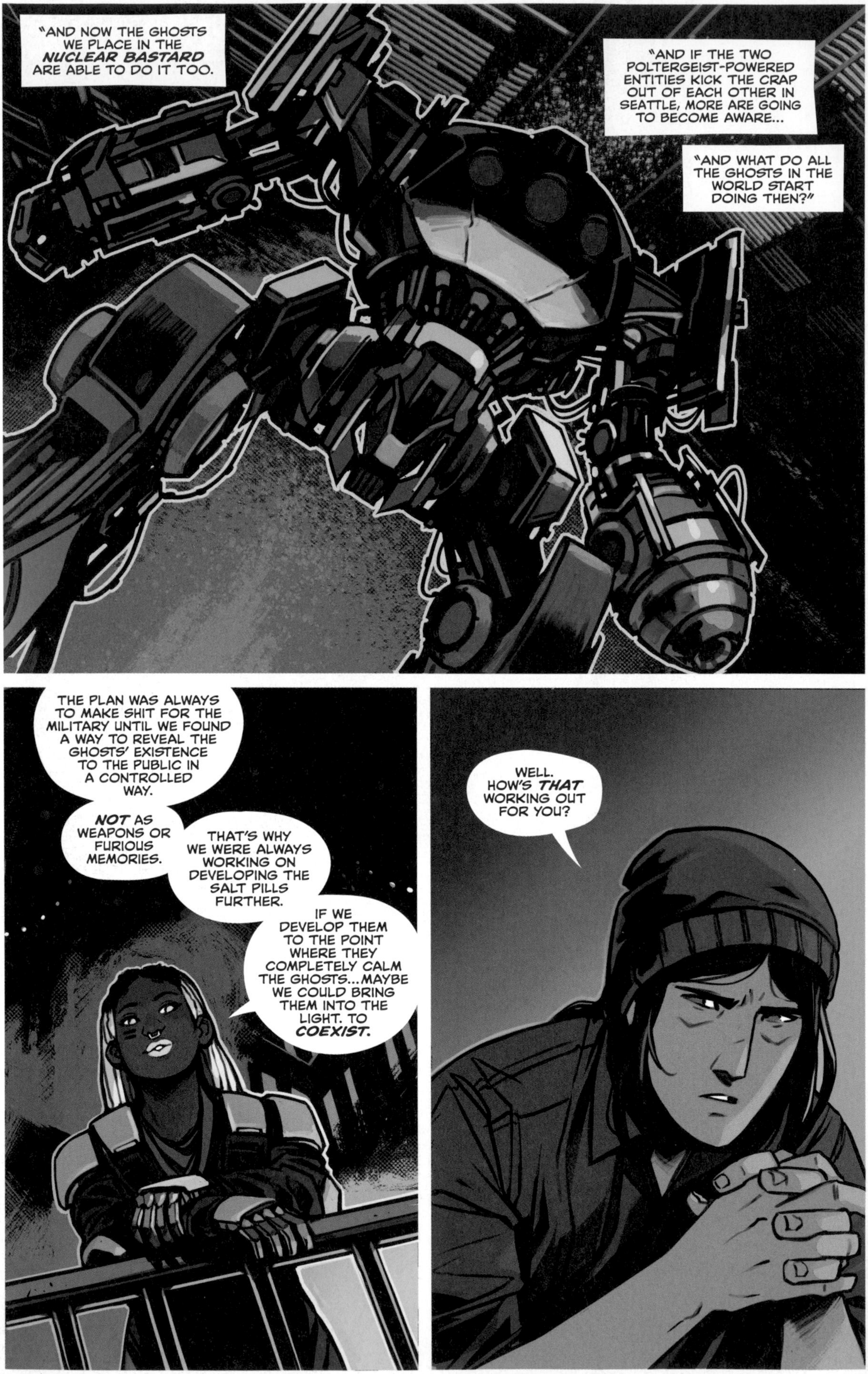
"AND NOW THE GHOSTS WE PLACE IN THE NUCLEAR BASTARD ARE ABLE TO DO IT TOO.
"AND IF THE TWO POLTERGEIST-POWERED ENTITIES KICK THE CRAP OUT OF EACH OTHER IN SEATTLE, MORE ARE GOING TO BECOME AWARE...
"AND WHAT DO ALL THE GHOSTS IN THE WORLD START DOING THEN?"
THE PLAN WAS ALWAYS TO MAKE SHIT FOR THE MILITARY UNTIL WE FOUND A WAY TO REVEAL THE GHOSTS' EXISTENCE TO THE PUBLIC IN A CONTROLLED WAY.
NOT AS WEAPONS OR FURIOUS MEMORIES.
THAT'S WHY WE WERE ALWAYS WORKING ON DEVELOPING THE SALT PILLS FURTHER.
IF WE DEVELOP THEM TO THE POINT WHERE THEY COMPLETELY CALM THE GHOSTS...MAYBE WE COULD BRING THEM INTO THE LIGHT. TO COEXIST.
WELL. HOW'S THAT WORKING OUT FOR YOU?

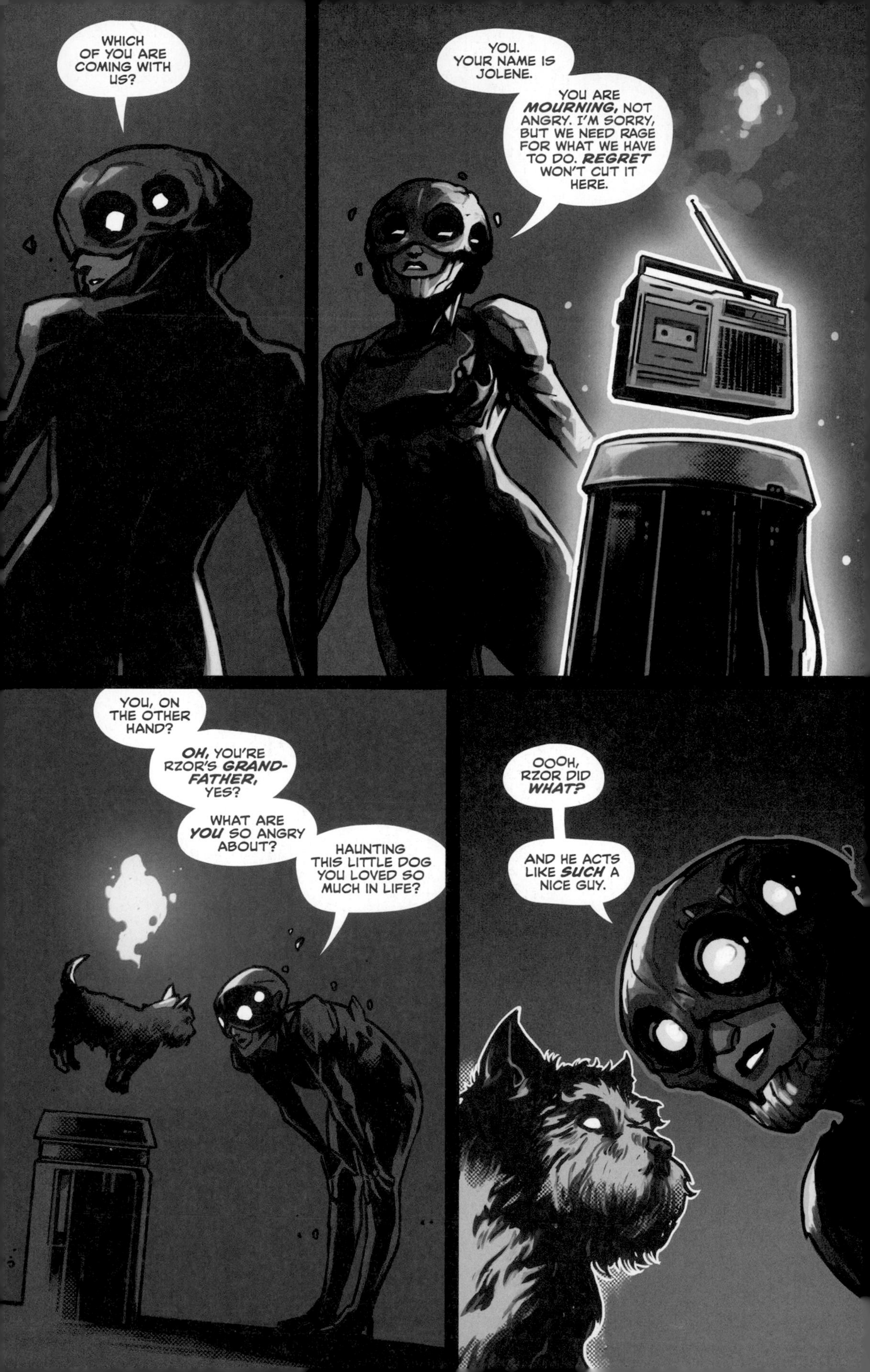
WHICH OF YOU ARE COMING WITH US?
YOU. YOUR NAME IS JOLENE.
YOU ARE MOURNING, NOT ANGRY. I'M SORRY, BUT WE NEED RAGE FOR WHAT WE HAVE TO DO. REGRET WON'T CUT IT HERE.
YOU, ON THE OTHER HAND?
OH, YOU'RE RZOR'S GRAND-FATHER, YES?
WHAT ARE YOU SO ANGRY ABOUT?
HAUNTING THIS LITTLE DOG YOU LOVED SO MUCH IN LIFE?
OOOH, RZOR DID WHAT?
AND HE ACTS LIKE SUCH A NICE GUY.

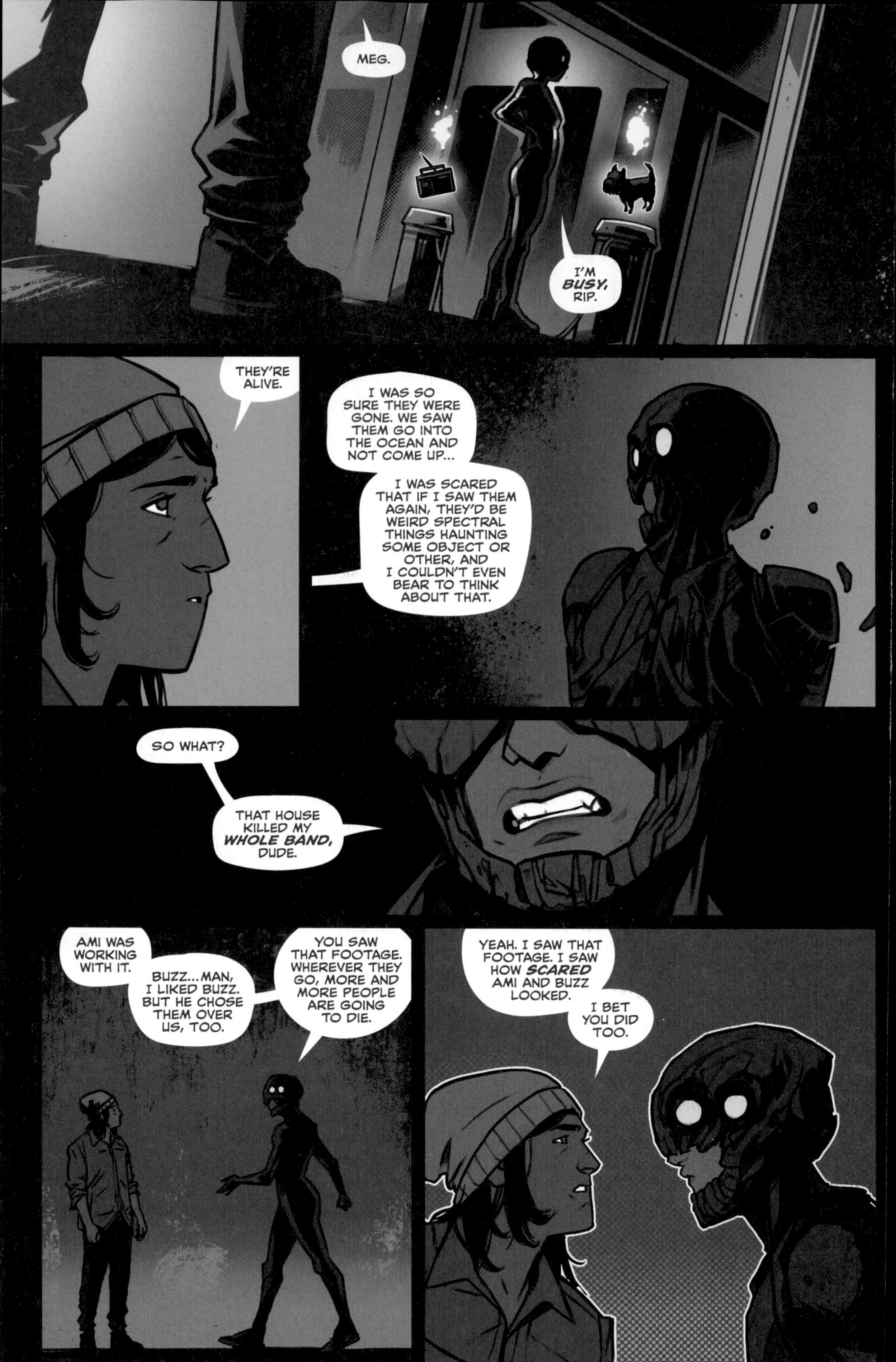
MEG.
I'M BUSY, RIP.
THEY'RE ALIVE.
I WAS SO SURE THEY WERE GONE. WE SAW THEM GO INTO THE OCEAN AND NOT COME UP...
I WAS SCARED THAT IF I SAW THEM AGAIN, THEY'D BE WEIRD SPECTRAL THINGS HAUNTING SOME OBJECT OR OTHER, AND I COULDN'T EVEN BEAR TO THINK ABOUT THAT.
SO WHAT?
THAT HOUSE KILLED MY *WHOLE BAND,* DUDE.
AMI WAS WORKING WITH IT.
BUZZ...MAN, I LIKED BUZZ. BUT HE CHOSE THEM OVER US, TOO.
YOU SAW THAT FOOTAGE. WHEREVER THEY GO, MORE AND MORE PEOPLE ARE GOING TO DIE.
YEAH. I SAW THAT FOOTAGE. I SAW HOW *SCARED* AMI AND BUZZ LOOKED.
I BET YOU DID TOO.

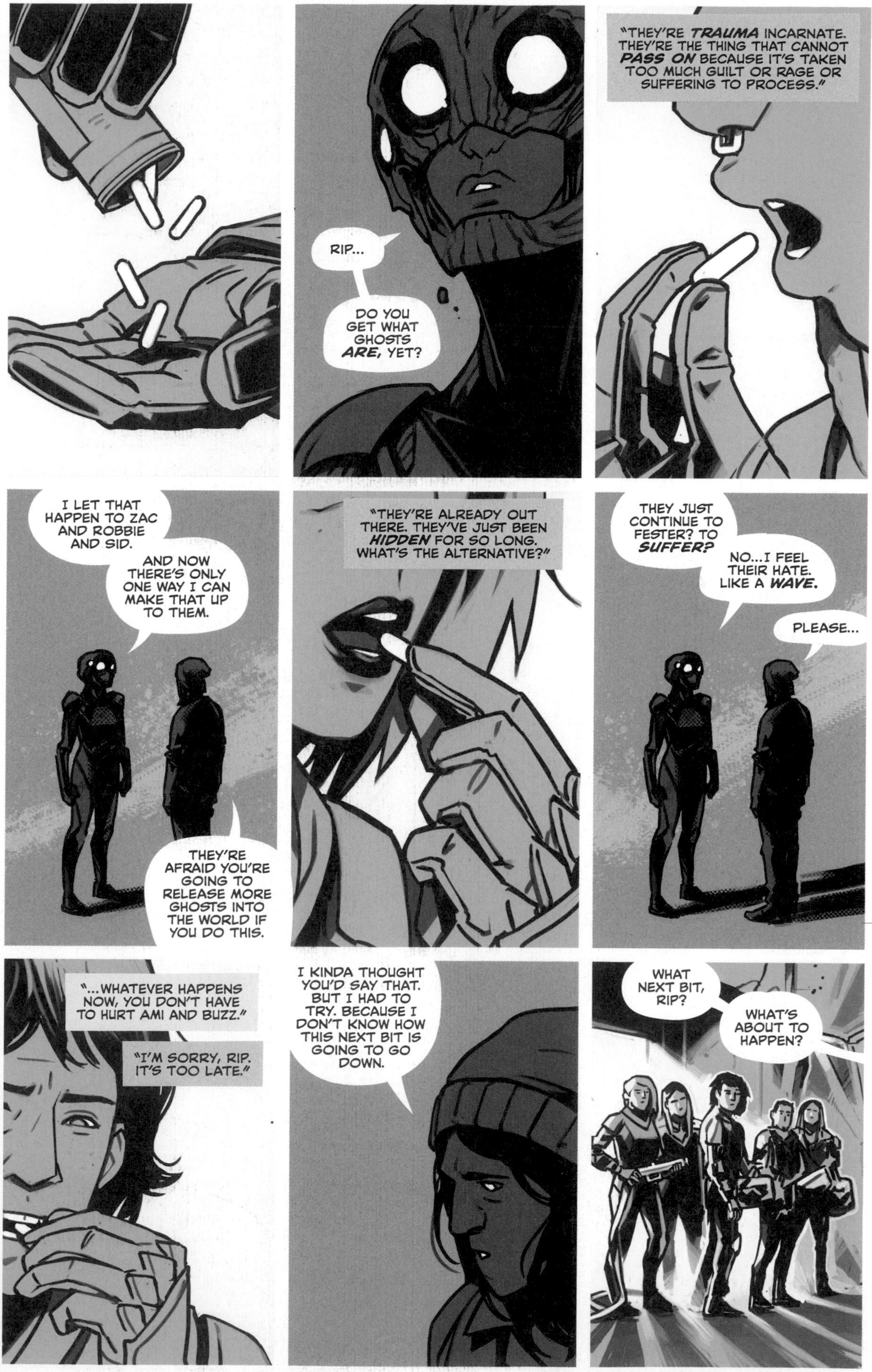
RIP...
DO YOU GET WHAT GHOSTS ARE, YET?
"THEY'RE TRAUMA INCARNATE. THEY'RE THE THING THAT CANNOT PASS ON BECAUSE IT'S TAKEN TOO MUCH GUILT OR RAGE OR SUFFERING TO PROCESS."
I LET THAT HAPPEN TO ZAC AND ROBBIE AND SID.
AND NOW THERE'S ONLY ONE WAY I CAN MAKE THAT UP TO THEM.
THEY'RE AFRAID YOU'RE GOING TO RELEASE MORE GHOSTS INTO THE WORLD IF YOU DO THIS.
"THEY'RE ALREADY OUT THERE. THEY'VE JUST BEEN HIDDEN FOR SO LONG. WHAT'S THE ALTERNATIVE?"
THEY JUST CONTINUE TO FESTER? TO SUFFER?
NO...I FEEL THEIR HATE. LIKE A WAVE.
PLEASE...
"...WHATEVER HAPPENS NOW, YOU DON'T HAVE TO HURT AMI AND BUZZ."
"I'M SORRY, RIP. IT'S TOO LATE."
I KINDA THOUGHT YOU'D SAY THAT. BUT I HAD TO TRY. BECAUSE I DON'T KNOW HOW THIS NEXT BIT IS GOING TO GO DOWN.
WHAT NEXT BIT, RIP?
WHAT'S ABOUT TO HAPPEN?

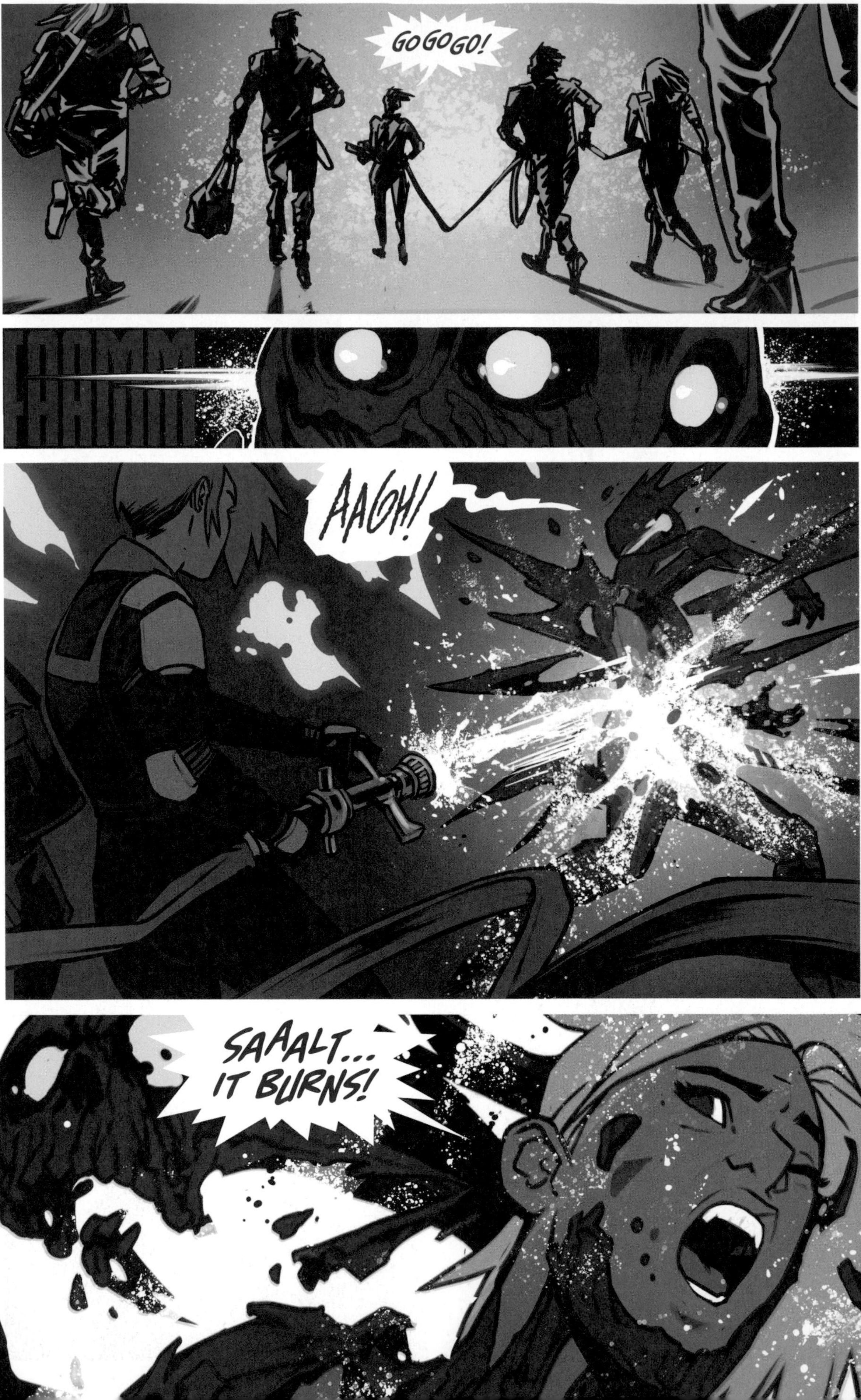
GOGOGO!
AAGH!
SAAALT... IT BURNS!

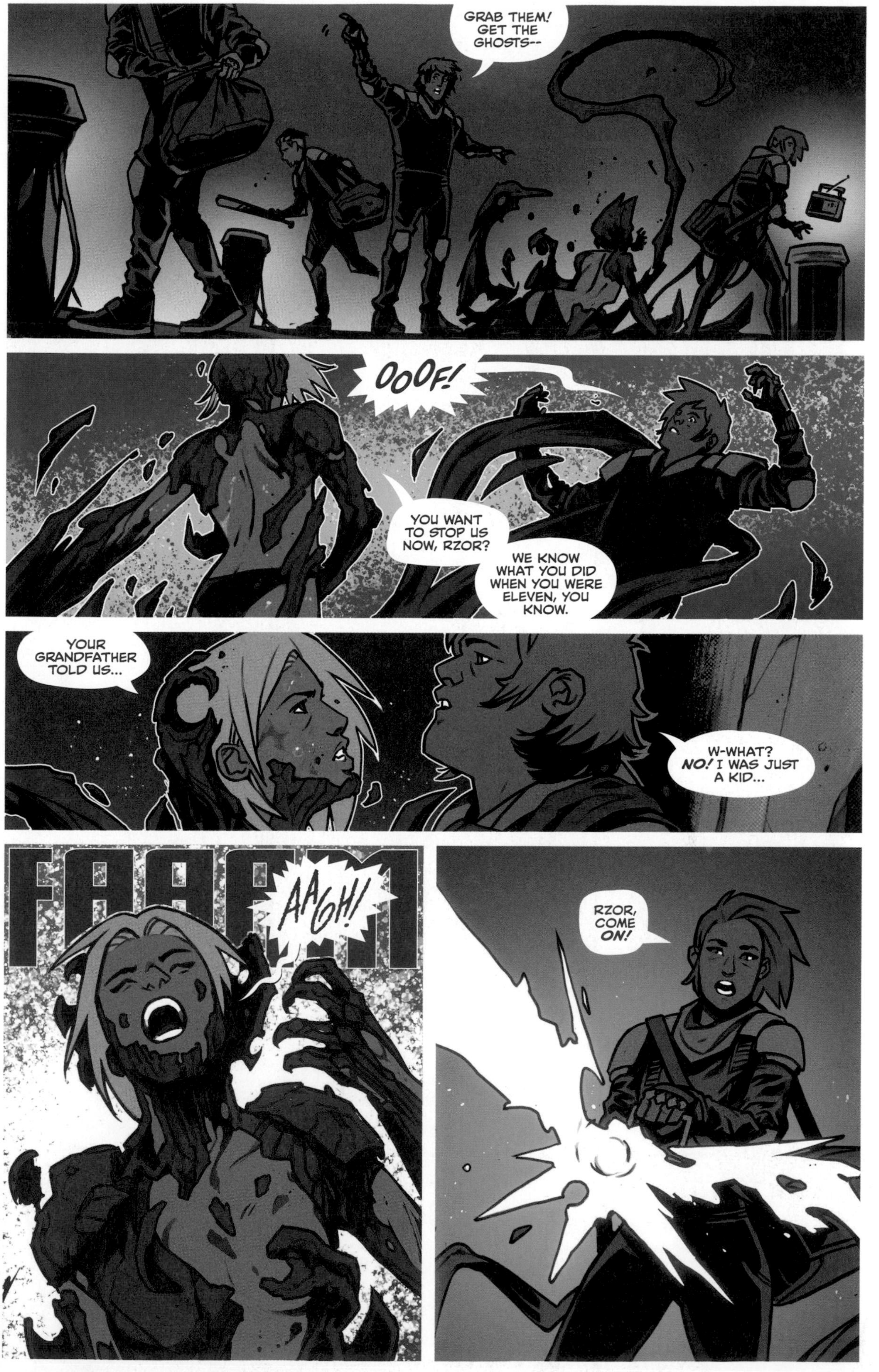
GRAB THEM! GET THE GHOSTS--
OOOF!
YOU WANT TO STOP US NOW, RZOR?
WE KNOW WHAT YOU DID WHEN YOU WERE ELEVEN, YOU KNOW.
YOUR GRANDFATHER TOLD US...
W-WHAT? NO! I WAS JUST A KID...
FAAAM
AAGH!
RZOR, COME ON!

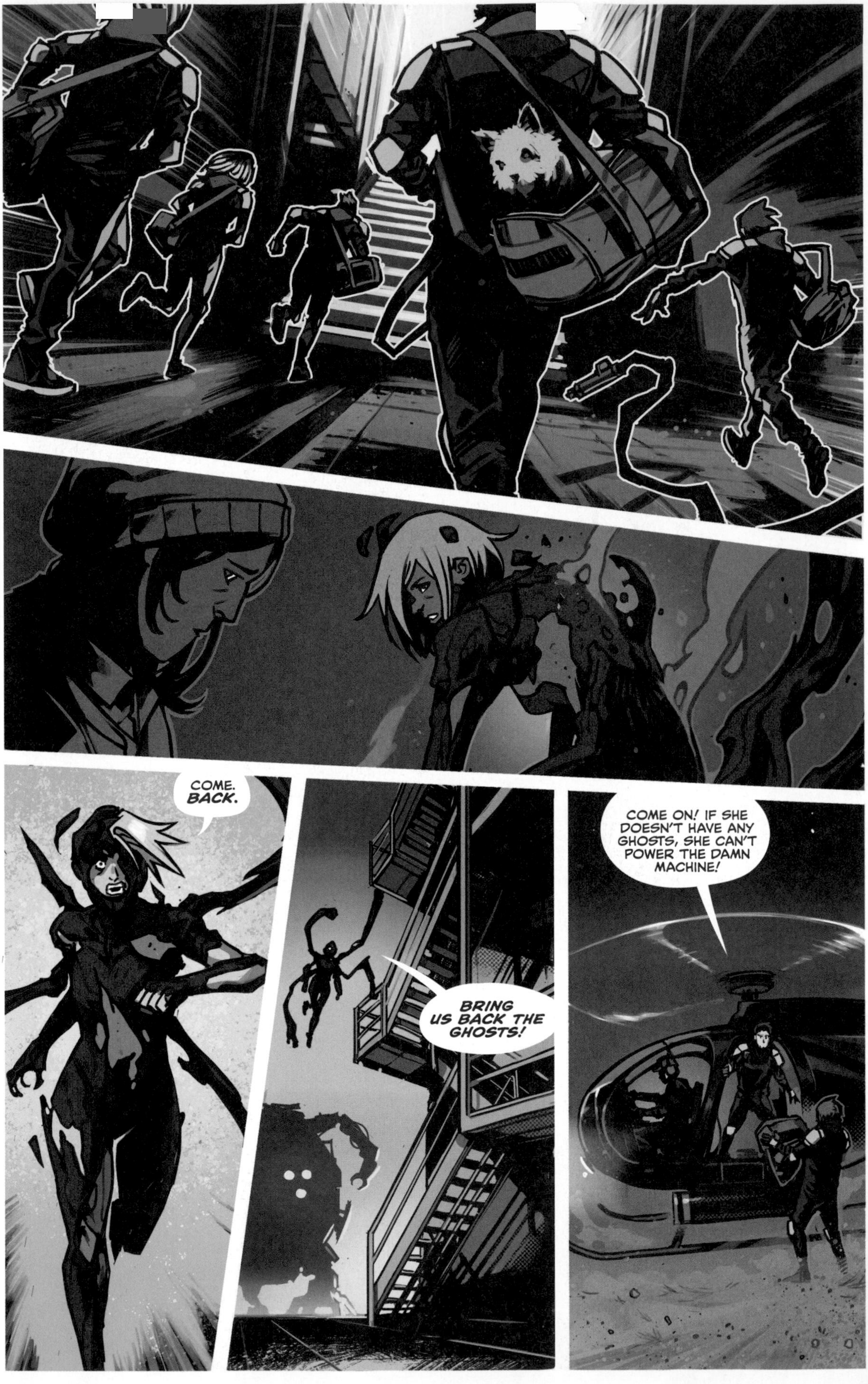
COME. BACK.
BRING US BACK THE GHOSTS!
COME ON! IF SHE DOESN'T HAVE ANY GHOSTS, SHE CAN'T POWER THE DAMN MACHINE!

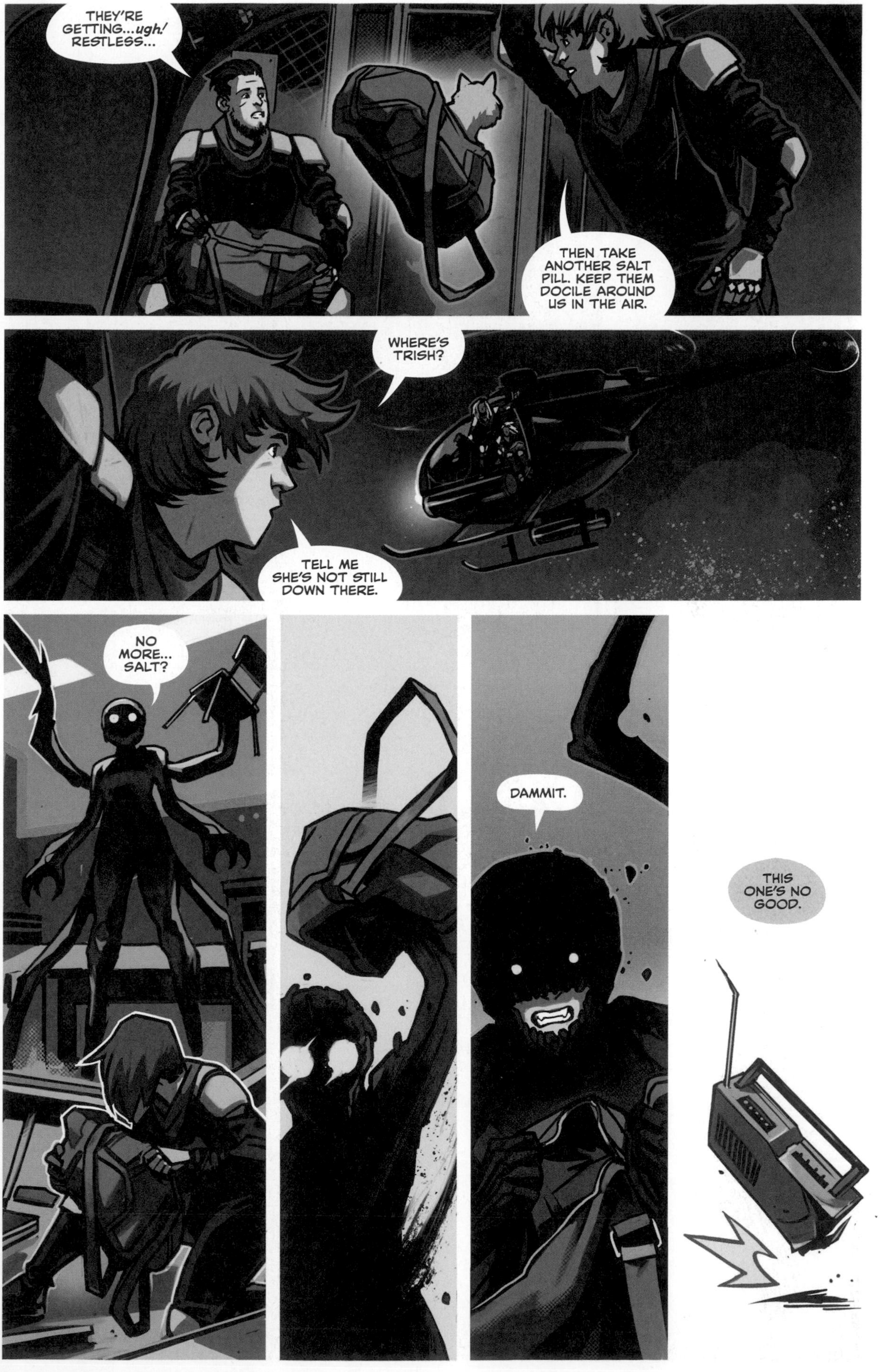
THEY'RE GETTING...*ugh!* RESTLESS...
THEN TAKE ANOTHER SALT PILL. KEEP THEM DOCILE AROUND US IN THE AIR.
WHERE'S TRISH?
TELL ME SHE'S NOT STILL DOWN THERE.
NO MORE... SALT?
DAMMIT.
THIS ONE'S NO GOOD.

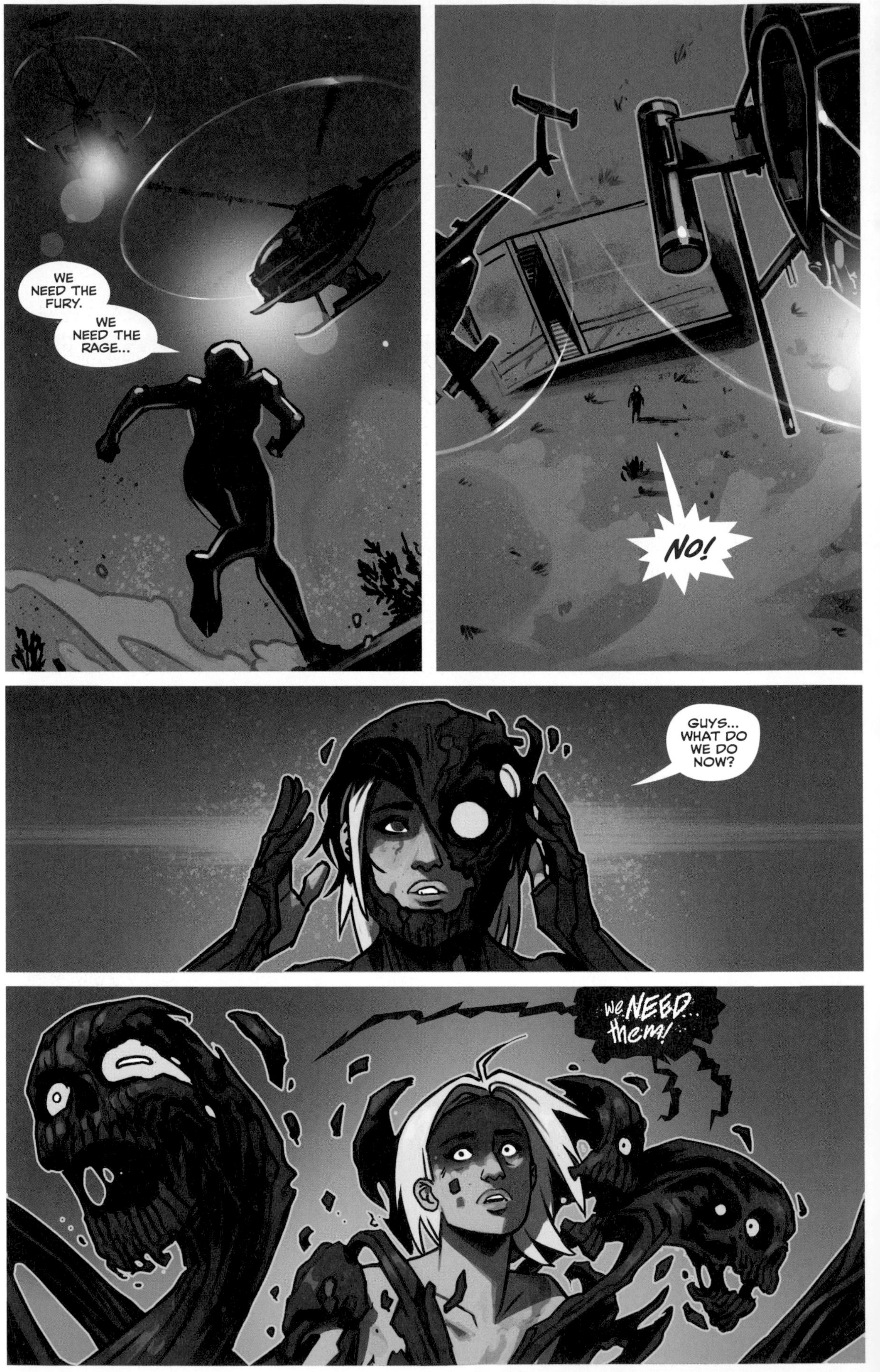
WE NEED THE FURY.
WE NEED THE RAGE...
NO!
GUYS... WHAT DO WE DO NOW?
we NEED... them!

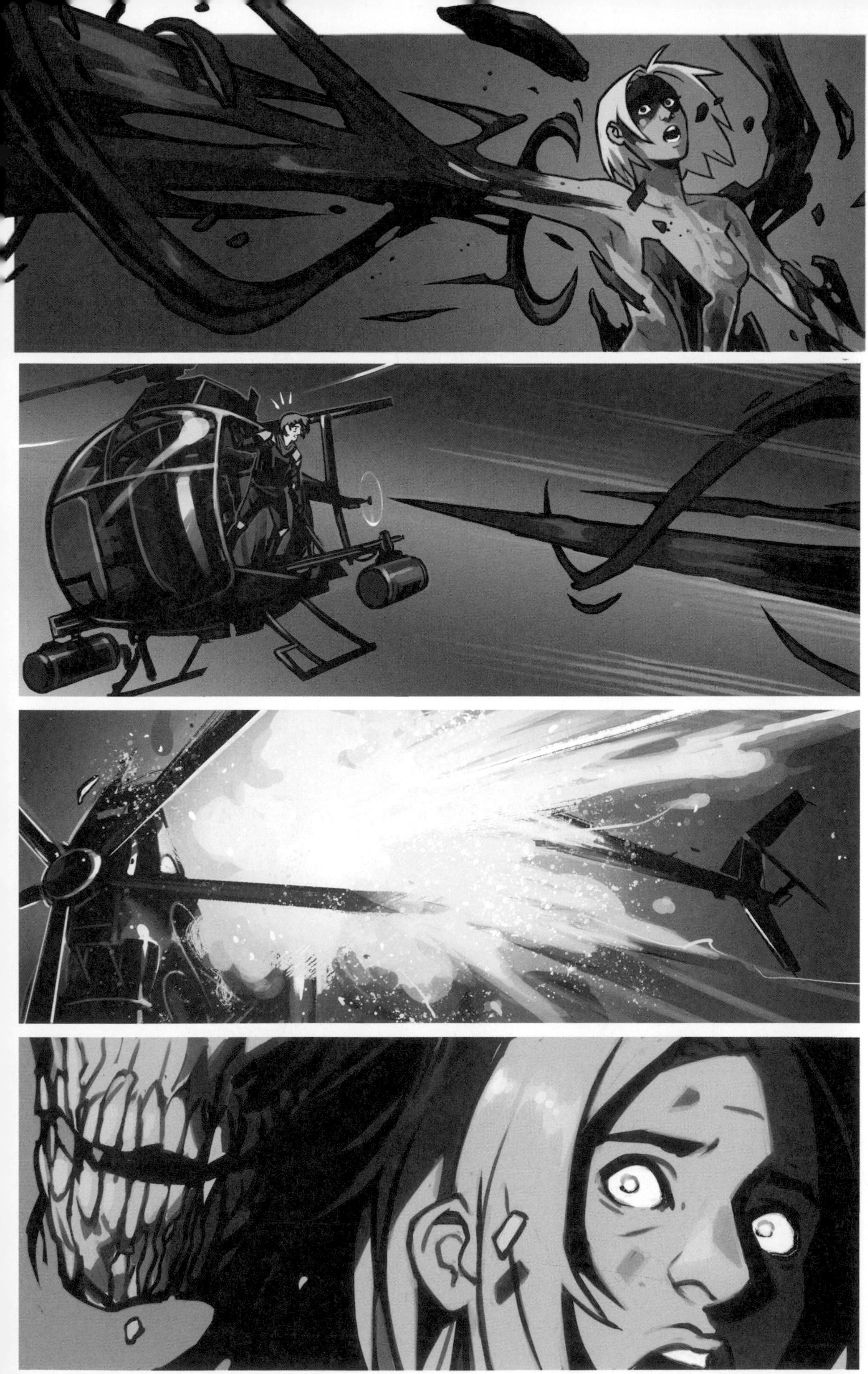

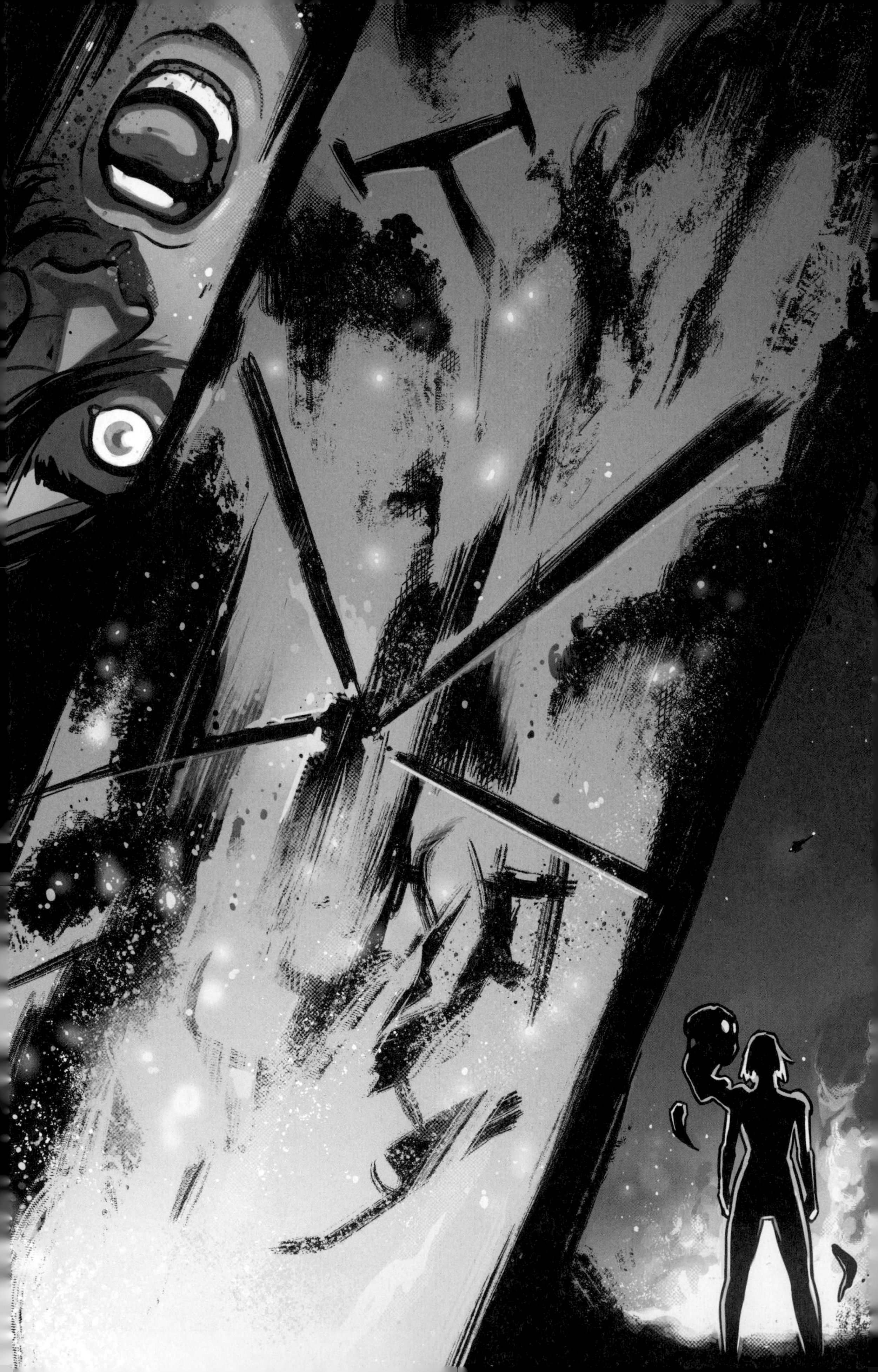

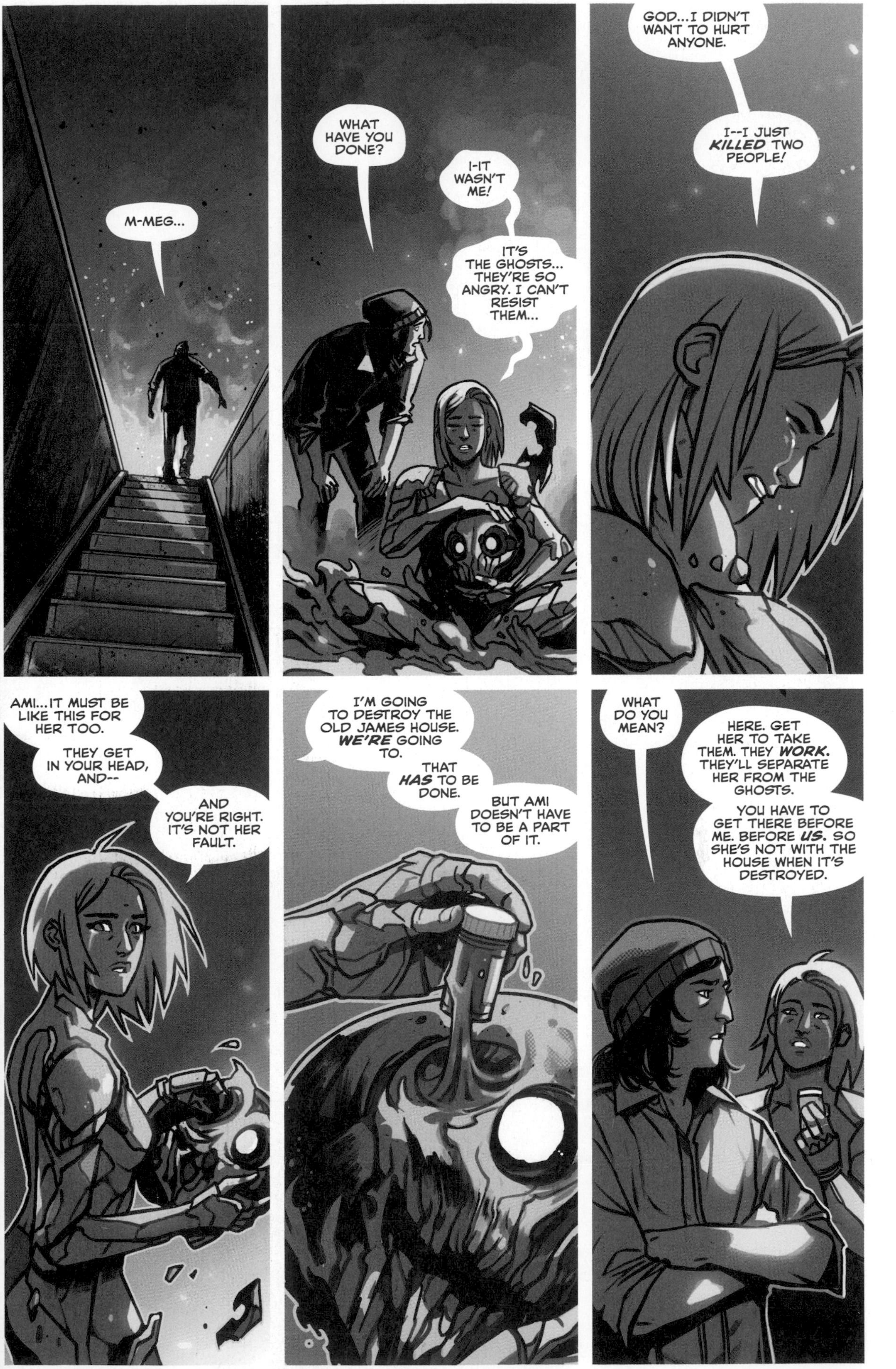
M-MEG...
WHAT HAVE YOU DONE?
I-IT WASN'T ME!
IT'S THE GHOSTS... THEY'RE SO ANGRY. I CAN'T RESIST THEM...
GOD...I DIDN'T WANT TO HURT ANYONE.
I--I JUST KILLED TWO PEOPLE!
AMI...IT MUST BE LIKE THIS FOR HER TOO.
THEY GET IN YOUR HEAD, AND--
AND YOU'RE RIGHT. IT'S NOT HER FAULT.
I'M GOING TO DESTROY THE OLD JAMES HOUSE. WE'RE GOING TO.
THAT HAS TO BE DONE.
BUT AMI DOESN'T HAVE TO BE A PART OF IT.
WHAT DO YOU MEAN?
HERE. GET HER TO TAKE THEM. THEY WORK. THEY'LL SEPARATE HER FROM THE GHOSTS.
YOU HAVE TO GET THERE BEFORE ME. BEFORE US. SO SHE'S NOT WITH THE HOUSE WHEN IT'S DESTROYED.

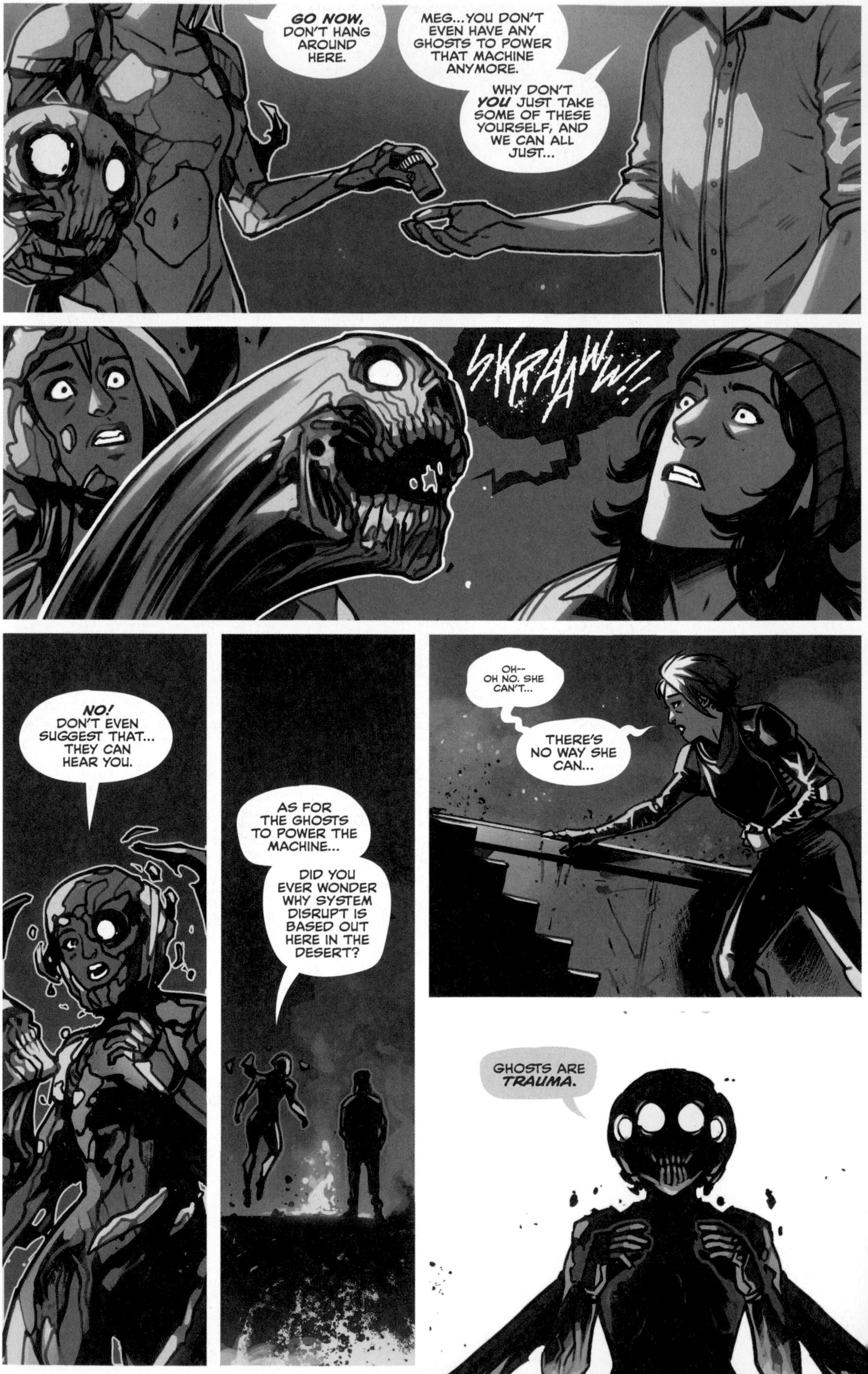
GO NOW, DON'T HANG AROUND HERE.
MEG...YOU DON'T EVEN HAVE ANY GHOSTS TO POWER THAT MACHINE ANYMORE.
WHY DON'T YOU JUST TAKE SOME OF THESE YOURSELF, AND WE CAN ALL JUST...
SKRAAWW!!
NO! DON'T EVEN SUGGEST THAT... THEY CAN HEAR YOU.
AS FOR THE GHOSTS TO POWER THE MACHINE...
DID YOU EVER WONDER WHY SYSTEM DISRUPT IS BASED OUT HERE IN THE DESERT?
OH-- OH NO. SHE CAN'T...
THERE'S NO WAY SHE CAN...
GHOSTS ARE TRAUMA.

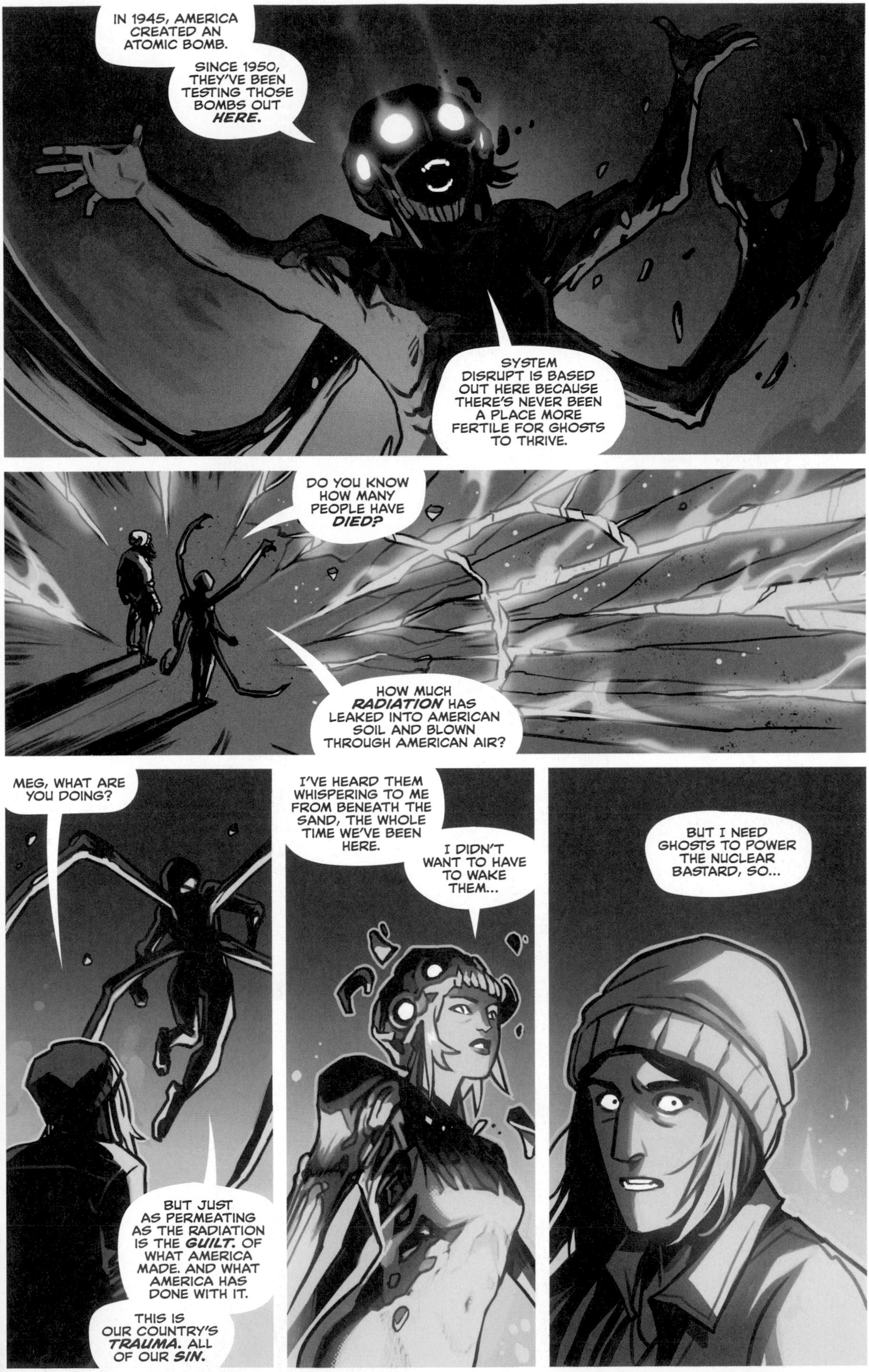
IN 1945, AMERICA CREATED AN ATOMIC BOMB.
SINCE 1950, THEY'VE BEEN TESTING THOSE BOMBS OUT HERE.
SYSTEM DISRUPT IS BASED OUT HERE BECAUSE THERE'S NEVER BEEN A PLACE MORE FERTILE FOR GHOSTS TO THRIVE.
DO YOU KNOW HOW MANY PEOPLE HAVE DIED?
HOW MUCH RADIATION HAS LEAKED INTO AMERICAN SOIL AND BLOWN THROUGH AMERICAN AIR?
MEG, WHAT ARE YOU DOING?
BUT JUST AS PERMEATING AS THE RADIATION IS THE GUILT. OF WHAT AMERICA MADE. AND WHAT AMERICA HAS DONE WITH IT.
THIS IS OUR COUNTRY'S TRAUMA. ALL OF OUR SIN.
I'VE HEARD THEM WHISPERING TO ME FROM BENEATH THE SAND, THE WHOLE TIME WE'VE BEEN HERE.
I DIDN'T WANT TO HAVE TO WAKE THEM...
BUT I NEED GHOSTS TO POWER THE NUCLEAR BASTARD, SO...

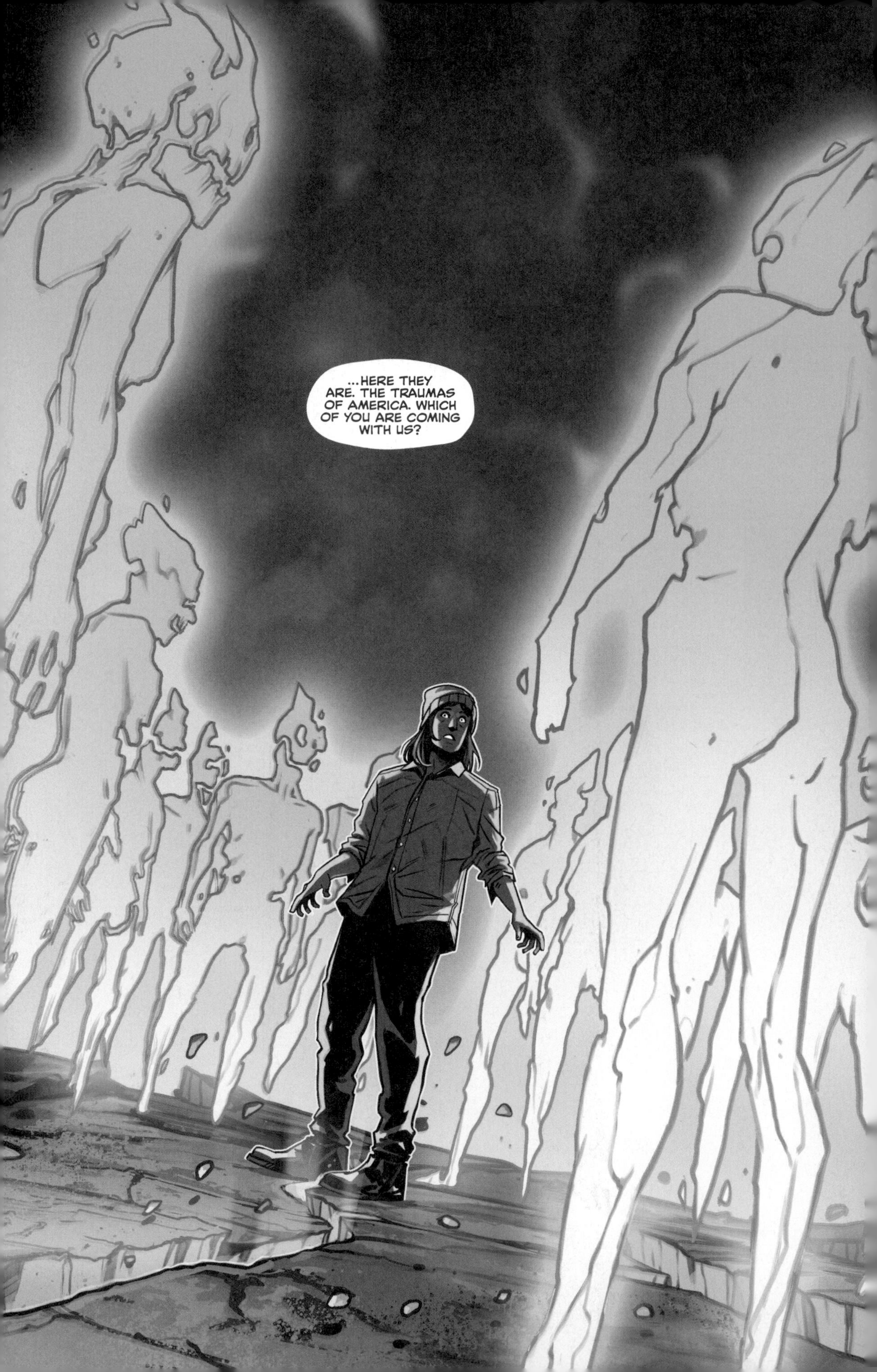
...HERE THEY ARE. THE TRAUMAS OF AMERICA. WHICH OF YOU ARE COMING WITH US?

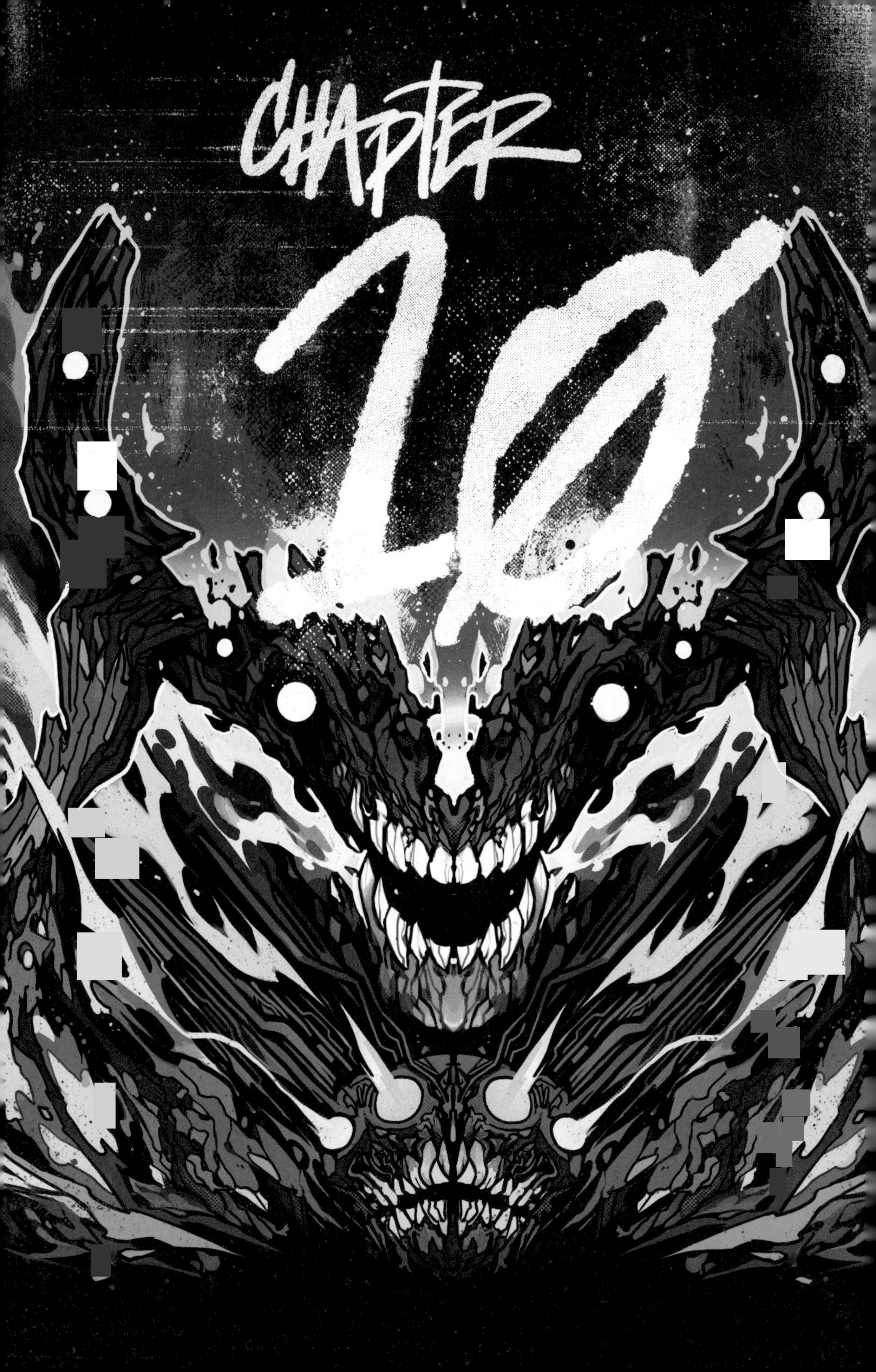
CHAPTER
10

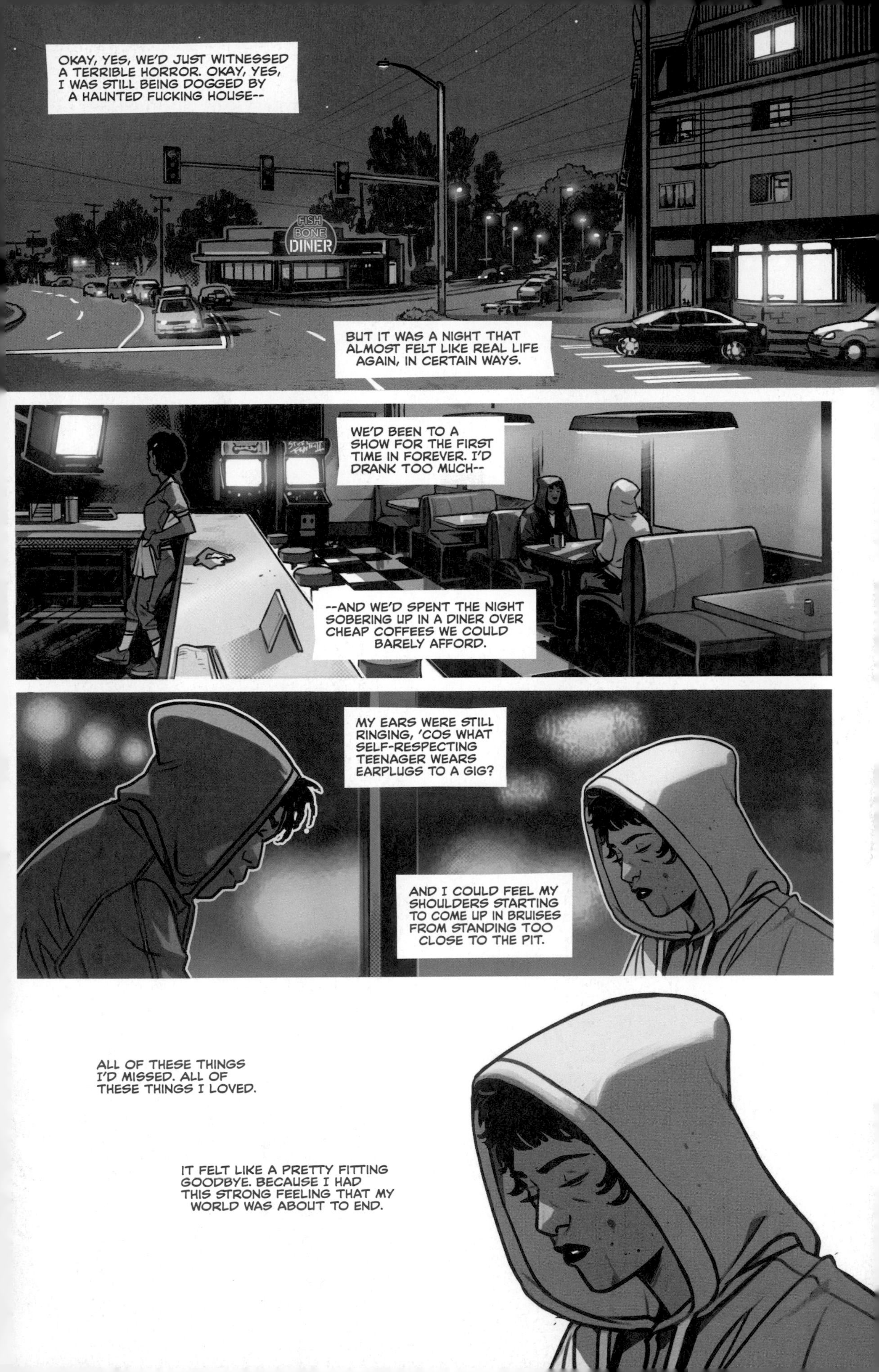

OKAY, YES, WE'D JUST WITNESSED A TERRIBLE HORROR. OKAY, YES, I WAS STILL BEING DOGGED BY A HAUNTED FUCKING HOUSE--
FISH BONE DINER
BUT IT WAS A NIGHT THAT ALMOST FELT LIKE REAL LIFE AGAIN, IN CERTAIN WAYS.
WE'D BEEN TO A SHOW FOR THE FIRST TIME IN FOREVER. I'D DRANK TOO MUCH--
--AND WE'D SPENT THE NIGHT SOBERING UP IN A DINER OVER CHEAP COFFEES WE COULD BARELY AFFORD.
MY EARS WERE STILL RINGING, 'COS WHAT SELF-RESPECTING TEENAGER WEARS EARPLUGS TO A GIG?
AND I COULD FEEL MY SHOULDERS STARTING TO COME UP IN BRUISES FROM STANDING TOO CLOSE TO THE PIT.
ALL OF THESE THINGS I'D MISSED. ALL OF THESE THINGS I LOVED.
IT FELT LIKE A PRETTY FITTING GOODBYE. BECAUSE I HAD THIS STRONG FEELING THAT MY WORLD WAS ABOUT TO END.

TWO HOURS BEFORE
THE NUCLEAR BASTARD
REACHED ME.

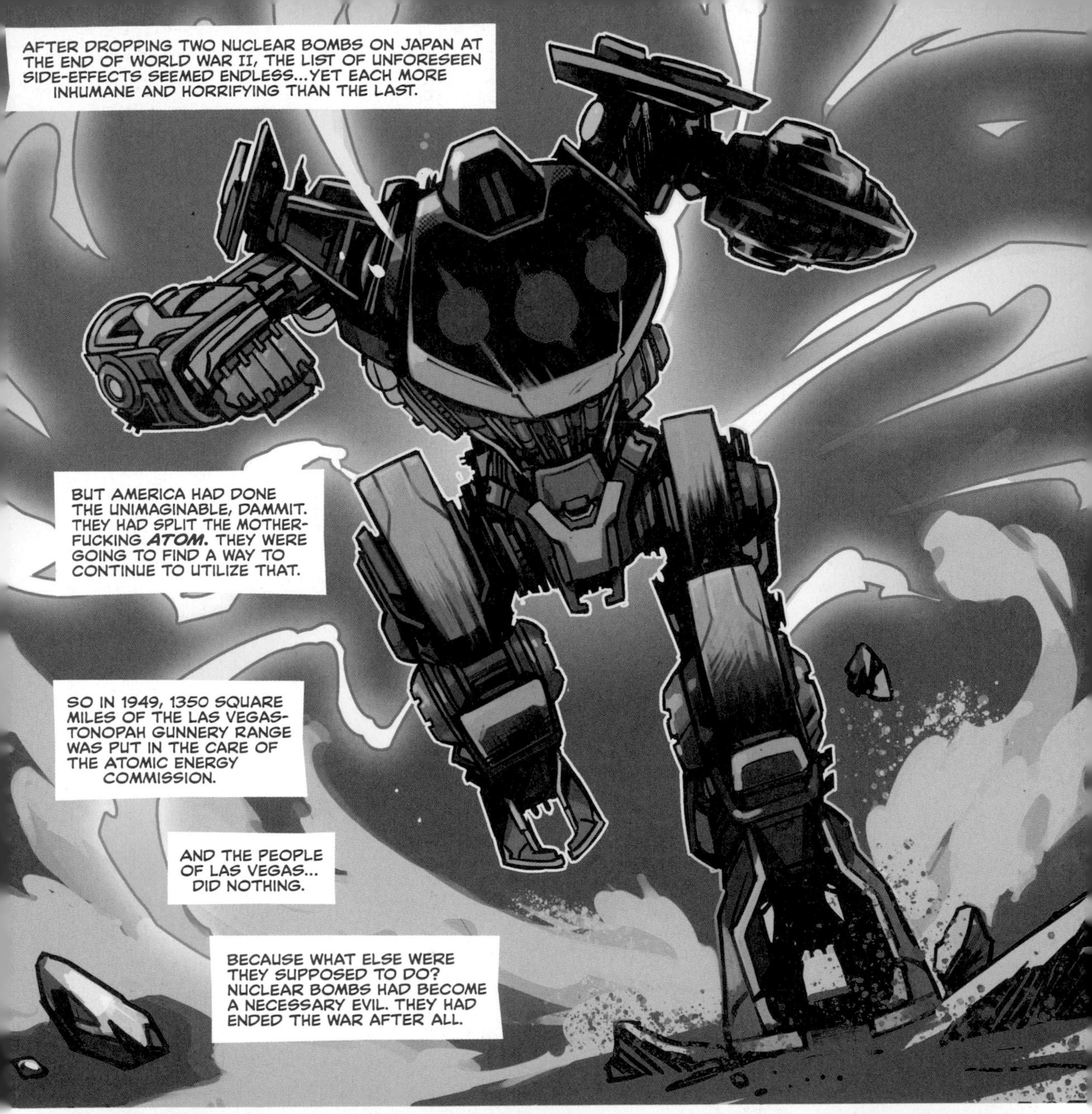
AFTER DROPPING TWO NUCLEAR BOMBS ON JAPAN AT THE END OF WORLD WAR II, THE LIST OF UNFORESEEN SIDE-EFFECTS SEEMED ENDLESS...YET EACH MORE INHUMANE AND HORRIFYING THAN THE LAST.
BUT AMERICA HAD DONE THE UNIMAGINABLE, DAMMIT. THEY HAD SPLIT THE MOTHER-FUCKING ***ATOM***. THEY WERE GOING TO FIND A WAY TO CONTINUE TO UTILIZE THAT.
SO IN 1949, 1350 SQUARE MILES OF THE LAS VEGAS-TONOPAH GUNNERY RANGE WAS PUT IN THE CARE OF THE ATOMIC ENERGY COMMISSION.
AND THE PEOPLE OF LAS VEGAS... DID NOTHING.
BECAUSE WHAT ELSE WERE THEY SUPPOSED TO DO? NUCLEAR BOMBS HAD BECOME A NECESSARY EVIL. THEY HAD ENDED THE WAR AFTER ALL.

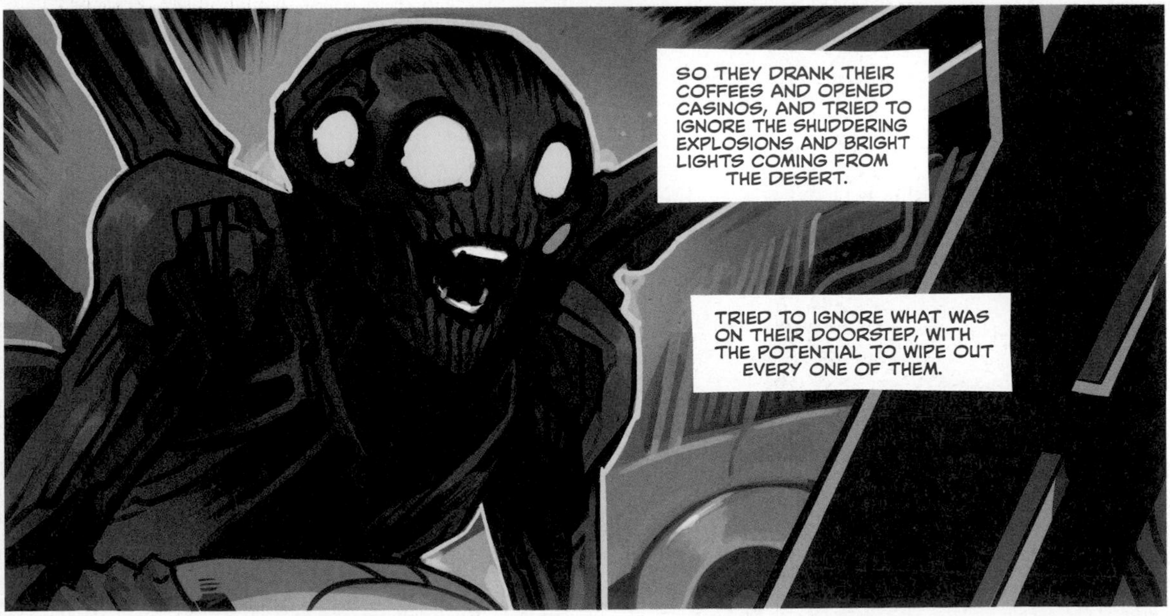
SO THEY DRANK THEIR COFFEES AND OPENED CASINOS, AND TRIED TO IGNORE THE SHUDDERING EXPLOSIONS AND BRIGHT LIGHTS COMING FROM THE DESERT.
TRIED TO IGNORE WHAT WAS ON THEIR DOORSTEP, WITH THE POTENTIAL TO WIPE OUT EVERY ONE OF THEM.

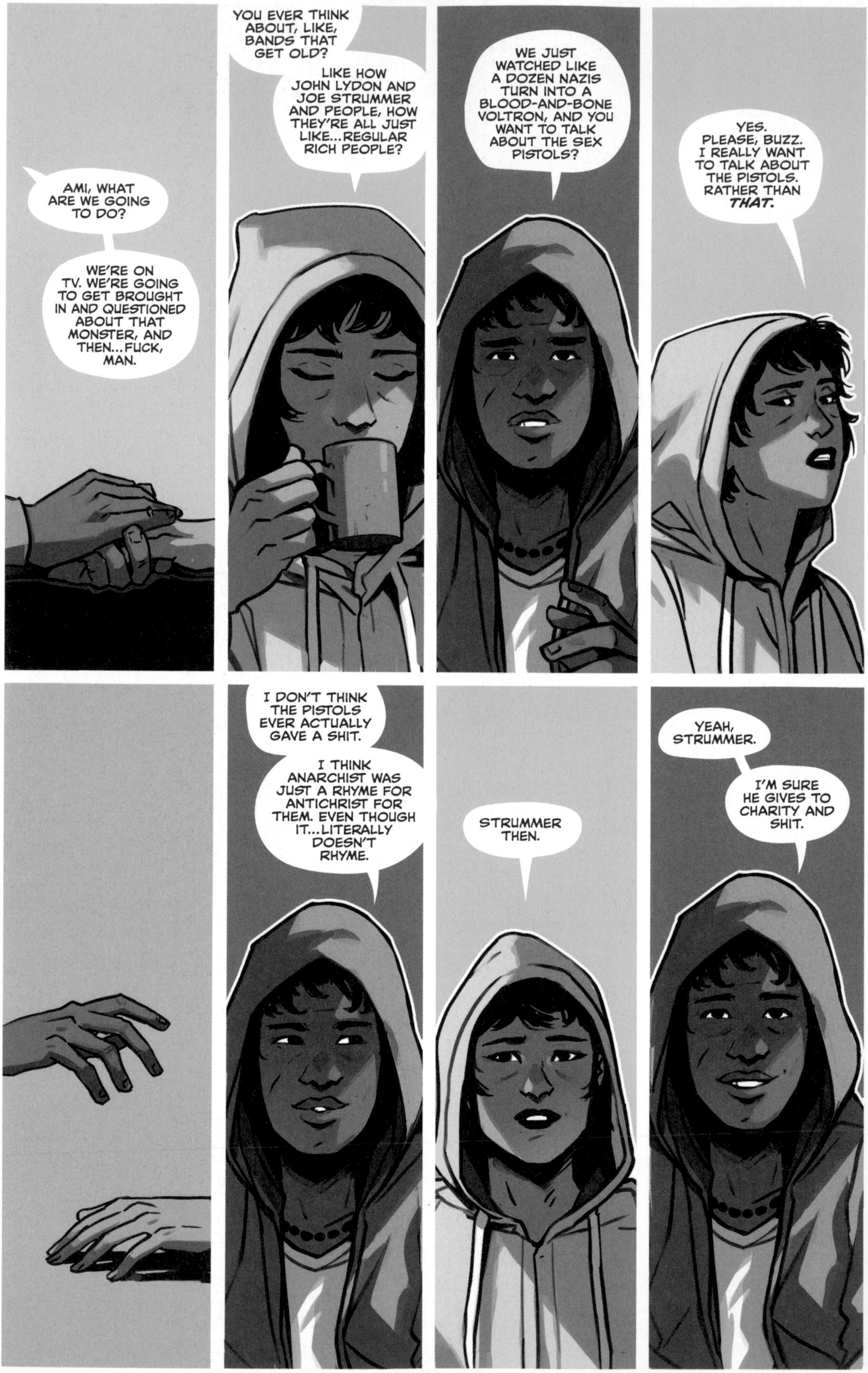
AMI, WHAT ARE WE GOING TO DO?
WE'RE ON TV. WE'RE GOING TO GET BROUGHT IN AND QUESTIONED ABOUT THAT MONSTER, AND THEN...FUCK, MAN.
YOU EVER THINK ABOUT, LIKE, BANDS THAT GET OLD?
LIKE HOW JOHN LYDON AND JOE STRUMMER AND PEOPLE, HOW THEY'RE ALL JUST LIKE...REGULAR RICH PEOPLE?
WE JUST WATCHED LIKE A DOZEN NAZIS TURN INTO A BLOOD-AND-BONE VOLTRON, AND YOU WANT TO TALK ABOUT THE SEX PISTOLS?
YES. PLEASE, BUZZ. I REALLY WANT TO TALK ABOUT THE PISTOLS. RATHER THAN *THAT.*
I DON'T THINK THE PISTOLS EVER ACTUALLY GAVE A SHIT.
I THINK ANARCHIST WAS JUST A RHYME FOR ANTICHRIST FOR THEM. EVEN THOUGH IT...LITERALLY DOESN'T RHYME.
STRUMMER THEN.
YEAH, STRUMMER.
I'M SURE HE GIVES TO CHARITY AND SHIT.

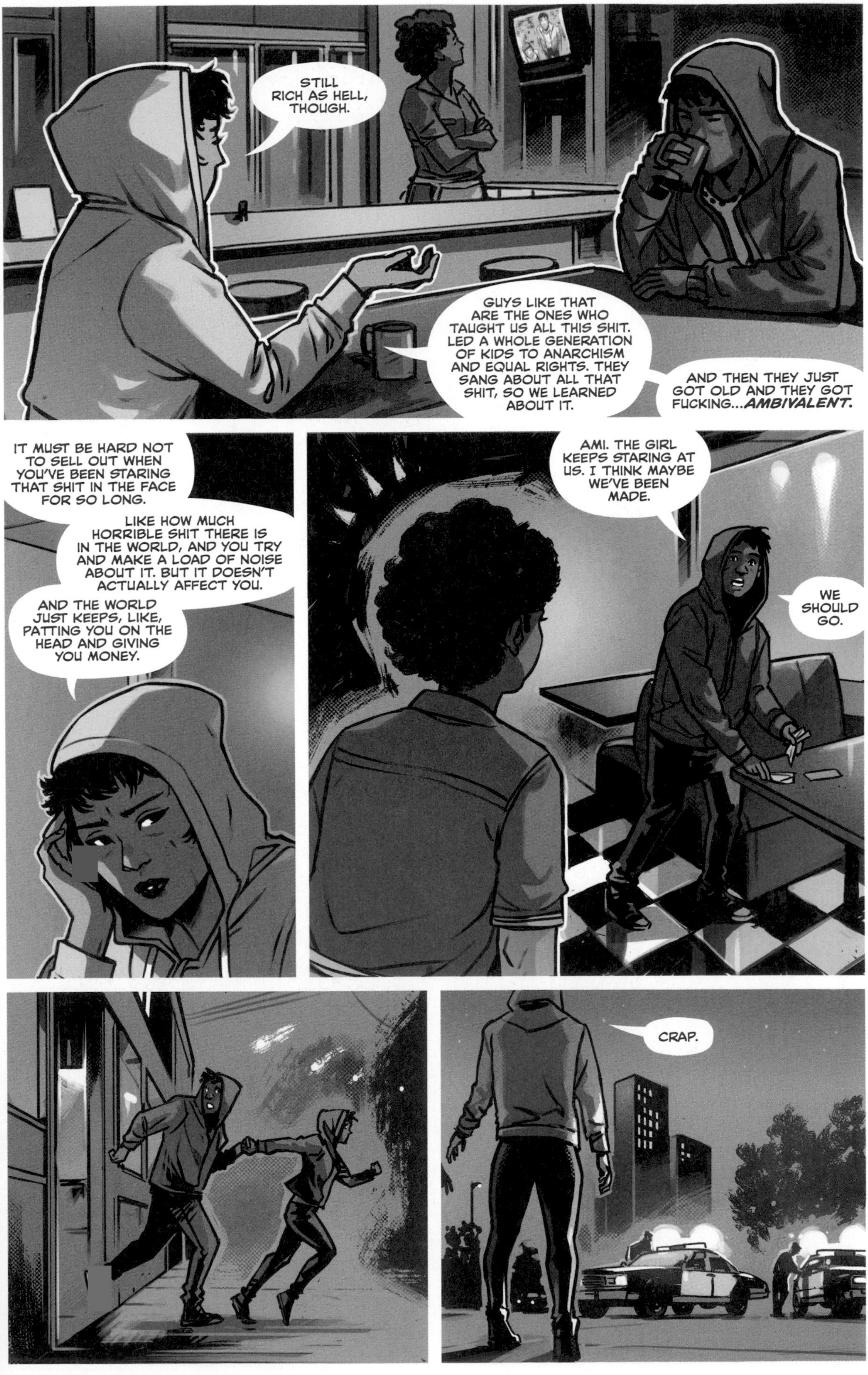
STILL RICH AS HELL, THOUGH.
GUYS LIKE THAT ARE THE ONES WHO TAUGHT US ALL THIS SHIT. LED A WHOLE GENERATION OF KIDS TO ANARCHISM AND EQUAL RIGHTS. THEY SANG ABOUT ALL THAT SHIT, SO WE LEARNED ABOUT IT.
AND THEN THEY JUST GOT OLD AND THEY GOT FUCKING...*AMBIVALENT.*
IT MUST BE HARD NOT TO SELL OUT WHEN YOU'VE BEEN STARING THAT SHIT IN THE FACE FOR SO LONG.
LIKE HOW MUCH HORRIBLE SHIT THERE IS IN THE WORLD, AND YOU TRY AND MAKE A LOAD OF NOISE ABOUT IT. BUT IT DOESN'T ACTUALLY AFFECT YOU.
AND THE WORLD JUST KEEPS, LIKE, PATTING YOU ON THE HEAD AND GIVING YOU MONEY.
AMI. THE GIRL KEEPS STARING AT US. I THINK MAYBE WE'VE BEEN MADE.
WE SHOULD GO.
CRAP.

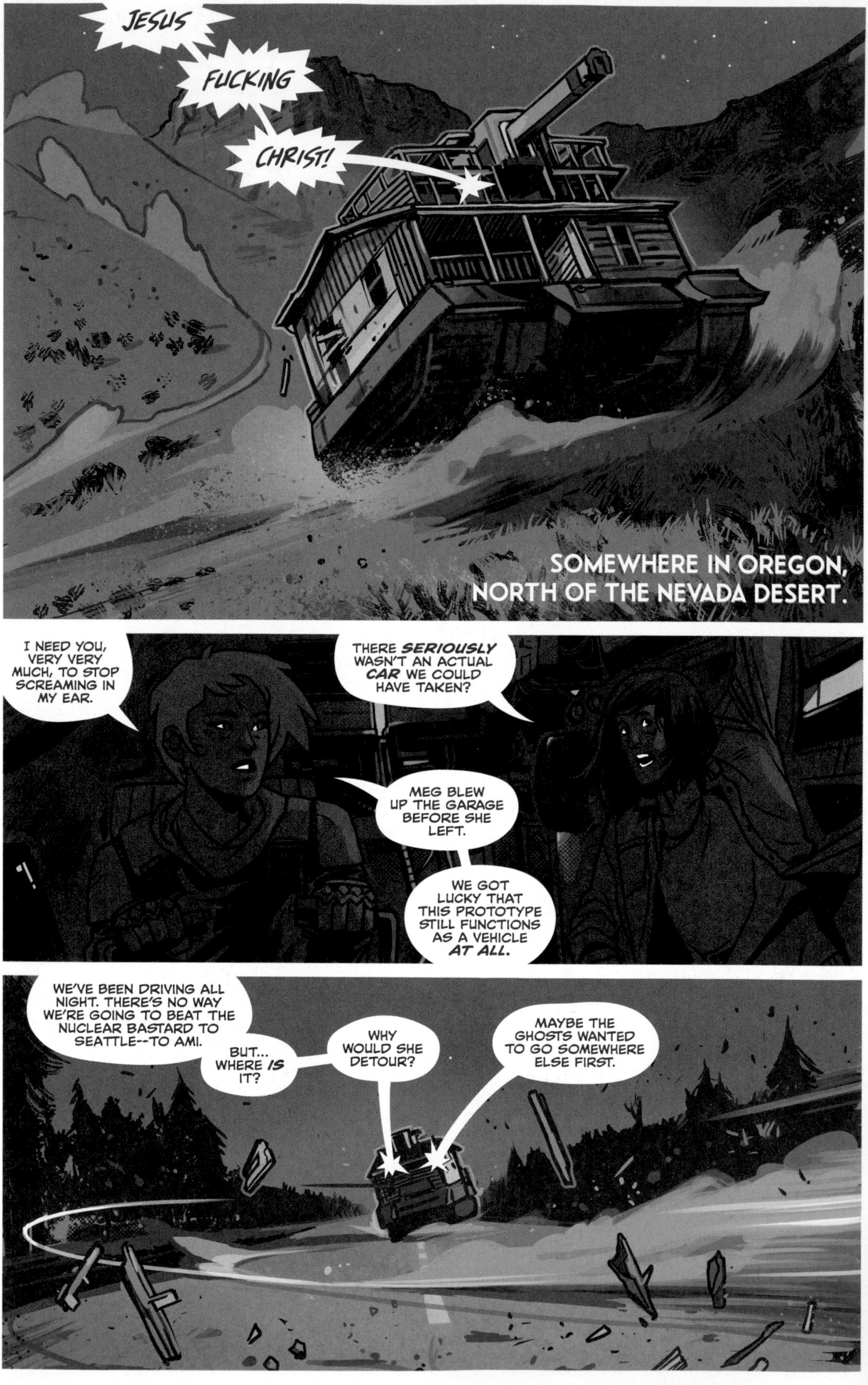
JESUS
FUCKING
CHRIST!
SOMEWHERE IN OREGON, NORTH OF THE NEVADA DESERT.
I NEED YOU, VERY VERY MUCH, TO STOP SCREAMING IN MY EAR.
THERE *SERIOUSLY* WASN'T AN ACTUAL *CAR* WE COULD HAVE TAKEN?
MEG BLEW UP THE GARAGE BEFORE SHE LEFT.
WE GOT LUCKY THAT THIS PROTOTYPE STILL FUNCTIONS AS A VEHICLE *AT ALL.*
WE'VE BEEN DRIVING ALL NIGHT. THERE'S NO WAY WE'RE GOING TO BEAT THE NUCLEAR BASTARD TO SEATTLE--TO AMI.
BUT... WHERE *IS* IT?
WHY WOULD SHE DETOUR?
MAYBE THE GHOSTS WANTED TO GO SOMEWHERE ELSE FIRST.

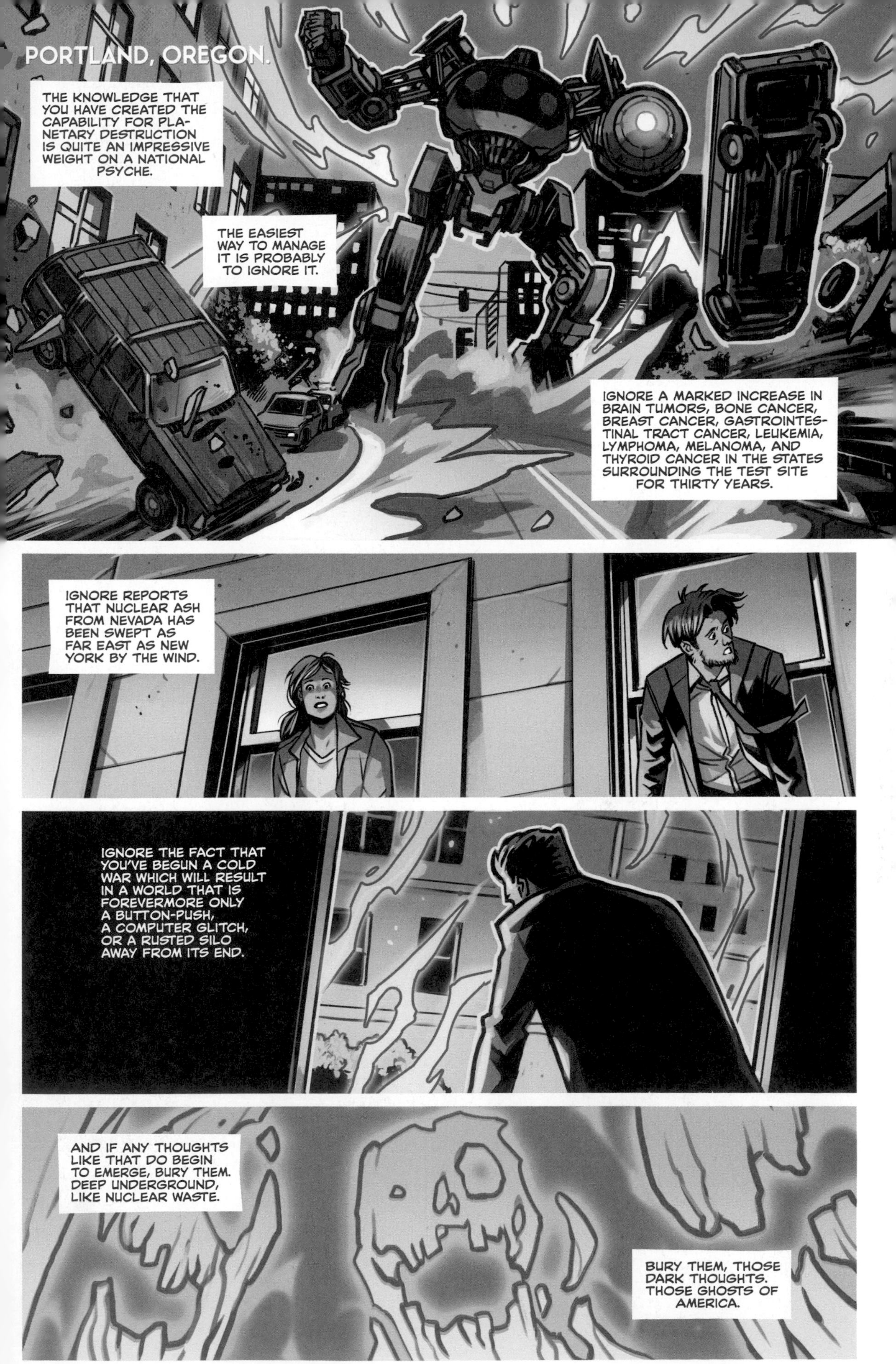
PORTLAND, OREGON.
THE KNOWLEDGE THAT YOU HAVE CREATED THE CAPABILITY FOR PLANETARY DESTRUCTION IS QUITE AN IMPRESSIVE WEIGHT ON A NATIONAL PSYCHE.
THE EASIEST WAY TO MANAGE IT IS PROBABLY TO IGNORE IT.
IGNORE A MARKED INCREASE IN BRAIN TUMORS, BONE CANCER, BREAST CANCER, GASTROINTESTINAL TRACT CANCER, LEUKEMIA, LYMPHOMA, MELANOMA, AND THYROID CANCER IN THE STATES SURROUNDING THE TEST SITE FOR THIRTY YEARS.
IGNORE REPORTS THAT NUCLEAR ASH FROM NEVADA HAS BEEN SWEPT AS FAR EAST AS NEW YORK BY THE WIND.
IGNORE THE FACT THAT YOU'VE BEGUN A COLD WAR WHICH WILL RESULT IN A WORLD THAT IS FOREVERMORE ONLY A BUTTON-PUSH, A COMPUTER GLITCH, OR A RUSTED SILO AWAY FROM ITS END.
AND IF ANY THOUGHTS LIKE THAT DO BEGIN TO EMERGE, BURY THEM. DEEP UNDERGROUND, LIKE NUCLEAR WASTE.
BURY THEM, THOSE DARK THOUGHTS. THOSE GHOSTS OF AMERICA.

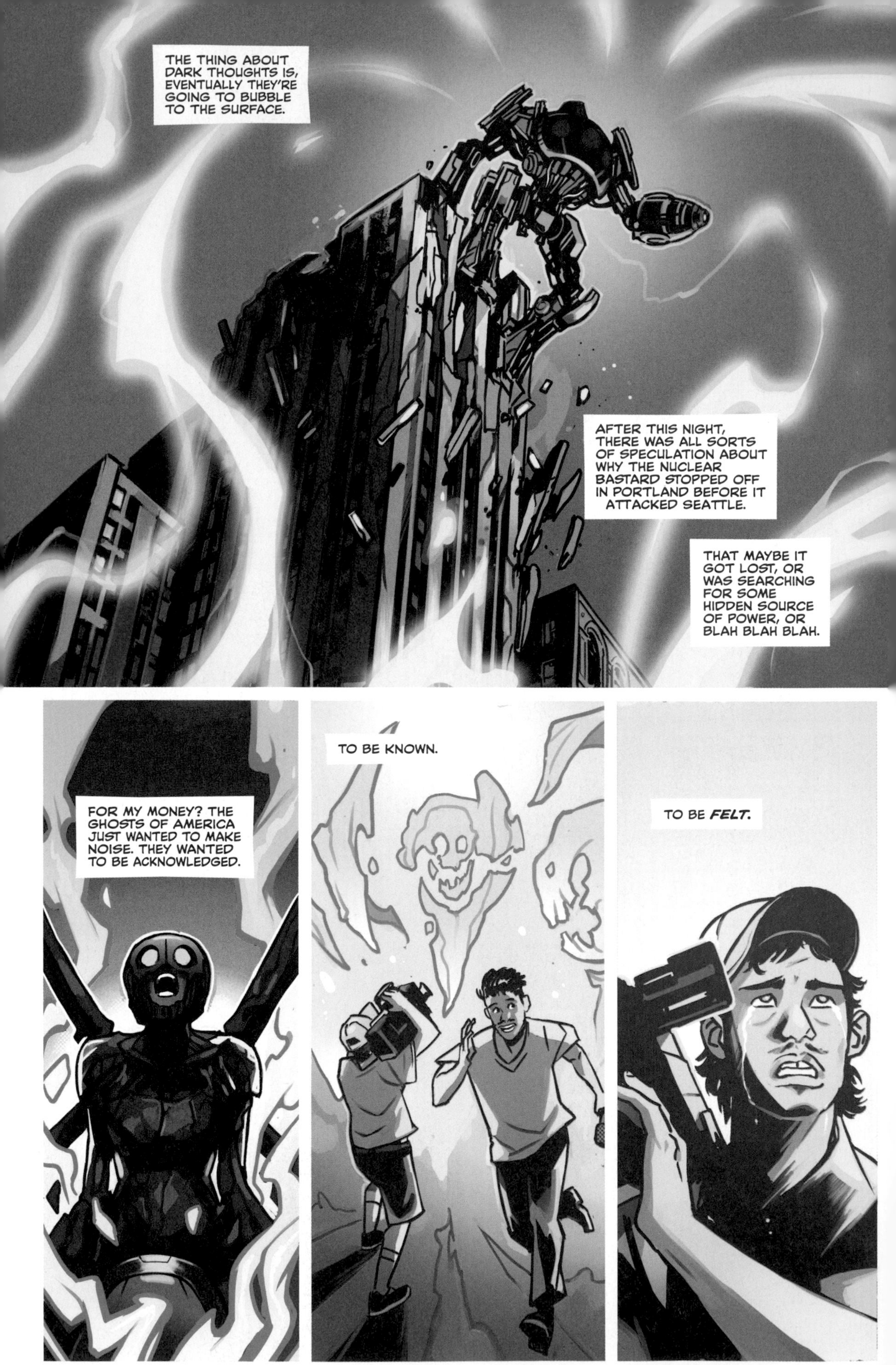
THE THING ABOUT DARK THOUGHTS IS, EVENTUALLY THEY'RE GOING TO BUBBLE TO THE SURFACE.
AFTER THIS NIGHT, THERE WAS ALL SORTS OF SPECULATION ABOUT WHY THE NUCLEAR BASTARD STOPPED OFF IN PORTLAND BEFORE IT ATTACKED SEATTLE.
THAT MAYBE IT GOT LOST, OR WAS SEARCHING FOR SOME HIDDEN SOURCE OF POWER, OR BLAH BLAH BLAH.
FOR MY MONEY? THE GHOSTS OF AMERICA JUST WANTED TO MAKE NOISE. THEY WANTED TO BE ACKNOWLEDGED.
TO BE KNOWN.
TO BE *FELT*.

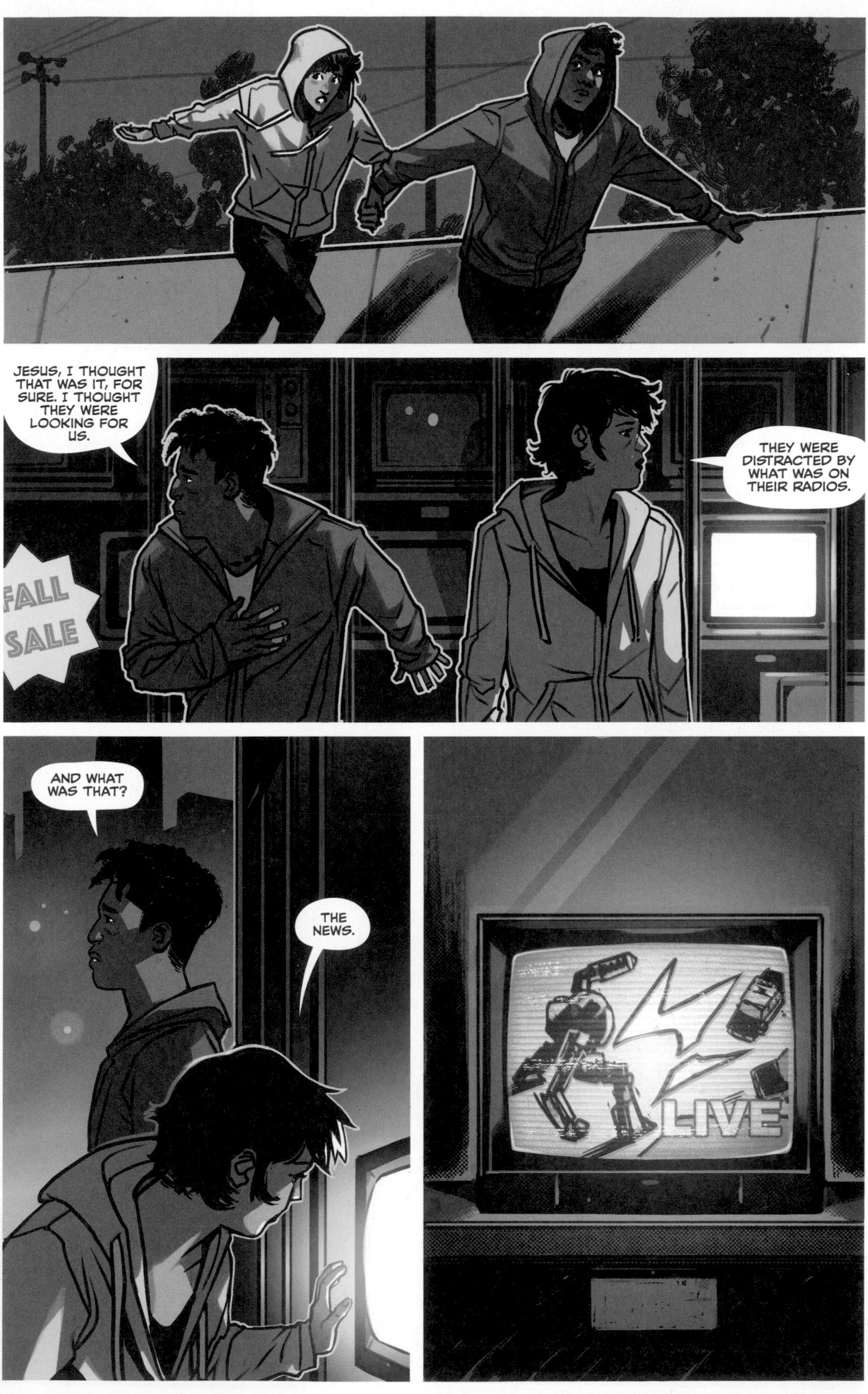
JESUS, I THOUGHT THAT WAS IT, FOR SURE. I THOUGHT THEY WERE LOOKING FOR US.
THEY WERE DISTRACTED BY WHAT WAS ON THEIR RADIOS.
FALL SALE
AND WHAT WAS THAT?
THE NEWS.
LIVE

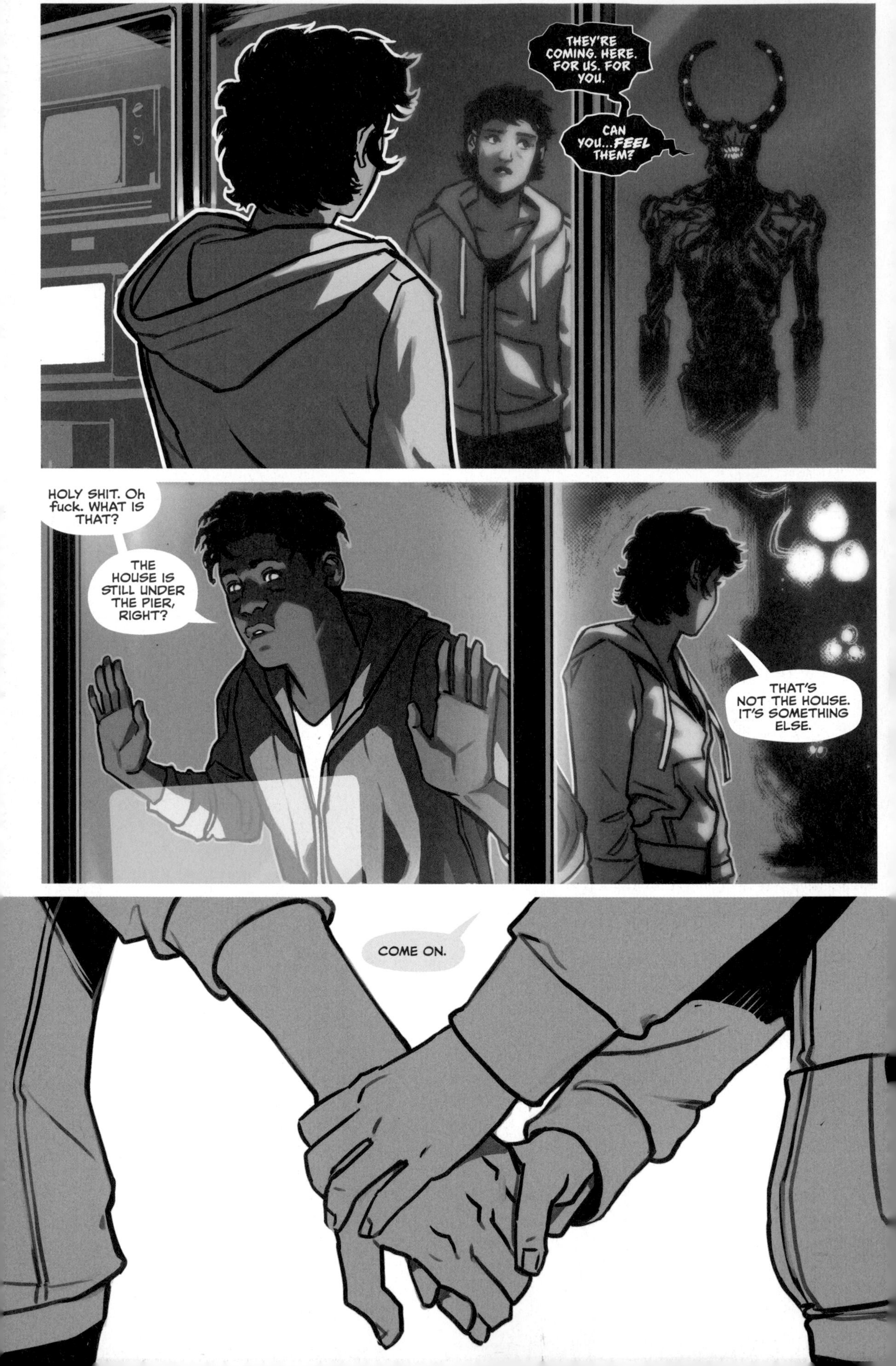
THEY'RE COMING. HERE. FOR US. FOR YOU.
CAN YOU...FEEL THEM?
HOLY SHIT. Oh fuck. WHAT IS THAT?
THE HOUSE IS STILL UNDER THE PIER, RIGHT?
THAT'S NOT THE HOUSE. IT'S SOMETHING ELSE.
COME ON.

ONE HOUR BEFORE
THE NUCLEAR BASTARD
REACHED ME.

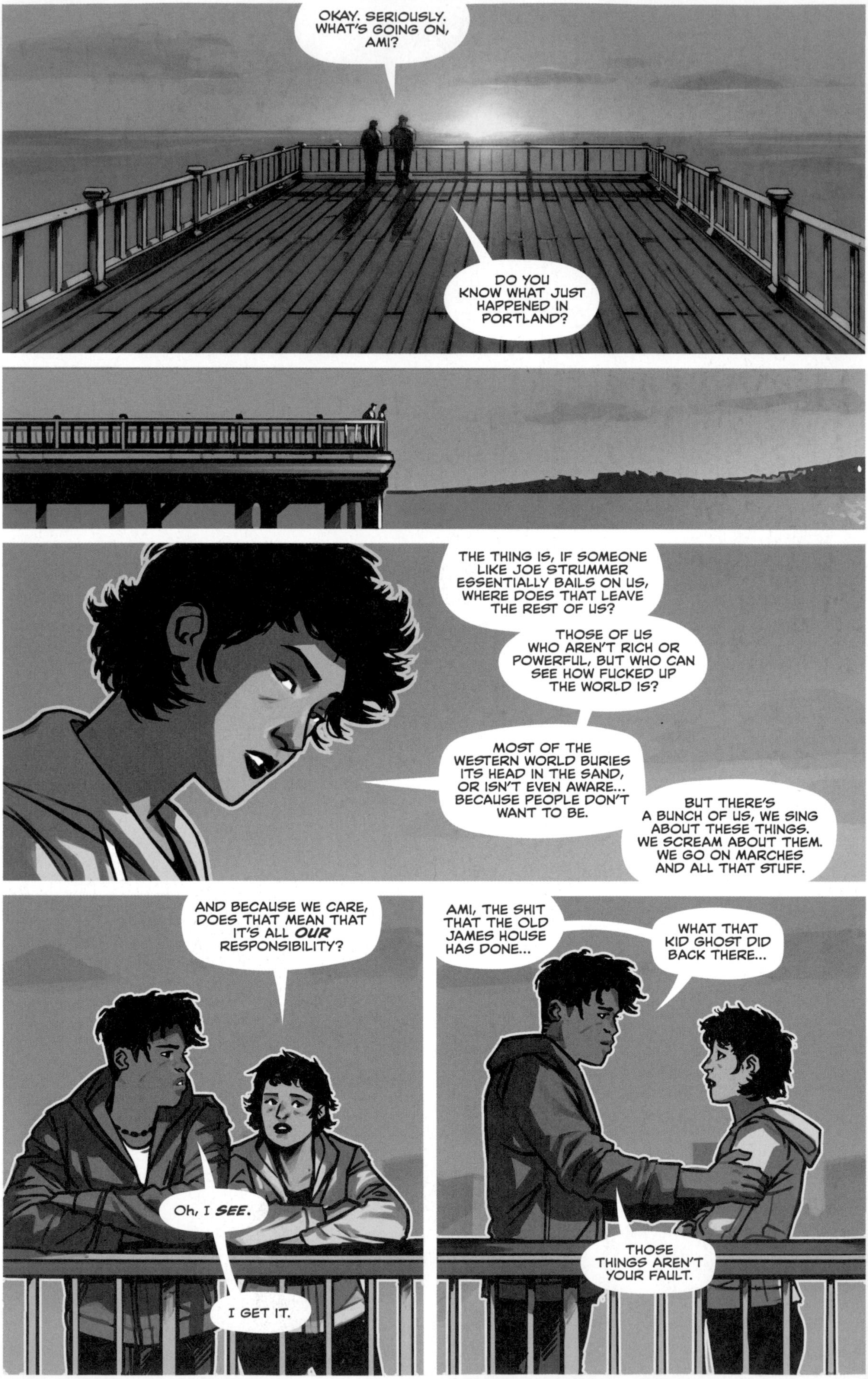
OKAY. SERIOUSLY. WHAT'S GOING ON, AMI?
DO YOU KNOW WHAT JUST HAPPENED IN PORTLAND?
THE THING IS, IF SOMEONE LIKE JOE STRUMMER ESSENTIALLY BAILS ON US, WHERE DOES THAT LEAVE THE REST OF US?
THOSE OF US WHO AREN'T RICH OR POWERFUL, BUT WHO CAN SEE HOW FUCKED UP THE WORLD IS?
MOST OF THE WESTERN WORLD BURIES ITS HEAD IN THE SAND, OR ISN'T EVEN AWARE... BECAUSE PEOPLE DON'T WANT TO BE.
BUT THERE'S A BUNCH OF US, WE SING ABOUT THESE THINGS. WE SCREAM ABOUT THEM. WE GO ON MARCHES AND ALL THAT STUFF.
AND BECAUSE WE CARE, DOES THAT MEAN THAT IT'S ALL ***OUR*** RESPONSIBILITY?
Oh, I ***SEE.***
I GET IT.
AMI, THE SHIT THAT THE OLD JAMES HOUSE HAS DONE...
WHAT THAT KID GHOST DID BACK THERE...
THOSE THINGS AREN'T YOUR FAULT.

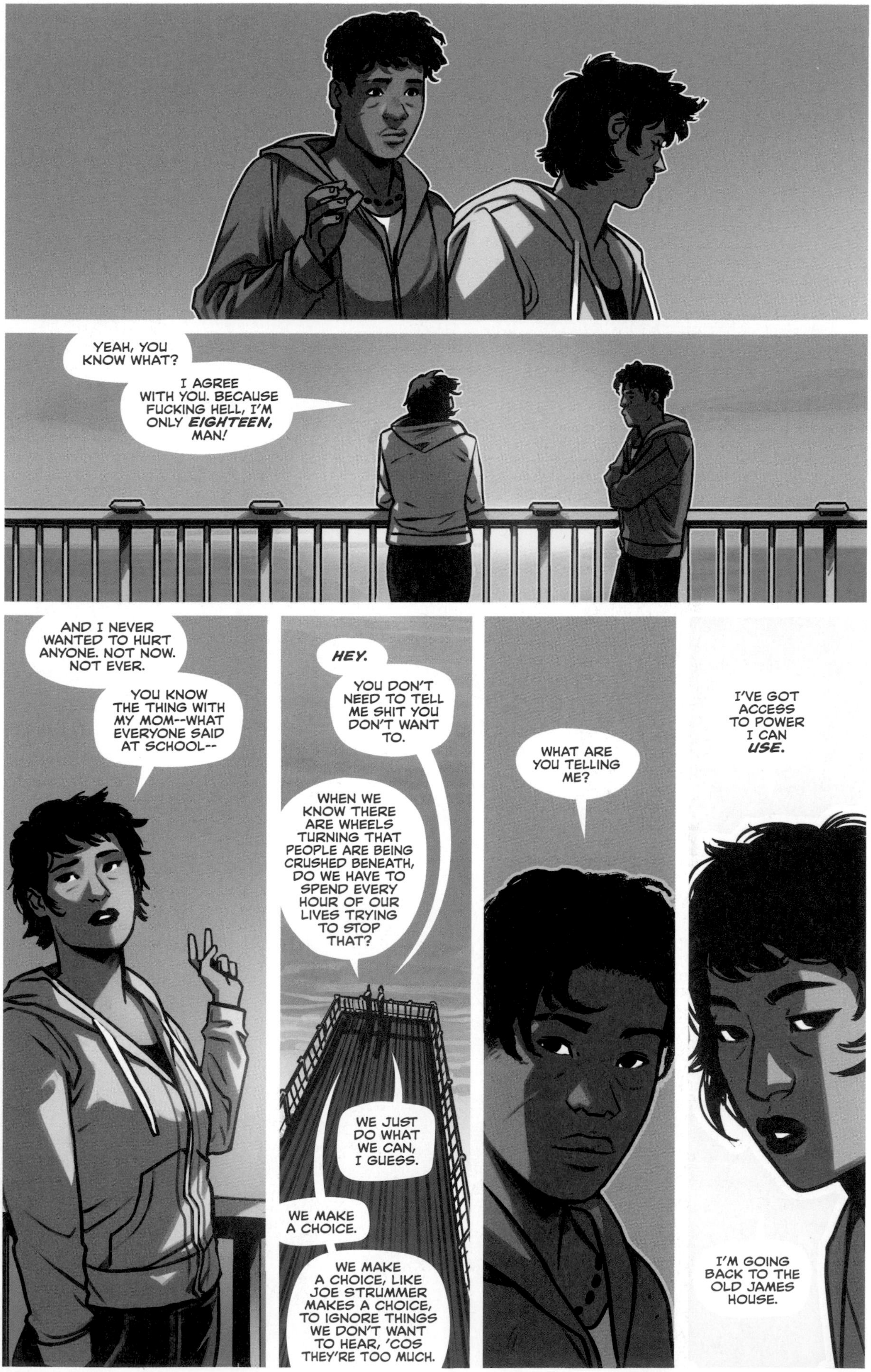

YEAH, YOU KNOW WHAT?
I AGREE WITH YOU. BECAUSE FUCKING HELL, I'M ONLY ***EIGHTEEN,*** MAN!
AND I NEVER WANTED TO HURT ANYONE. NOT NOW. NOT EVER.
YOU KNOW THE THING WITH MY MOM--WHAT EVERYONE SAID AT SCHOOL--
HEY.
YOU DON'T NEED TO TELL ME SHIT YOU DON'T WANT TO.
WHEN WE KNOW THERE ARE WHEELS TURNING THAT PEOPLE ARE BEING CRUSHED BENEATH, DO WE HAVE TO SPEND EVERY HOUR OF OUR LIVES TRYING TO STOP THAT?
WE JUST DO WHAT WE CAN, I GUESS.
WE MAKE A CHOICE.
WE MAKE A CHOICE, LIKE JOE STRUMMER MAKES A CHOICE, TO IGNORE THINGS WE DON'T WANT TO HEAR, 'COS THEY'RE TOO MUCH.
WHAT ARE YOU TELLING ME?
I'VE GOT ACCESS TO POWER I CAN ***USE.***
I'M GOING BACK TO THE OLD JAMES HOUSE.

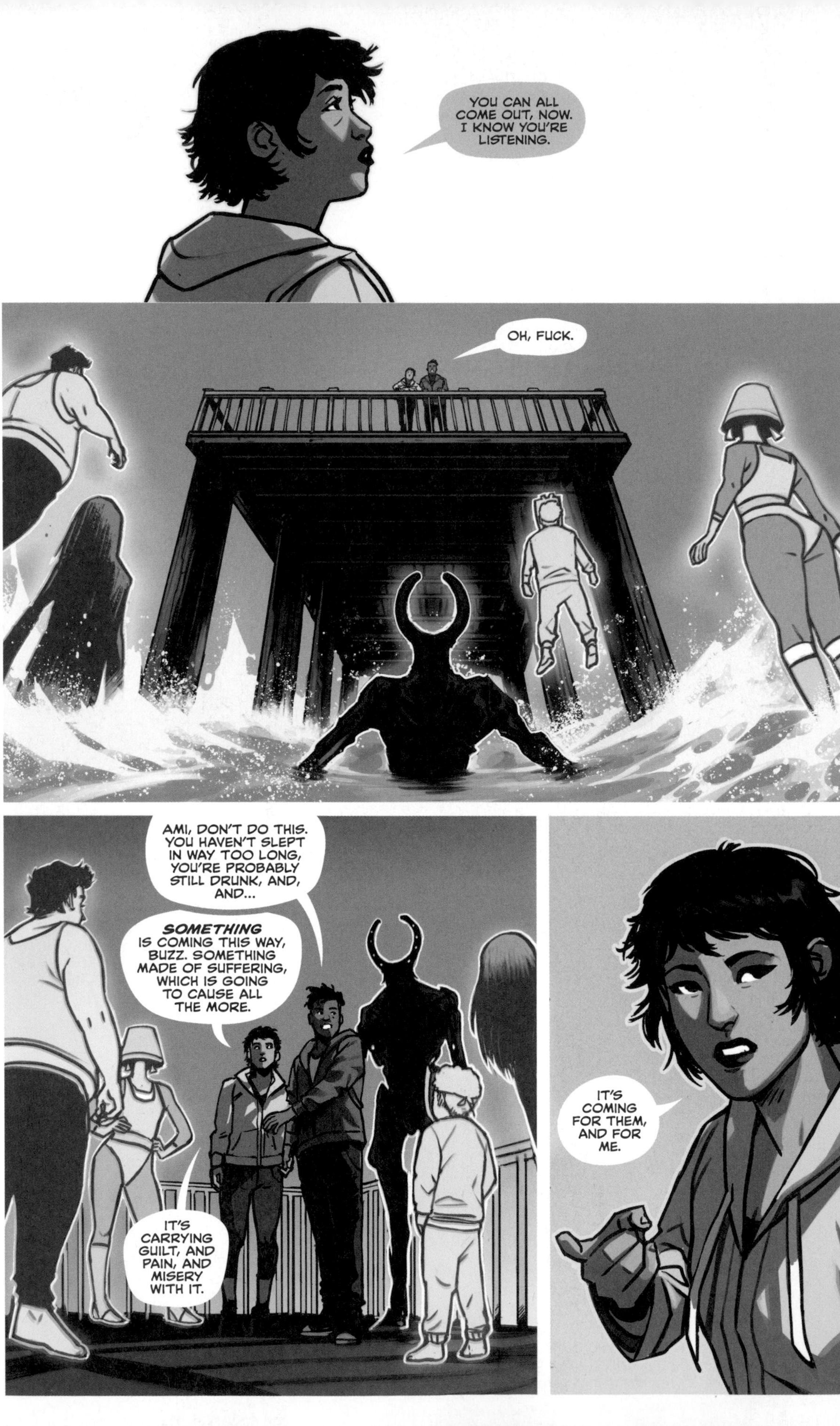
YOU CAN ALL COME OUT, NOW. I KNOW YOU'RE LISTENING.
OH, FUCK.
AMI, DON'T DO THIS. YOU HAVEN'T SLEPT IN WAY TOO LONG, YOU'RE PROBABLY STILL DRUNK, AND, AND...
SOMETHING IS COMING THIS WAY, BUZZ. SOMETHING MADE OF SUFFERING, WHICH IS GOING TO CAUSE ALL THE MORE.
IT'S CARRYING GUILT, AND PAIN, AND MISERY WITH IT.
IT'S COMING FOR THEM, AND FOR ME.

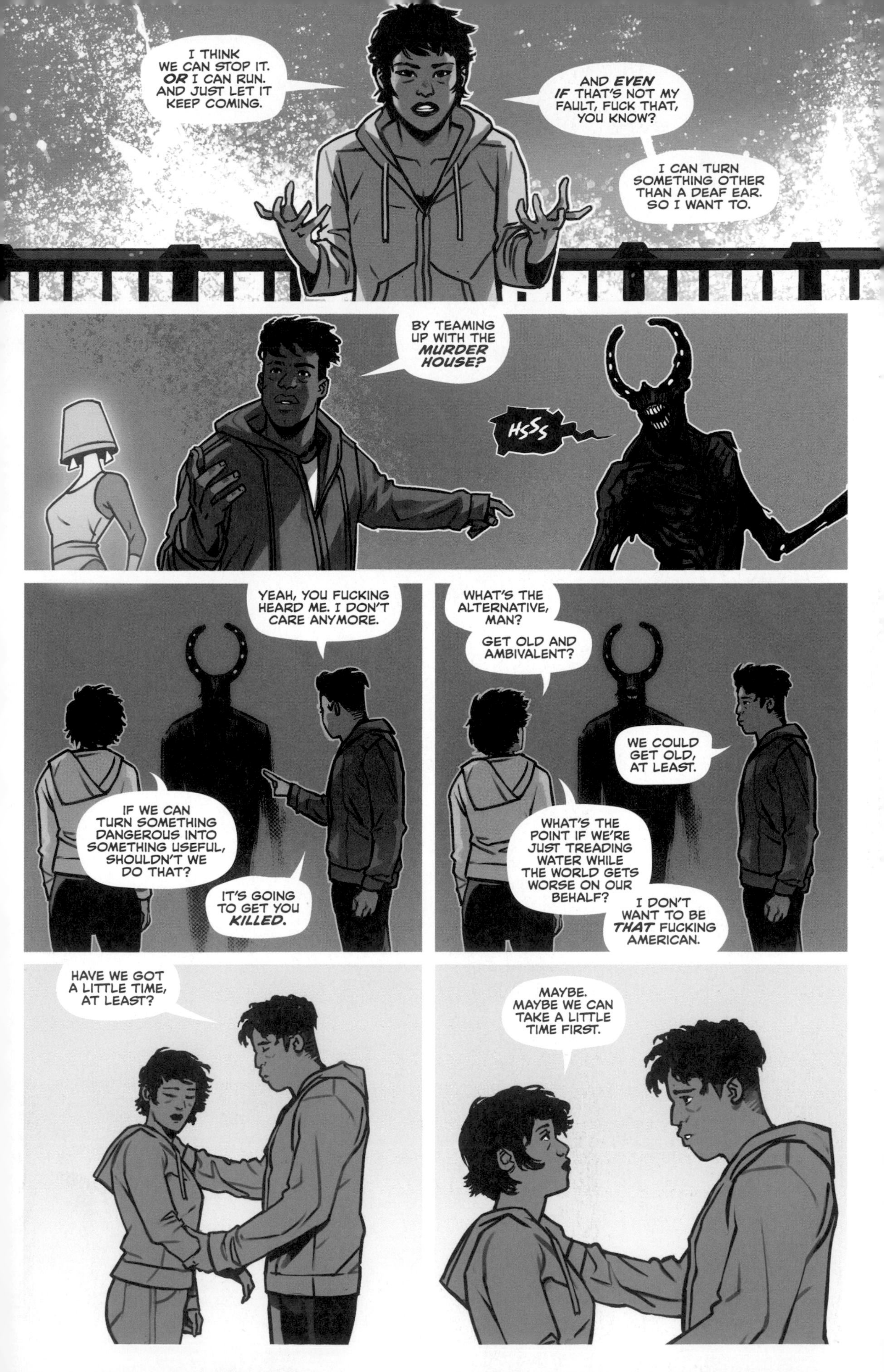
I THINK WE CAN STOP IT. OR I CAN RUN. AND JUST LET IT KEEP COMING.
AND EVEN IF THAT'S NOT MY FAULT, FUCK THAT, YOU KNOW?
I CAN TURN SOMETHING OTHER THAN A DEAF EAR. SO I WANT TO.
BY TEAMING UP WITH THE MURDER HOUSE?
HSSS
YEAH, YOU FUCKING HEARD ME. I DON'T CARE ANYMORE.
IF WE CAN TURN SOMETHING DANGEROUS INTO SOMETHING USEFUL, SHOULDN'T WE DO THAT?
IT'S GOING TO GET YOU KILLED.
WHAT'S THE ALTERNATIVE, MAN?
GET OLD AND AMBIVALENT?
WE COULD GET OLD, AT LEAST.
WHAT'S THE POINT IF WE'RE JUST TREADING WATER WHILE THE WORLD GETS WORSE ON OUR BEHALF?
I DON'T WANT TO BE THAT FUCKING AMERICAN.
HAVE WE GOT A LITTLE TIME, AT LEAST?
MAYBE. MAYBE WE CAN TAKE A LITTLE TIME FIRST.

A FEW MINUTES BEFORE
THE NUCLEAR BASTARD
REACHED ME.

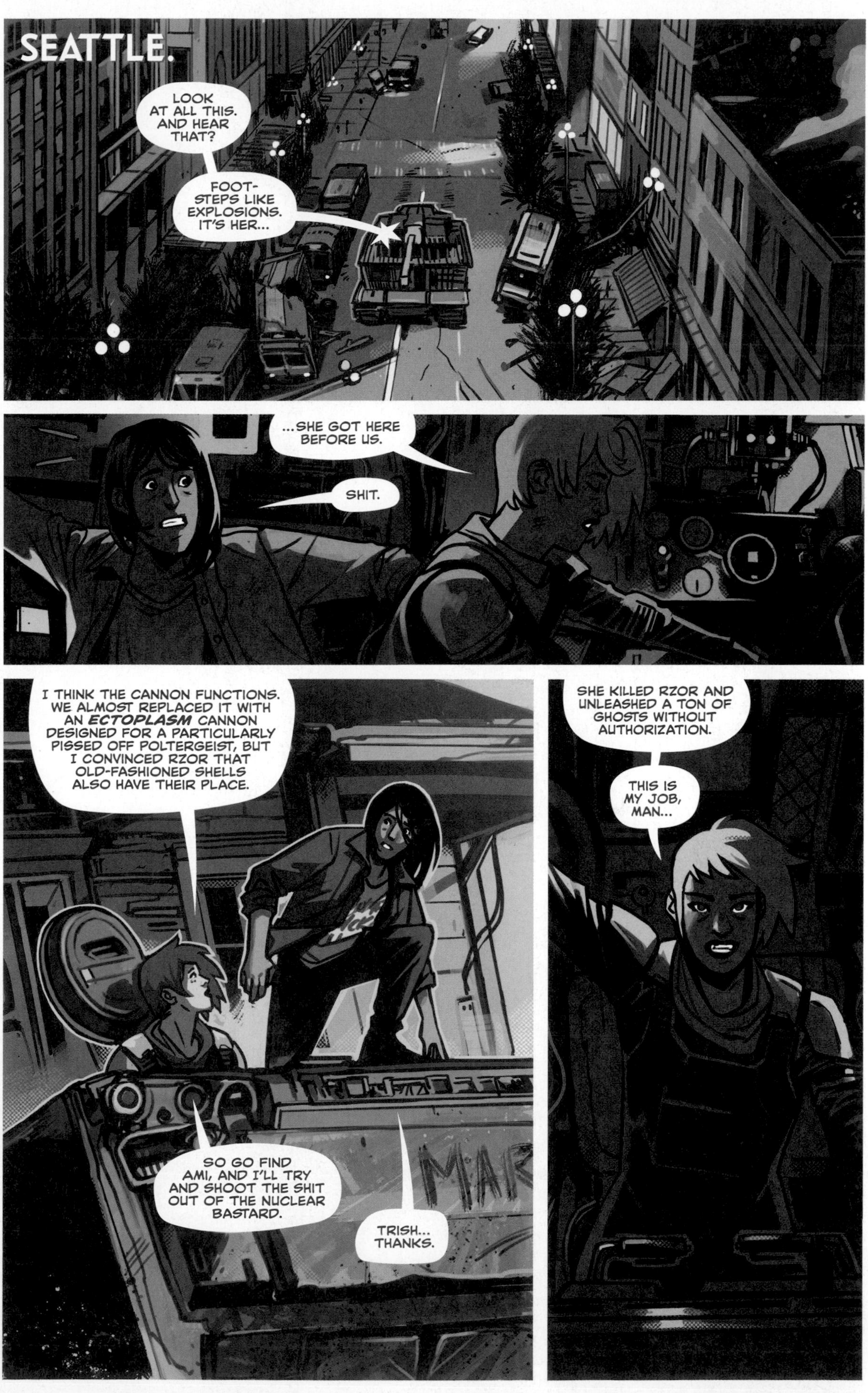
SEATTLE.
LOOK AT ALL THIS. AND HEAR THAT?
FOOT-STEPS LIKE EXPLOSIONS. IT'S HER...
...SHE GOT HERE BEFORE US.
SHIT.
I THINK THE CANNON FUNCTIONS. WE ALMOST REPLACED IT WITH AN *ECTOPLASM* CANNON DESIGNED FOR A PARTICULARLY PISSED OFF POLTERGEIST, BUT I CONVINCED RZOR THAT OLD-FASHIONED SHELLS ALSO HAVE THEIR PLACE.
SO GO FIND AMI, AND I'LL TRY AND SHOOT THE SHIT OUT OF THE NUCLEAR BASTARD.
TRISH... THANKS.
SHE KILLED RZOR AND UNLEASHED A TON OF GHOSTS WITHOUT AUTHORIZATION.
THIS IS MY JOB, MAN...

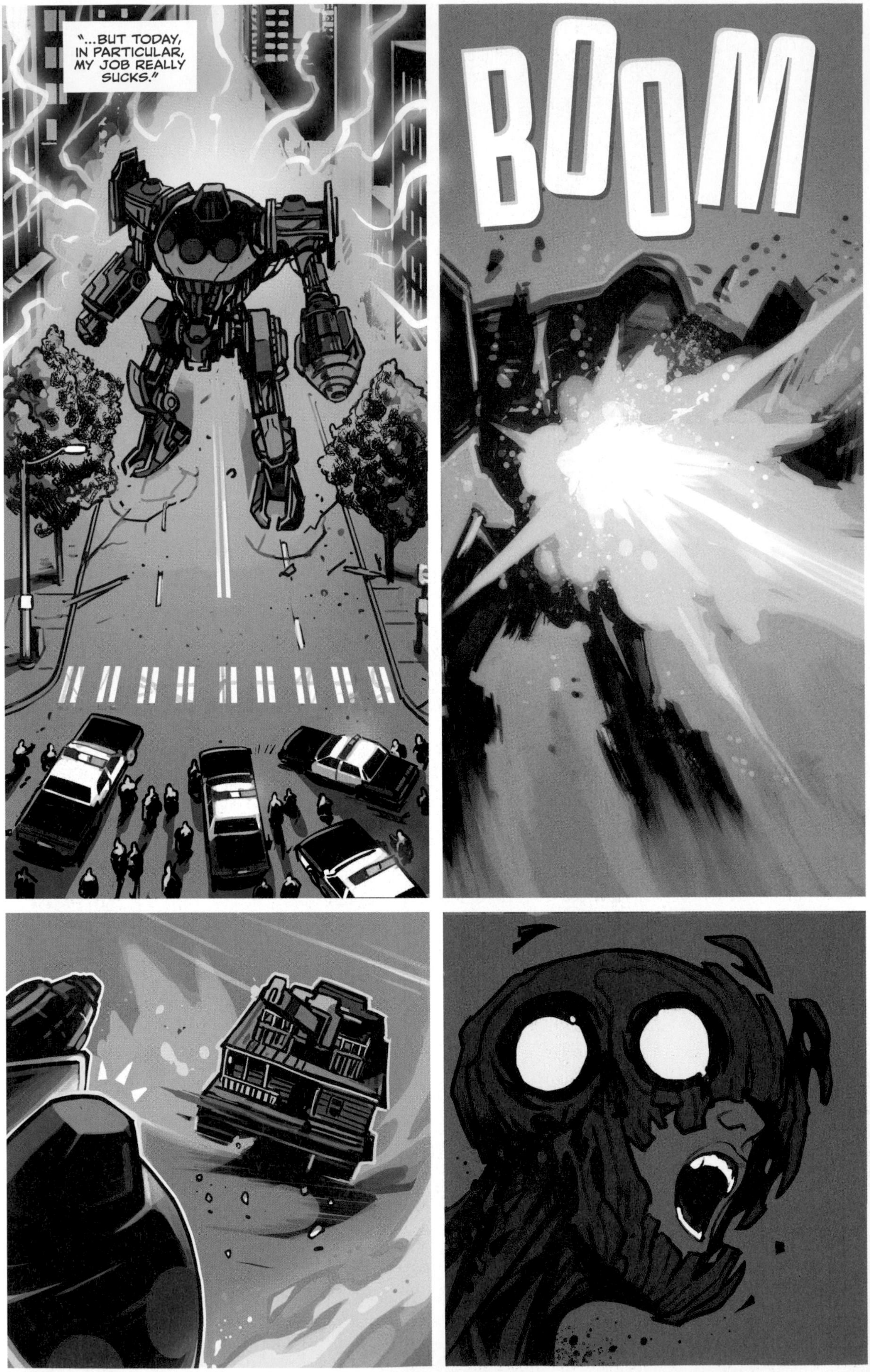
"...BUT TODAY, IN PARTICULAR, MY JOB REALLY SUCKS."
BOOM

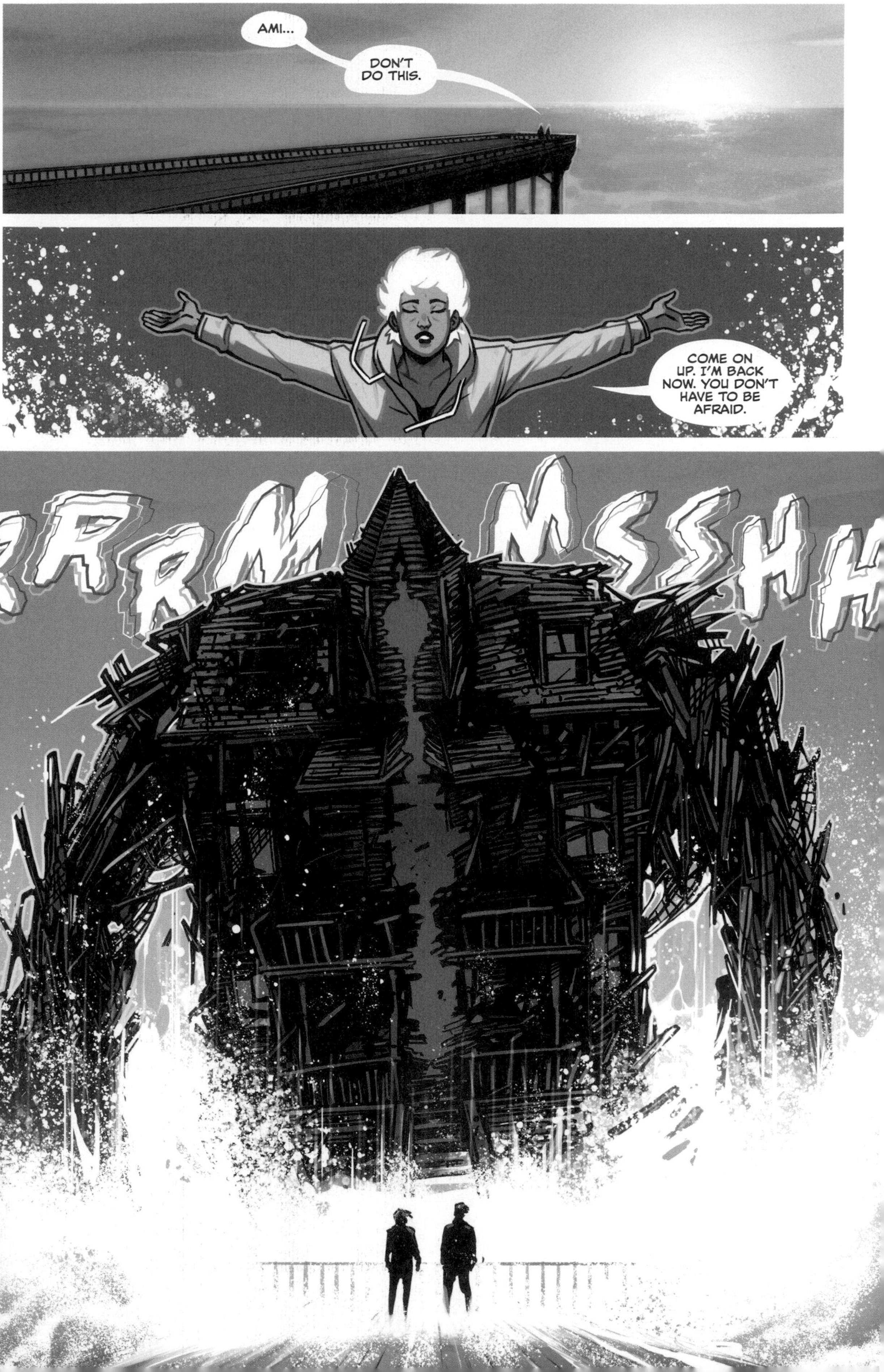
AMI...
DON'T DO THIS.
COME ON UP. I'M BACK NOW. YOU DON'T HAVE TO BE AFRAID.
RRMMMSSHH

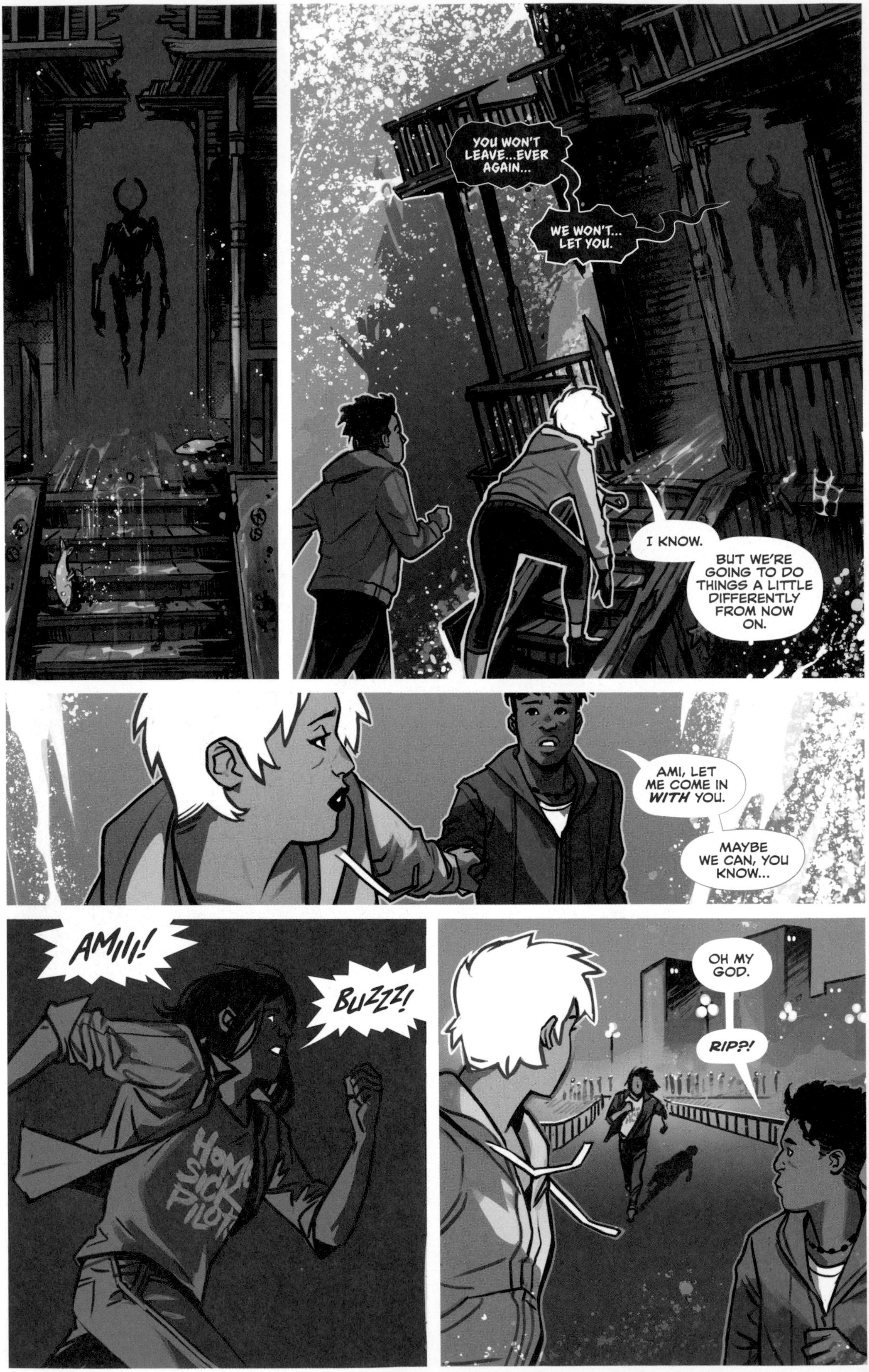
YOU WON'T LEAVE...EVER AGAIN...
WE WON'T... LET YOU.
I KNOW.
BUT WE'RE GOING TO DO THINGS A LITTLE DIFFERENTLY FROM NOW ON.
AMI, LET ME COME IN *WITH* YOU.
MAYBE WE CAN, YOU KNOW...
AMIII!
BUZZZ!
HOME SICK PILOT
OH MY GOD.
RIP?!

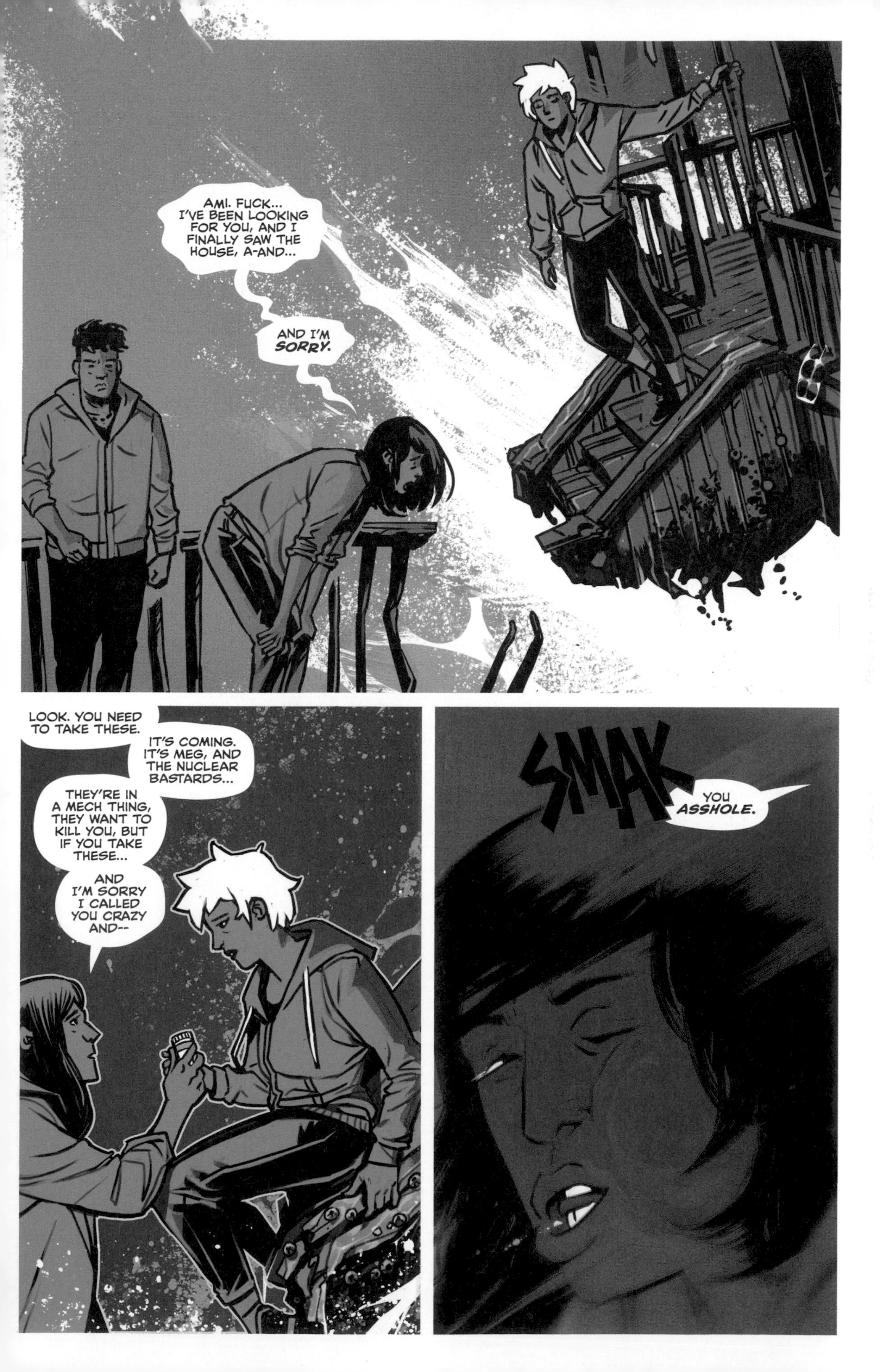
AMI. FUCK... I'VE BEEN LOOKING FOR YOU, AND I FINALLY SAW THE HOUSE, A-AND...
AND I'M SORRY.
LOOK. YOU NEED TO TAKE THESE.
IT'S COMING. IT'S MEG, AND THE NUCLEAR BASTARDS...
THEY'RE IN A MECH THING, THEY WANT TO KILL YOU, BUT IF YOU TAKE THESE...
AND I'M SORRY I CALLED YOU CRAZY AND--
SMAK
YOU ASSHOLE.

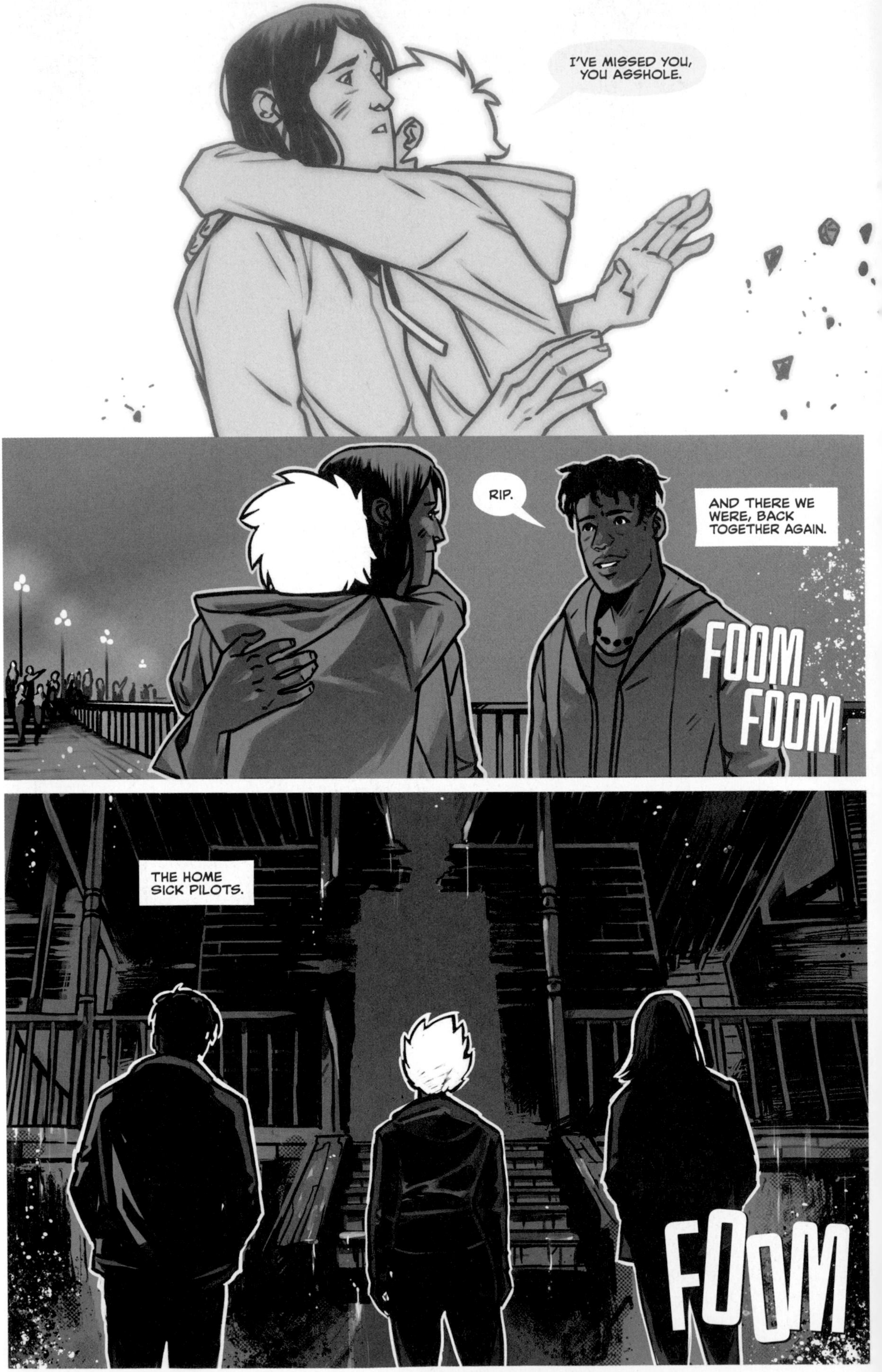
I'VE MISSED YOU, YOU ASSHOLE.
RIP.
AND THERE WE WERE, BACK TOGETHER AGAIN.
FOOM FOOM
THE HOME SICK PILOTS.
FOOM

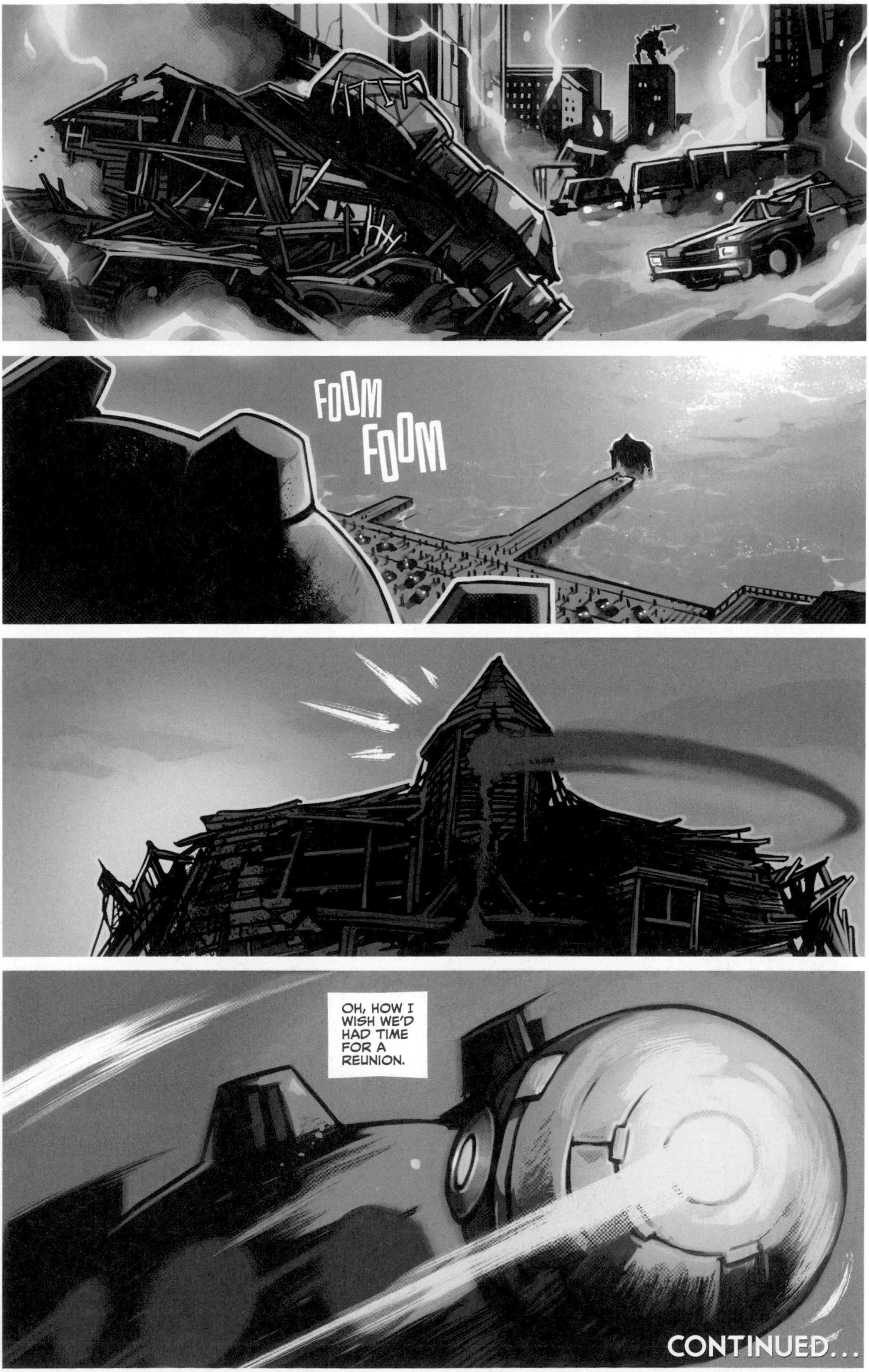
FOOM
FOOM
OH, HOW I WISH WE'D HAD TIME FOR A REUNION.
CONTINUED...

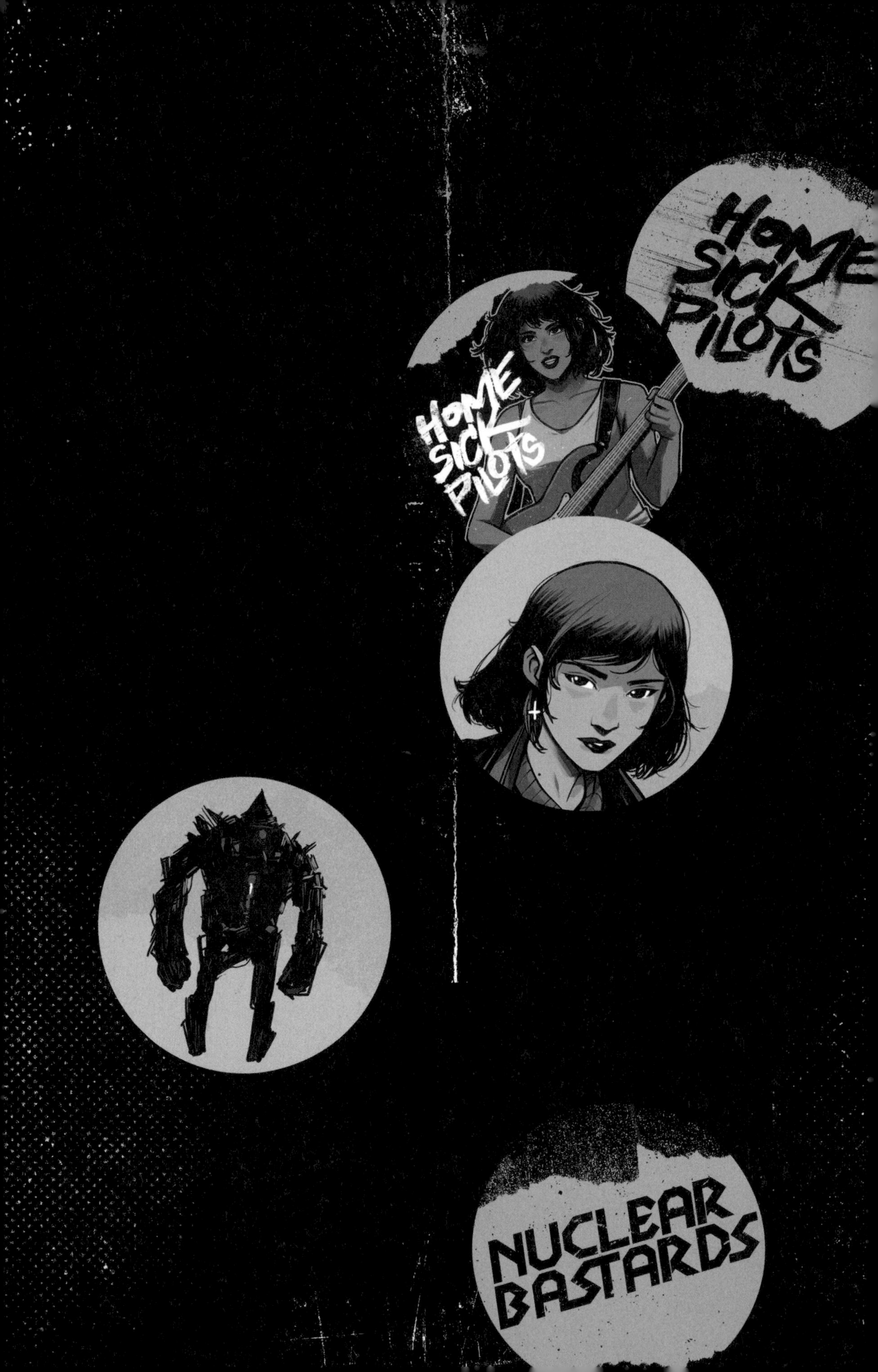
HOME SICK PILOTS
HOME SICK PILOTS
NUCLEAR BASTARDS

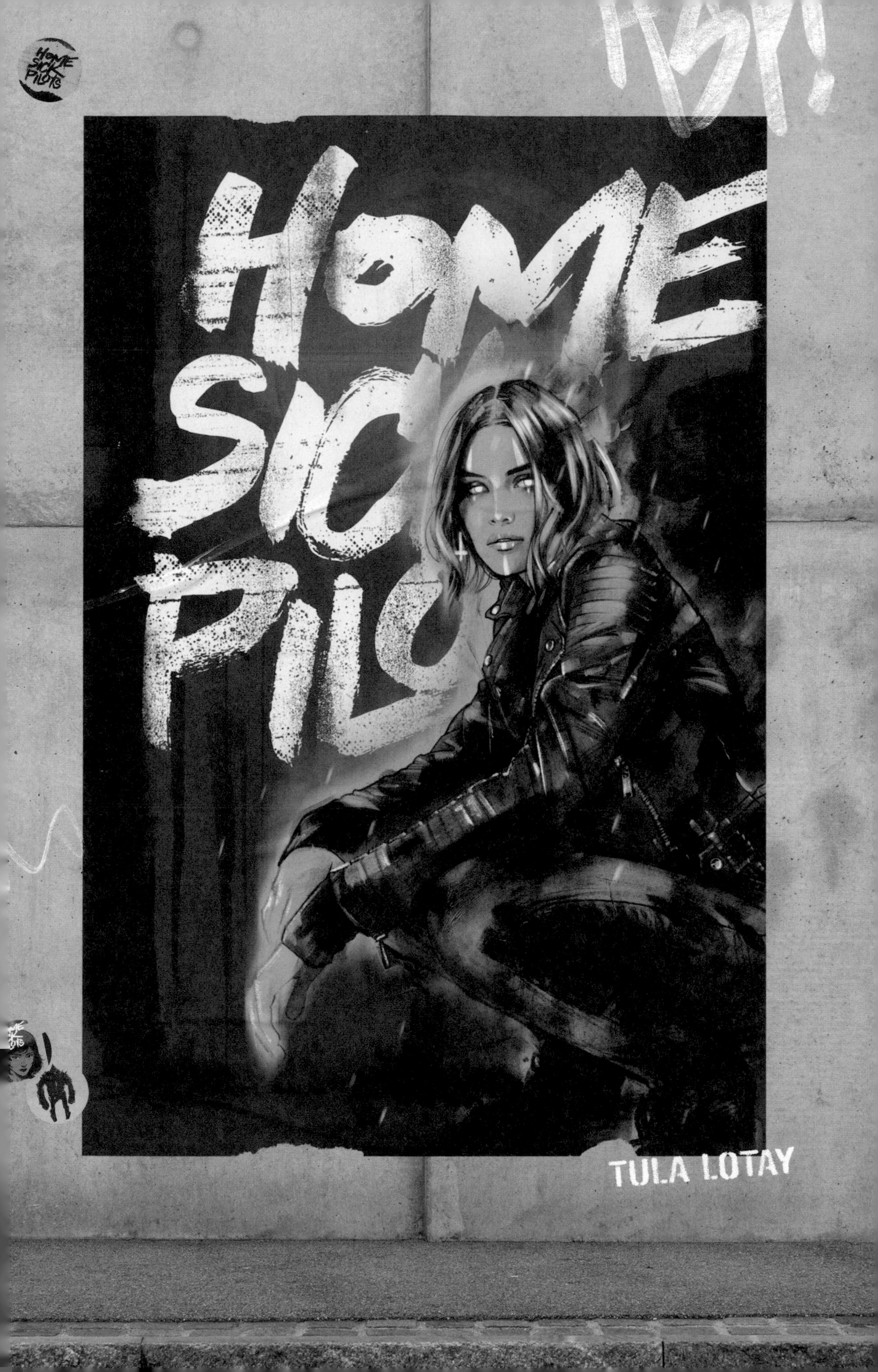
HOME SICK PILOTS
HSP!
HOME
SIC
PILO
TULA LOTAY

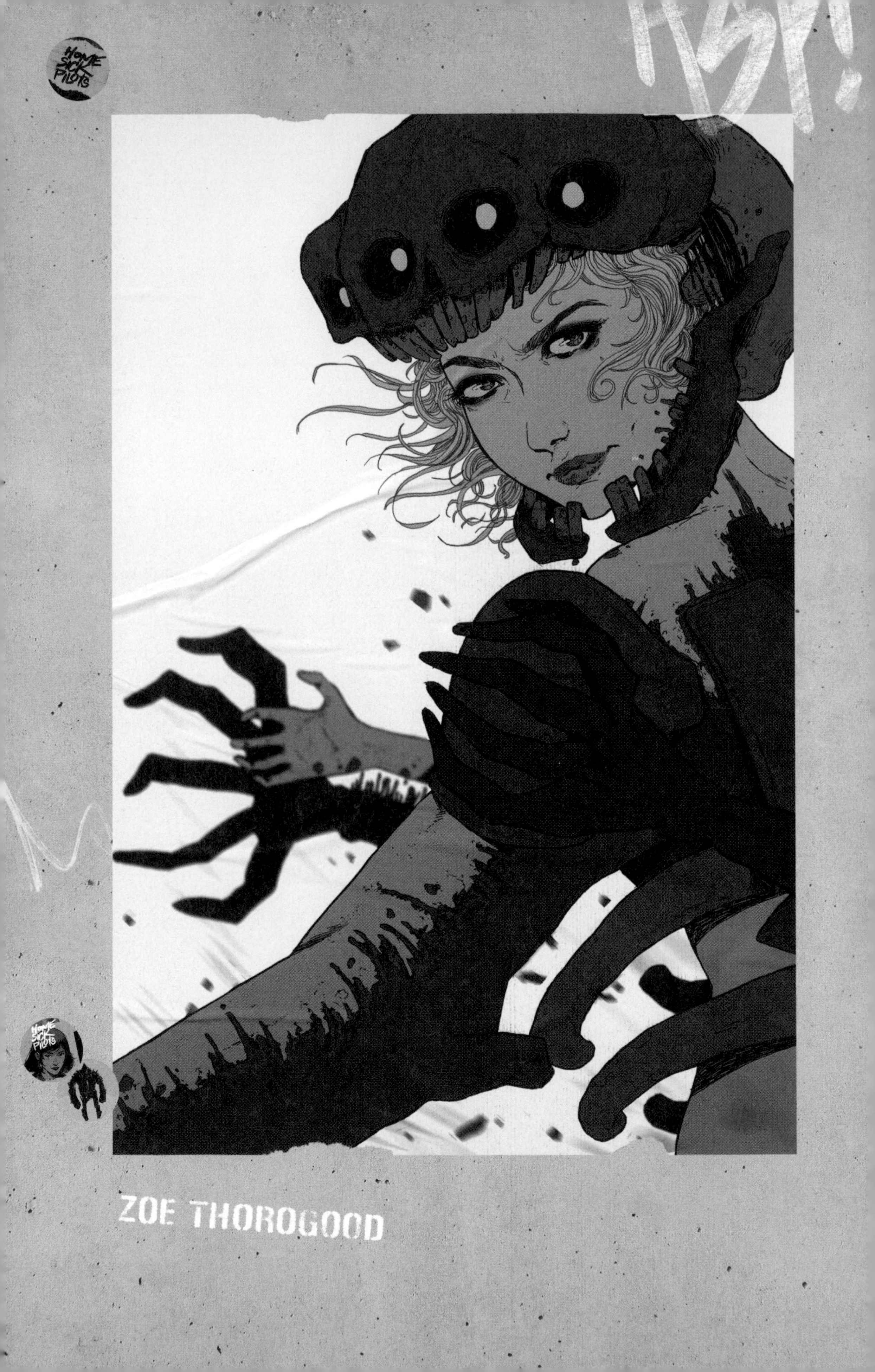

ZOE THOROGOOD

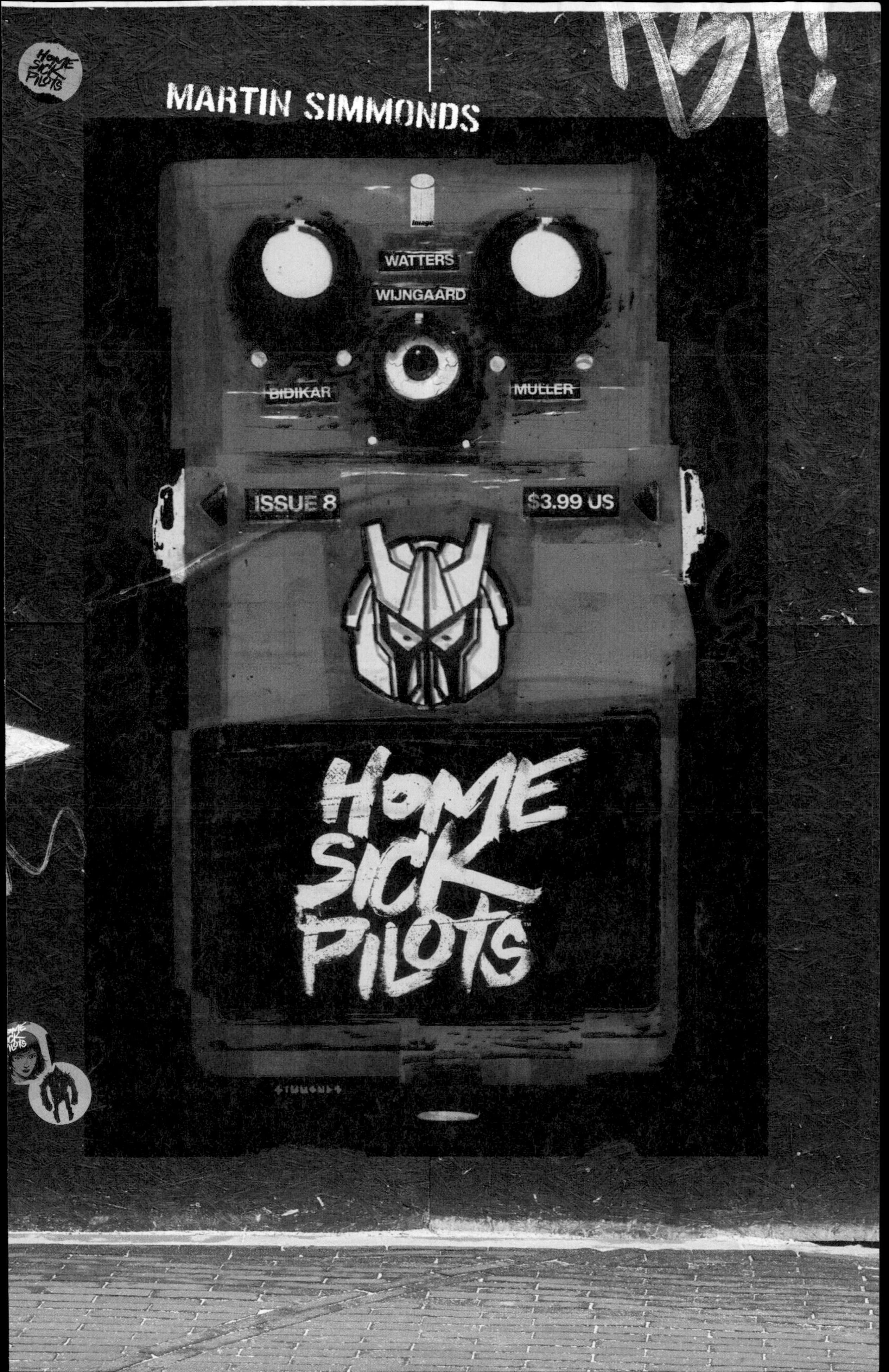
MARTIN SIMMONDS
WATTERS
WIJNGAARD
BIDIKAR
MULLER
ISSUE 8
$3.99 US
HOME SICK PILOTS™
SIMMONDS

ADAM GORHAM

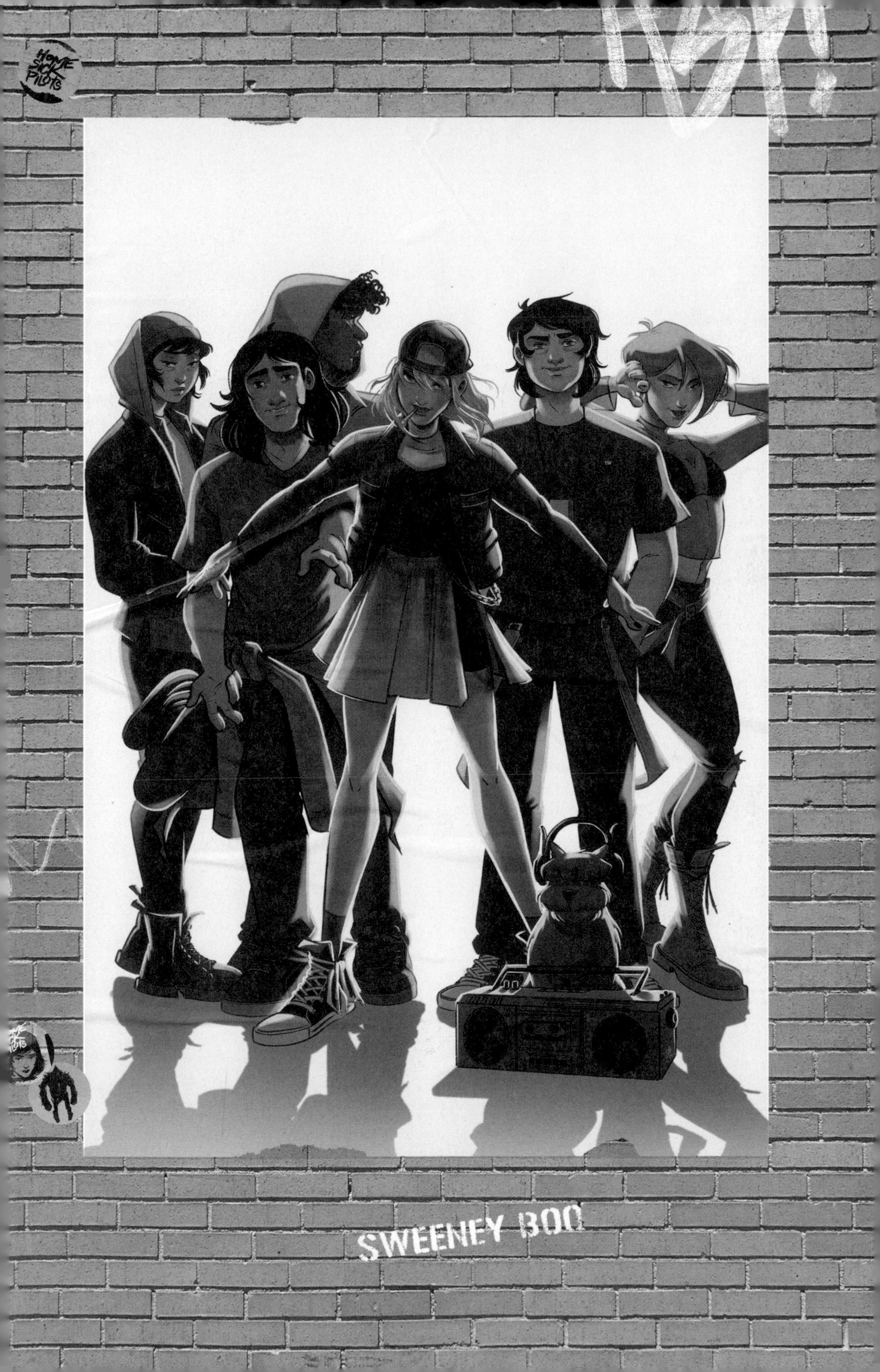
HOME SICK PILOTS
SWEENEY BOO